See:
Gerhard Loewenberg,
"Influence of Parliamentary
Behavior on Regime Stability"
Comparative Politics 3 (1971):
177 - 200.

America's Congress

DAVID R. MAYHEW

America's Congress

Actions in the Public Sphere,
James Madison Through Newt Gingrich

YALE UNIVERSITY PRESS / NEW HAVEN & LONDON

To my wife, Judith

Set in Scala type by Tseng Information Systems.
Printed in the United States of America by/Vail-Ballou Press, Binghamton, New York.

Library of Congress Cataloging-in-Publication Data
Mayhew, David R.
America's Congress : actions in the public sphere, James Madison through Newt Gingrich / David R. Mayhew.
    p.   cm.
Includes bibliographical references and index.
ISBN 0-300-08049-2 (cloth : alk. paper)
1. United States. Congress—History.   2. Legislators—United States—History.   I. Title.
JK1021 .M39   2000
328.73'09—dc21   99-086055

A catalogue record for this book is available from the British Library.
The paper in this book meets the guidelines for permanence and durability of the Committee on Production Guidelines for Book Longevity of the Council on Library Resources.

10 9 8 7 6 5 4 3 2 1

CONTENTS

ACKNOWLEDGMENTS

I have had a great deal of help in preparing this work. For their criticism at various stages, I am grateful to Joseph LaPalombara, my most faithful and helpful reader over the years, and to Robert Dahl, Jacob Hacker, Rogan Kersh, Andrew Rich, Harvey Schantz, Eric Schickler, and Andrew Spejewski. Akhil R. Amar, Manfred Brocker, Greg Forster, Hung Bo, Steven Jiang, John McCormick, Garrison Nelson, Eric Patashnik, and Ian Shapiro offered useful tips and comments. Many thanks to Clint Hermes for verifying my data on member careers so adeptly, and to Barry McMillion for doing the same for my references. Sid Milkis allowed me to deliver an address based on the project's dataset at his 1996 conference at Brandeis University on "Progressivism—Then and Now." For research materials, I relied on the fine libraries at Yale, Stanford, and Boston University. Yale supported me with a senior faculty fellowship and a triennial leave, and the Center for Advanced Study in the Behavioral Sciences (CASBS) with a wonderful year in residence in 1995–96 where I assembled my dataset, mastered (sufficiently) Microsoft Excel, and started writing. My financial support from CASBS came from National Science Foundation Grant #SES-9022192. At CASBS, I profited greatly from the intellectual companionship of Keith Krehbiel, who was pursuing his own recent congressional project then. My project differs from his in theoretical grounding but not entirely, I would like to think, in spirit. My dataset and a coding guide to it are available at http://pantheon.yale. edu/~dmayhew/

INTRODUCTION

"If Newt Gingrich had been run over by a truck in 1993, it is almost certain that there would not be a Republican majority in the House today. Few other congressional politicians have made such a difference in partisan history."
—Michael Barone, November 1997

On Capitol Hill, like it or not, the 1990s was Newt Gingrich's decade. Certainly he made a major public splash as GOP House leader, and who would deny that many of his much-noticed moves in that role were consequential? "Gingrich's articulation of a Republican agenda, culminating in the September 1994 Contract with America; his avid recruitment of candidates; his continual assertion since his election to the leadership by two votes in March 1989, that Republicans could win a majority—without all these, Republicans would probably have made gains in the House elections in 1994, but would have fallen well short of a majority. And, with Bill Clinton winning re-election, they would not have made further gains in 1996."[1] These claims are at least plausible, as would be others about the policy results of the Republican congressional takeover in 1994. In Gingrich, we have as good a case as we are likely to see of a member of Congress operating in the public sphere with consequence.[2]

1. The opening epigraph and this quotation are from Michael Barone, "Slender Is the Newt," *National Review*, November 24, 1997, p. 28.
2. See David S. Broder, "Newt Gingrich's Legacy: He'll Be Gone, But the House of Representatives Is Unlikely to Ever Be the Same Again," *Washington Post National*

For me, Gingrich's and other Capitol Hill performances in the 1990s — Henry J. Hyde's in the impeachment of President Clinton, for example — have been a wake-up call to take seriously the idea of congressional politicians operating in the public sphere with, arguably, consequence. This may seem an obvious idea to emphasize in studying congressional politics, but it is a recessive one in contemporary political science. There, in a deductively flavored kind of analysis, public officials are routinely cast as agents or instruments of societal interests or preferences — of interest groups, for example, or of opinion distributions residing in electorates — and, for the most part, that's that. There is much good sense in this analytic motif, which has infused the scholarship about Congress from the days of pluralism and group theory in the 1950s and 1960s through the rational-choice formulations of recent times. Writers in the latter genre have brought a signal sharpness to the discussion, thus exhibiting the motif's power and utility yet also, I believe, as a side effect, showing some of its limits. Key aspects of congressional politics, including analytically orderable ones that anyone trying to understand American politics and government should be interested in, are being downplayed or ignored.

Hence this book, an interpretation of congressional politics rooted in a different motif, or rather a pair of motifs — the idea of a "public sphere" and the idea of "actions" engaged in by members of Congress. By "public sphere" I mean a realm of shared American consciousness in which government officials and others make moves before an attentive stratum of the public, and in which society's preference formation, politics, and policymaking all substantially take place; they are substantially endogenous to it. "Actions" are, in principle, moves by members of Congress that are to a significant degree autonomous and consequential — or at least potentially consequential — and that are noticed by an alert stratum of

---

Weekly Edition, November 16, 1998, p. 11. This was an article marking Gingrich's resignation from the Speakership in 1998.

the public exactly because of their perceived current or potential conse-quentiality. Gingrich and his Contract with America are a notable recent instance. This is a world of politics that we experience in our lives but, for some reason, tend to skirt in our scholarship.

In Chapter 1, I make a case for analyzing congressional politics in this way. I lead off with a general question that frames the discussion and points it in an empirical direction: If a legislature is set down in a constitu-tional environment, what sorts of actions will its members engage in that win public notice? I introduce, consider, and argue for the idea of a "pub-lic sphere," a necessary move given my purposes, but then I stop on that front. To flesh out empirically an American "public sphere," especially one extending back two centuries as this book's content otherwise does, would be a daunting task for which supporting secondary scholarship is sparse, and I pass up that task here. An American "public sphere" is as-sumed. The bulk of Chapter 1 is devoted to crystallizing and advancing the idea of "actions" by members of Congress—the empirical keynote of the rest of the book.

The conceptual discussion in Chapter 1 is followed by a methodologi-cal one in Chapter 2. Here, I elaborate and defend a way of documenting "actions" by members of the House and Senate, starting at the beginning in the First Congress of 1789–91, when James Madison dominated the proceedings as a freshman House member from Virginia. In a nutshell, what I do is to itemize moves made by members of Congress that are mentioned in any of thirty-eight selected works of American "public af-fairs" history covering the past two centuries. The result, at the close of the chapter, is an overall dataset of 2,304 member "actions," which are sorted into forty-three categories in Table 2.6—a supply of materials for use in later chapters. Truth in advertising requires an upfront announce-ment that the dataset in fact ends, for reasons of source availability that will become evident in Chapter 2, in 1988. Still, the discussion through-out the book encompasses the 1990s, and I do not believe that readers will have any difficulty interpolating events, even if they are trying now to forget them, from this most recent decade.

Once past these preparations, I draw on the 2,304-item dataset in Chapters 3, 4, and 5 to present three separate treatments of congressional politics during the two-centuries-long U.S. national regime. My general concern is: What do patterns of "action" by members of Congress reveal about the nature of this regime—about both its constant features and its evolving ones? Looked at one way, each of the three chapters is itself a series of distinct, though related, presentations each centering on one or more data-based tables or graphs. Looked at another way, each chapter develops a theme. In Chapter 3, the theme is Congress's signature *mix* of certain basic kinds of member "actions." Taken up under this rubric are legislating, investigating, impeaching, taking public stands, intruding into foreign policy, and, as important as anything else, staging opposition to presidential administrations. The chapter closes with some reflections about this "action" mix as well as a backward glance at a seventeenth-century English antecedent of it.

In Chapter 4, the theme is *relations and balance* among the basic elective institutions of American government—the House, the Senate, the presidency, and state and local governments—that are illuminated by certain patterns of member "action." How have senators stacked up against House members as producers of "actions"? In what patterns during what eras have members of Congress moved up to cabinet appointments, served on the side as heads of state or local party organizations, been influential in selecting presidents or vice presidents, or run for those two top offices themselves? A good deal of change comes to light across the two centuries. In some respects, as shown in these "action" trends, the various governmental institutions have at once distanced themselves from each other and democratized their ties to the public—a double victory for a view of representation expressed by Thomas Jefferson two centuries ago—yet they have also stayed in place as formidable check and balance of each other—a victory for James Madison's view back then. The result has implications, which are discussed, for conducting politics and policymaking in the "public sphere."

In Chapter 5, the theme is *careers within Congress*. What has been the pattern of notable "action careers"—those of the likes of Henry Clay, Robert F. Wagner, Robert A. Taft, and Edward M. Kennedy? In the twentieth century, did "action" performance center distinctively among committee chairs, and among southerners? When during their careers have members tended to perform "actions"? Have early performers differed in interesting ways from late performers? During the twentieth century, where did "actions" associated with a series of powerful ideological impulses—La Follette Progressivism, the New Deal, pre–World War II isolationism, and anti–Vietnam War sentiment, for example—register in Congress's career structure—among newcomers or old-timers? In light of these various patterns, how might a term-limits reform cut into Congress's "action" performance? The chapter points to a particular, relatively unnoticed pattern of checks and balances introduced into the American system during the twentieth century, then closes with a discussion of the indexing potential of congressional careers—why do we hear of an age of Franklin D. Roosevelt but not an age of Robert F. Wagner?

In Chapter 6, I close with some thoughts on the striking stability of the American regime and how Congress's "action" patterns may have contributed to that property of it, on the present and possible future of member "actions," and on certain features of congressional politics during the 1990s.

One of my objectives in this book is to comment, implicitly or explicitly, on the treatment of Congress by contemporary political science. But that is done in passing. In general, the work is aimed at a broad audience—at anyone interested in the subject, reasonably aware of American political history, and willing to tolerate simple graphs. The discussion of methodology and statistical data is all, I hope, common sense.

I alert the reader that this study is (at least, I have tried to frame it to be) both disciplined and positive. That is, I try to use data sources carefully and stick close to them, and, for the most part, I try to illuminate or explain rather than to judge or appraise. The latter assignment can be difficult, and its execution may come across as exasperating or even surprising, on a subject where we have become accustomed to partisan or interpretive tilting of one variety or another in professional as well as popular writing, and where we need to make judgments in order to live our lives as citizens. Why treat Senator Joseph McCarthy (a major producer of member "actions") as a specimen rather than a villain? Here, he is a specimen, along with Daniel Webster, Huey Long (who was a senator, not a governor, during his prime "share our wealth" days), Thaddeus Stevens, the pre–vice presidential Richard M. Nixon, Sam Rayburn, Newt Gingrich, J. W. Fulbright, Edward M. Kennedy, and the rest. My chief objective is to illuminate how the American regime has worked, and that has required a mobilization of specimens. A further aim of the book, though, is to provide food for thought and judgment not about particular politicians, ideologies, or issue tendencies — all of which come and go — but about the regime itself.

the regime itself

Member Actions in the Public Sphere

If a legislature is set down in a constitutional environment, what sorts of actions will its members engage in that win public notice? For reasons elaborated below, I believe this is a useful question to ask, and I rely on it as an underpinning for this book about the U.S. Congress. By "public notice," I mean notice by at least a politically aware stratum of the population. For a sense of what I mean by "sorts of actions," consider the following account of congressional politics during Clinton's first two controversy-laden years in 1993–94. I wrote this stylized sketch for the occasion of this book, but probably any of several million witnesses of U.S. politics during those years composing a brief narrative of widely noticed events involving Congress or its members would have written something like it.

Exhilarated by their party's 1992 election victory, President Clinton and Democratic House and Senate leaders Tom Foley (D-Wash.)[1] and George Mitchell (D-Maine) set out to build Capitol Hill coalitions "from the left in"—that is, the Republican minority party would be largely ignored. Joining the new cabinet were

1. The first time the name of a member of Congress appears, here and throughout text, it is followed by a party-state designation such as "D-Wash."

veteran legislators Les Aspin (D-Wis.) at Defense, Lloyd Bentsen (D-Tex.) at Treasury, Mike Espy (D-Miss.) at Agriculture, and Leon Panetta (D-Calif.) at the Office of Management and Budget. African-Americans rose to new prominence on the Hill as Kweisi Mfume (D-Md.) invigorated the Congressional Black Caucus and Carol Moseley-Braun (D-Ill.) spoke out as the first black woman senator. Clinton's February 1993 budget plan, unveiled to considerable public and Capitol Hill acclaim, headed to Congressman Dan Rostenkowski's (D-Ill.) Ways and Means Committee for expeditious treatment.

But troubles loomed. Senator Sam Nunn (D-Ga.) derailed Clinton's so-called gays-in-the-military initiative. Senator Joseph Biden (D-Del.) presided over the demise of key White House appointments. Daniel Patrick Moynihan (D-N.Y.), chairman of the Senate Finance Committee, began grousing publicly about Administration stances. Senators David Boren (D-Okla.) and John Breaux (D-La.), both thought to be needed for a Senate victory on the budget, took advantage of their marginal coalitional position to kill the White House's proposed BTU tax. The Republicans came alive again in April 1993 as Senate Minority Leader Bob Dole (R-Kans.) staged a successful filibuster against Clinton's economic stimulus bill. House backbenchers Tim Penny (D-Minn.) and John Kasich (R-Ohio) hatched their own competing plan to reduce the deficit. Eventually, in August 1993, the White House budget plan won narrow victories in both houses, albeit only after much of its content had been diluted or dropped. Bob Kerrey (D-Nebr.) drove a bargain as the key marginal voter in the Senate; first-termer Marjorie Margolies-Mezvinsky (D-Pa.) was put on the spot in that role in the House.

In a landmark policy move in November 1993, Congress approved NAFTA—the North American Free Trade Agreement—through an odd coalition that saw House Republican Whip Newt Gingrich (R-Ga.) assisting the White House and House Democratic leaders Dick Gephardt

(D-Mo.) and David Bonior (D-Mich.) leading the opposition. But after that it was all downhill for the White House through 1994 as, most important, the Clintons' ambitious health-care plan foundered and died. John Dingell (D-Mich.) could not assemble a majority for any version of it on the House Energy and Commerce Committee. Rostenkowski tried on Ways and Means but then had to step aside after being indicted for defrauding the government. Compromise plans promoted by Congressman Jim Cooper (D-Tenn.) and Senator John Chafee (R-R.I.) came to nothing. The Republicans dug in hostilely under Gingrich and Dole. At the end, Democratic compromise bills shaped by leaders Gephardt and Mitchell went nowhere. Meanwhile, the White House had to endure damaging Whitewater hearings run by Senator Donald Riegle (D-Mich.). In August 1994, the Democrats' omnibus crime bill, attacked by Gingrich as being loaded with "social pork," surprisingly fell short of a House majority (though a revised version later passed). Many other legislative items died as adjournment approached, although first-term Senator Dianne Feinstein (D-Calif.) managed to salvage a major bill protecting the California desert. House Republican leaders Gingrich and Dick Armey (R-Tex.), in a striking September 1994 initiative, put forth an elaborate "Contract with America" program that became the GOP's November election centerpiece and then, in January 1995, that winning party's legislative agenda.

Consider too, for variety if not necessarily for contrast, the following sketch of Congress-related politics two centuries ago during the second term of George Washington. The same U.S. regime is on exhibit:[2]

Shock waves from the radical phase of the French Revolution stirred U.S. domestic unrest and a foreign policy crisis during 1793–97. In

2. This sketch is my product also, although of course in this case I relied on secondary sources.

1793, House Republican spokesman James Madison (DR-Va.),[3] spotting an unwelcome pro-British tilt in the Washington Administration's proclamation of neutrality vis-à-vis France and Britain, wrote a series of public essays as "Helvidius" claiming foreign policy powers for Congress. In January 1794, he brought to the House a series of anti-British "Commercial Propositions" that were countered by Congressman William L. Smith (Federalist-S.C.). Madison also balked at President Washington's condemnation of the effervescent new "democratic societies." In June 1795, the Federalist-controlled Senate voted 20 to 10 in secret session to approve the Jay Treaty—the Administration's new move to establish peace terms and trade relations with Britain. Senator Pierce Butler (DR-S.C.) leaked the treaty page-by-page to Madison, then Senator S.T. Mason (DR-Va.) leaked the full text to the public, and popular outrage ensued. Republicans in the House, the dominant party there, eventually moved to put their stamp on policy. Edward Livingston (DR-N.Y.) engineered a resolution asking Washington to turn over the Jay Treaty documents. The President refused. Madison argued that the House had a right to see the documents, and, beyond that, notwithstanding the Senate's assigned constitutional role as ratifier of treaties, to nullify a treaty by withholding appropriations. The strategy worked. A House majority-vote showdown kicked into place as inevitable. Both sides took to mobilizing public support, Treasury Secretary Alexander Hamilton and Senator Rufus King (F-N.Y.), for example, through writing essays as "Camillus" backing the treaty. A drawn-out, high-stakes endgame [rather like the one involving NAFTA in 1993] culminated in April 1796 in a moving House speech by the veteran Federalist spokesman Fisher Ames (F-Mass.) and a 49–49 tie

3. In parenthetical designations here and throughout, I refer to the early Jeffersonian Republican party as "Democratic Republican" or "DR" so as to distinguish it from the later, more familiar Republican party of Lincoln's time and since.

vote broken in the treaty's favor by Frederick Muhlenberg (DR-Pa.), chairing the House's Committee of the Whole.[4] The treaty survived. Otherwise in the mid-1790s, Albert Gallatin (DR-Pa.) joined the House as a Republican leader—a key acquisition since no one else in the party approached Federalist policy leader Hamilton in fiscal expertise. Senator Aaron Burr (DR-N.Y.) aspired to the vice presidency in 1796 but lost. Senator William Blount (DR-Tenn.), like Congressman Thomas Scott (Pa.) a few years earlier, brought trouble on himself by conspiring with the British over western lands.

Public affairs in a democracy is, among other things, a stream of collective consciousness in which certain actions by individuals, including legislators like those cited above, come to be noticed and remembered. Individuals' actions seem to reach this standing if they are widely thought to be consequential, potentially consequential, or otherwise significant. They are observed by politically aware citizens trying to size up events in their environment. It is a good bet, for example, that millions of politics watchers considered Moynihan's grousing, Boren's footdragging on the budget, Rostenkowski's stepping aside as Ways and Means chair, and Gingrich's Contract with America initiative to be politically significant actions during 1993–94. When actions register as significant like this among an aware sector of the public, I want to argue here, they should be regarded as significant by any scholar who takes public affairs seriously. In the case of 1993–94, for anyone trying to track, examine, or characterize U.S. politics during those years, the moves by Rostenkowski, Gingrich, and the rest that were putatively widely judged to be politically

---

4. For a comprehensive account of Congress's handling of the Jay Treaty, see Stanley Elkins and Eric McKitrick, *The Age of Federalism: The Early American Republic, 1788–1800* (New York: Oxford University Press, 1993), pp. 415–49. On Ames's speech: "He proceeded to show that he could still perform the part, without notes to prompt him, of the wiliest demagogue in the House" (p. 448).

significant can be taken, for analytic purposes, to have *been* politically significant.[5] The widely recognized is, in this sense, the real. The standard for significance is immanent.

For this approach to be useful, the realm of public affairs has to amount to something, and I want to argue that it does. I see it as a busy timestream of events featuring uncertainty, open deliberation and discussion, opinion formation, strutting and ambition, surprises, endless public moves and countermoves by politicians and other actors, rising and falling issues, and an attentive and sometimes participating audience of large numbers of citizens. Health-care politics in 1993–94 and Jay Treaty politics in 1795–96 provide cases in point. Public affairs, moreover, is a highly important realm in that much of what virtually anybody by any standard would consider to be politically important originates, is substantially caused, and happens within it—that is, is endogenous to it. This may be a commonsense view, but it is not all that common within the boundaries of modern social science, where politics tends to be seen as driven or determined by exogenous forces such as classes, interest groups, interests, or otherwise pre-politically caused preferences. In one limiting-case analysis, the economist George J. Stigler's well-known account of regulatory politics, public affairs shrinks to zero; all an analyst needs to examine or reckon with are imputed policy preferences (indus-

---

5. For James G. March and Johan P. Olsen, public affairs narratives would seem to have a place in an "institutional," as opposed to an "exchange," understanding of politics. In an institutional analysis, "Politics depends on *accounts* of political events and responsibility for them, interpretations of political history. Accounts form the basis for defining situations within which identities are relevant. Meanings and histories are socially constructed. Political myths are developed and transmitted. Accountability is established. It is possible to study the processes by which a current situation is defined or history is understood and by which political events and possibilities are interpreted, as well as the possibilities for transmission, retention, and retrieval of the lessons of history" (p. 259). March and Olsen, "Institutional Perspectives on Political Institutions," *Governance* 9 (1996), 247–64.

tries want self-serving regulations) and policy results (they get them); the realm of public affairs does not enter the picture at all.[6] For purposes of this book, I want to shake free from this idea of exogenous determination. Public affairs can matter; if so, it is worth focusing on.

Backup for such a focus can be found in political theory, though it needs to be assembled. One idea is that of the "public sphere" as it has been proposed and given empirical grounding by Jürgen Habermas. A kind of realm warranting that label, Habermas writes, appeared on the world scene in England in the late seventeenth and eighteenth century. It featured open and well-reported deliberation in Parliament, constant and open press criticism of the government, wide circulation of news, and attentiveness and sometimes assertiveness by a fairly broad public (the rising bourgeoisie, in Habermas's view).[7] It was a major new development. This is theorizing in the German tradition in which authors take pains to characterize forms of actual political life; in Habermas's case both the characterization and the catchphrase (as translated into English) seem apt for my purposes—hence this book's title.

Surprisingly, the main American tradition of political theorizing—Locke and Montesquieu as recast by Madison and others in the late eighteenth century—does not give much attention to public affairs, as I have used that term here, or a "public sphere."[8] Instead, interests, factions, and balancing among them are the familiar ingredients and emphases. Among those who have written about government by deliberation or by discussion, about public officials making moves before an

6. George J. Stigler, *The Citizen and the State: Essays on Regulation* (Chicago: University of Chicago Press, 1975), ch. 8.

7. Jürgen Habermas, *The Structural Transformation of the Public Sphere: An Inquiry into a Category of Bourgeois Society* (Cambridge: MIT Press, 1989), chs. 1–3. The original German edition was published in 1962.

8. A relevant discussion appears in Bernard Manin, *The Principles of Representative Government* (New York: Cambridge University Press, 1997), pp. 183–92.

attentive public, and about public opinion formation, the relevant authorities turn out to be a less prominent line extending from Harrington and Hume through—if anybody in the generation of the 1780s—James Wilson, though to some degree also Madison. Fortunately, this other tradition has been given new life in recent writings by Cass R. Sunstein and Samuel H. Beer.[9] "The central idea here," Sunstein writes, for example, "is that politics has a deliberative or transformative dimension. Its function is to select values, to implement 'preferences about preferences,' or to provide opportunities for preference formation rather than simply to implement existing desires. . . . Moreover, the systems of checks and balances, bicameralism, and federalism responded to the central republican understanding that disagreement can be a creative force. National institutions were set up so as to ensure a measure of competition and dialogue; the federal system would produce both experimentation and mutual controls. In all these ways, the constitutional framework created a kind of deliberative democracy."[10]

This is theory. How about practice? Has a "public sphere" existed and operated during the two centuries of American national history? My assumption here is yes. Obviously, media technology has changed immensely during that time, but a basic mix of openness, news coverage, moves by politicians, attentive strata of the public, and opinion fluidity has been there in the system from the start—well before the Contract with America, C-SPAN, or Larry King Live.[11] Anyone who doubts that

9. Cass R. Sunstein, "Beyond the Republican Revival," *Yale Law Journal* 97 (1988), 1539–90; Samuel H. Beer, *To Make a Nation: The Rediscovery of American Federalism* (Cambridge: Harvard University Press, 1993), ch. 3 and pp. 224–31, 261–78, 371–72.

10. Sunstein, "Beyond the Republican Revival," pp. 1545, 1562.

11. In the political realm in general, Samuel P. Huntington has argued, the United States has exhibited unique stability among countries of the world since the late eighteenth century. He states, "The expansion of political participation occurred earlier and far more extensively in America than in Europe," and continues, "The institutional

might consult, say, Stanley Elkins and Eric McKitrick's account of the handling of the Jay Treaty in 1795–96 or William Lee Miller's recent work on the campaign by Congressman John Quincy Adams (Whig-Mass.) and others, which caused a nationwide stir, to admit antislavery petitions to the House in the 1830s and 1840s.[12] Britain has arguably been stable in these same basic respects during the past two centuries, even though the British electorate was of course small in the nineteenth century—a "public sphere" can exist without universal suffrage or mass participatory democracy. Continental Europe is another matter.[13]

Such American stability makes possible the lineage described in this book from James Madison—as a member of the House—through Newt Gingrich. If a "public sphere" or a collective political consciousness does exist, elected legislators, of course, earn a wonderful chance to do things that register within it. With the member's job goes a license to persuade, connive, hatch ideas, propagandize, assail enemies, vote, build coalitions, shepherd legislation, and in general cut a figure in public affairs. A legislature can be a decision machine, a forum, an arena, a stage, or a springboard. One member of Congress may craft bills; another may make deals; another may conduct investigations; another may undertake issue cru-

---

framework established in 1787 has . . . changed remarkably little" (pp. 93, 98). Huntington, *Political Order in Changing Societies* (New Haven and London: Yale University Press, 1968).

12. Elkins and McKitrick, *The Age of Federalism,* pp. 415–49; William Lee Miller, *Arguing About Slavery: The Great Battle in the United States Congress* (New York: Knopf, 1996). For a revealing treatment of the role of public opinion during the enactment of President John Adams's defense policies in 1798, see Karen S. Hoffman, "Public Opinion Before the 20th Century: Measuring the President's Relationship with the People," manuscript presented at the Annual Meeting of the American Political Science Association, Atlanta, September 2–5, 1999.

13. In the Habermas canon, let it be said, the eighteenth century in Britain was something of a golden age. It has been downhill for the "public sphere" since. In his *Structural Transformation,* Habermas does not comment on the United States.

sades; another may run for president. A member may do more than one of these things at the same time. The mix of actual member activities is, in one sense, determined by the Constitution's job description for House and Senate members, but in another sense it is empirical. You have to look and see. What sorts of member actions register in the collective political consciousness? Elect people to Congress, and what will they noticeably do?

In this book, I argue that one good way to understand a legislature— including how it fits into a larger political system—is to examine conspicuous member actions like those presented in the two sketches that open this chapter.[14] My specific focus is acts by members of the U.S. Congress from 1789 through 1988 (no later than that, notwithstanding the first sketch here, for reasons explained in Chapter 2). On the high side of conspicuousness, that means such actions as: Congressman James Madison co-founded (with Thomas Jefferson) the Republican party in the early 1790s. Speaker Henry Clay (DR-Ky.) agitated as a "War Hawk" for war against England in 1811–12. Senator Charles Sumner (D,Free Soil-Mass.) hammered slavery in his "Crime against Kansas" speech in 1856. Senator Stephen A. Douglas (D-Ill.) supplied half the personnel for the Lincoln-Douglas debates in 1858 (Lincoln was an ex-House member then). Congressman George W. Norris (R-Nebr.) brought down Speaker Joseph "Czar" Cannon (R-Ill.) in 1910. Senator Henry Cabot Lodge (R-Mass.) masterminded the defeat of the League of Nations in 1919. Senator Robert M. La Follette (R-Wis.) ran for president as a Progressive in 1924. Senator Robert F. Wagner (D-N.Y.) shaped the National Labor Relations Act of 1935, Senator Robert A. Taft (R-Ohio) the counterbalancing Taft-Hartley Act of 1947. Senator Joseph R. McCarthy (R-Wis.)

14. All the individuals mentioned in the two sketches were members of the House or Senate at the times the recited actions occurred, except for the presidents and other executive officials (Alexander Hamilton and John Jay) whose roles needed to be referred to in order to frame the acts by the legislators.

helped bring on the Red Scare of 1950–54. Senator J. William Fulbright (D-Ark.) staged televised hearings on the Vietnam War in 1966–67. Senator Edmund S. Muskie (D-Maine) packaged the Clean Air Act of 1970. Senator Samuel J. Ervin, Jr. (D-N.C.), brought steel and southern charm to the Watergate investigation in 1973. If the dataset could be updated, I would include, for example, the following items: Congressman Gingrich launched the Contract with America in 1994–95, and Congressman Hyde managed the drive to impeach Clinton in 1998. Down a few notches in conspicuousness, though still drawing notice, are such actions as Senator Boren blocking the BTU tax in 1993 and Congressman Livingston angling after the Jay Treaty documents in 1796.

Using standard history books (see Chapter 2), I resolve U.S. congressional history into 2,304 items or "bits" by tracking such member actions, the result being a kind of substance or currency that I hope to show can be analytically useful. As of now, the chief substance most of us use for long-term congressional analysis is roll-call votes, which are ideal for arraying members on ideological dimensions but are not particularly illuminating for many other aspects of politics. The dataset in hand, I proceed to address questions like those broached in the Introduction: What *kinds* of actions do members of Congress (henceforth, "MCs") noticeably engage in?[15] How has the mix changed over time? How have MCs figured in the country's party structure and its office-to-office career ladder, sometimes called an "opportunity structure"? How about patterns of high-intensity opposition to presidential administrations? When during their careers have members conspicuously performed? How might a switch to congressional term limits influence performance patterns, and with what possible systemic consequences?

15. As with "MPs," for members of Parliament in Britain. The abbreviation here serves two ends. It degenderizes the prose by eliminating the generic "congressman," and it avoids the cumbersome "congresspeople" or "congresspersons."

In principle, the idea of noticed member actions, given suitable ways of tracking them, might be carried to other legislatures and thus allow comparative analysis. Here are some examples of what might be found: In a British-type Westminster system, many actions performed by members in their roles as cabinet ministers or in formal parliamentary question periods; in, say, eighteenth-century England or post–World War II Italy, maneuverings by factional leaders as they manage nationwide patronage networks; in Chicago's city council during that city's classic machine days of the mid–twentieth century, lavish servicing of ward constituencies accompanied by allegations of corruption. In all cases the operative question would be: What draws public notice? No doubt it is true (if decreasingly so) that in many twentieth-century European systems based on list proportional representation, the leaders of the tightly organized parliamentary parties tended to drown out all other members in their ability to draw public notice. But that, too, is a revelation about a kind of system.

Plainly, members of Congress need to possess a certain degree of autonomy for the study outlined here to make much sense. MCs cannot be mere devices for registering exogenously formed societal views (interest group demands, constituency preferences, and the like). As it happens, even analytic schools that accent the exogenous tend to leave a role for member initiative. In classical pluralist analysis, where politics is said to be driven by societal interest groups, MCs can at least be "brokers." In contemporary rational-choice theory, which emphasizes roll-call voting where members register "ideal points" ordinarily dictated by constituency views, certain members still have a sizable role as agenda-setters; they can play traffic cop, in effect, among issue dimensions imposed on Capitol Hill by society.[16] Vastly better is the case for autonomy

16. See, for example, William H. Riker, *The Art of Political Manipulation* (New Haven and London: Yale University Press, 1986); Riker, *Liberalism Against Populism: A Confron-*

if, following common sense, we allow a role for individual MCs' talent and drive, which in fact may be needed to make anything happen at all in Congress's maze of institutions and processes.[17] For one thing, in the sphere of legislating, the transaction costs associated with packaging bills, making deals, and mobilizing votes can be enormously high; they may or may not be paid by anybody.[18]

Still, it may be objected, don't members of Congress, through roll-call voting and otherwise, devote their main efforts to getting reelected? Doesn't the election incentive exactly guarantee that MCs will cater to societal preferences—those of voters or, for example, campaign bank-rollers—thus reducing themselves to agents of societal forces? It turns out that even James Madison, in piloting the Bill of Rights amendments

---

tation Between the Theory of Democracy and the Theory of Social Choice (San Francisco: W.H. Freeman, 1982), ch. 8.

17. "Every piece of legislation needs a champion," and "Persistence, patience, hustle, and a willingness to compromise are the essential characteristics of the willful agents who realize legislative success" (pp. 203, 206). These are conclusions from a recent, interview-based study of selected congressional successes of the early 1960s and early 1990s. Lewis G. Irwin, "Evaluating Change in Legislative Success: Actors, Procedures, Strategies, and Product in the U.S. House of Representatives," Ph.D. dissertation submitted to the Department of Political Science, Yale University, 1998, pp. 11, 203–6, 288–302.

18. Terry M. Moe and Scott A. Wilson argue: "More generally, these [rational-choice] models assume that legislative voting is costless, and thus entirely determined by the various players' ideal points. In a literature that prides itself on recognizing the pervasive consequences of transaction costs, this is a great oddity. The transaction costs of moving a bill through the entire legislative process are enormous. . . . [W]e cannot predict outcomes based on the ideal points of the players alone. The best prediction is that, for most issues most of the time, there will be no affirmative action on the part of Congress at all. The ideal points may logically support a given outcome, but in reality *nothing will happen.*" Moe and Wilson, "Presidents and the Politics of Structure," *Law and Contemporary Problems* 57 (1994), 26–27. On paying Capitol Hill transaction costs, see also David R. Mayhew, *Congress: The Electoral Connection* (New Haven and London: Yale University Press, 1974), pp. 110–40.

through the House in 1789, was attending to constituency sentiment.[19] Sumner's "Crime against Kansas" speech of 1856, which caused a national sensation during the struggle over slavery in that territory, was (among other things) a move to keep his Massachusetts Senate seat in 1857 by outdramatizing the anti-Catholic appeals of the Know Nothing Party.[20] Madison and the moralistic Sumner needed to win elections, too. Even so, for a number of reasons, obeying the electoral incentive does not necessarily bar a politician from being autonomous. First, to a certain degree an MC can choose what reelection constituency to cater to.[21] In the 1990s, for example, a senator could choose to take campaign contributions from well-heeled trial lawyers or, alternatively, from the industries those lawyers target in class-action suits. Second, for a politician facing electoral risk it may sometimes make sense to resort to bold innovation, as did Senator McCarthy in 1950 in charging that the State Department was riddled with Communists. This was a calculated, consequential innovation.[22]

Third—and of particular relevance to the argument here—insofar as

19. Thornton Anderson, *Creating the Constitution: The Convention of 1787 and the First Congress* (University Park: Pennsylvania State University Press, 1993), pp. 176–77. Previously, anti-Federalist Patrick Henry had thwarted a campaign for a Virginia Senate seat for Madison and "placed his House candidacy in such jeopardy that he felt constrained to promise his constituents that he would support amendments."

20. See Michael D. Pierson, " 'All Southern Society Is Assailed by the Foulest Charges': Charles Sumner's 'The Crime against Kansas' and the Escalation of Republican Antislavery Rhetoric," *New England Quarterly* 68 (1995), 531–57. Sumner's proximate constituency was the Massachusetts state legislature, which in fact returned him to the Senate.

21. See Raymond A. Bauer, Ithiel de Sola Pool, and Lewis Anthony Dexter, *American Business and Public Policy: The Politics of Foreign Trade* (Chicago: Aldine Atherton, 1972), Part V; Richard F. Fenno, Jr., *Home Style: House Members in Their Districts* (Boston: Little, Brown, 1978), ch. 1.

22. See Mayhew, *Congress: The Electoral Connection*, pp. 68–69.

politicians cater to public opinion, what does it mean to do that? The reality seems to be a long way from any model of lockstep obedience to fixed, distinct public attitudes. For the most part, such attitudes do not seem to exist. Instead, according to a recent work by John R. Zaller, voters tend to possess in their minds a jumble of possibly conflicting "considerations" about public matters.[23] Thus "The budget needs to be balanced" may coexist in the same mind with "Medicare shouldn't be cut." Whatever "considerations" prevail in any one mind at one time will determine a person's vote. Accordingly, politicians take on a key role as cue-givers or propagandists: To advance their own reelection or other ends, they need to feed, elicit, or highlight the right voter "considerations." Just before an election, Republicans run ads about budget-balancing, and Democrats run ads about Medicare cuts.

This is an oversimple portrayal of Zaller, in whose account voters' minds also possess, for example, "predispositions." But the idea of politicians as highlighters of voter "considerations" rings true. That is certainly one thing they do. What's more, I do not see anything wrong with viewing politicians as commonly *implanting* voter "considerations" (or components of them) rather than simply highlighting existing ones.[24] This also rings true, especially if we look beyond "issue dimensions" like the familiar one in political science that features a five- or seven-point scale, codable from strongly yes to strongly no, asking respondents whether

23. John R. Zaller, *The Nature and Origins of Mass Opinion* (New York: Cambridge University Press, 1992), chs. 2, 3. A consideration is "any reason that might induce an individual to decide a political issue one way or the other. Considerations, thus, are a compound of cognition and affect—that is, a belief concerning an object and an evaluation of the belief" (p. 40).

24. Zaller allows for this move but does not emphasize it. In his account, politicians may deliver "persuasive messages," which are "arguments or images providing a reason for taking a position or point of view; if accepted by an individual, they become considerations" (p. 41).

the government should guarantee everybody a job. Constructs like this can be vague and abstract, after all, even if they are central to political science analysis. It makes at least as much sense to examine real public life where politicians often serve up vivid arguments and locutions about times, places, and events. In the course of American history, here are some kinds of ideational material that members of Congress have aimed at citizens' heads: *Factual claims,* such as Senator McCarthy's charge that Communists were rife in the State Department, or Senator Fulbright's charge that the Johnson administration lied about who did what to whom in the Tonkin Gulf in 1964 (the senator thus helped open up a Vietnam "credibility gap"); *causal claims,* as in Senator Gerald P. Nye's (R-N.Dak.) in the 1930s that profit-hungry munitions makers had triggered World War I, Congressman Gingrich's that the welfare state itself causes crime and poverty, or the implicit one by the authors of the Humphrey-Hawkins Full Employment and Balanced Growth Act of 1978 that a measure anything like that could bear out the promise of its title (it was in fact a toothless instrument); *predictions,* as in Senator William H. Seward's (R-N.Y.) "irrepressible conflict" speech of 1858 shortly before that conflict came, or isolationist Senator Burton K. Wheeler's (D-Mont.) acid comment in 1941 that a result of lend lease aid for Europe, on the analogy of New Deal crop programs (which destroyed supply in order to raise prices), would be to "plow under every fourth American boy"; *characterizations,* as in Congresswoman Clare Boothe Luce's (R-Conn.) term of "globaloney" for Vice President Henry Wallace's left-tilting vision of world politics in the early 1940s, or Gingrich's devastating "social pork" for the 1994 crime bill; *pleasing scenarios,* as in Speaker (and then Senator) Henry Clay's "American System," Senator Stephen A. Douglas's "popular sovereignty," Senator Huey Long's (D-La.) "share our wealth," or Gingrich's "opportunity society"; *moral claims* bearing the message "I'm outraged and you should be, too" as in, again, Senator Sumner's "Crime against Kansas" speech or Senator George McGovern's (D-S.Dak.) "This chamber reeks of blood" speech attacking the Vietnam War in 1970.[25] In all these types of cases, MCs have unquestionably aimed to "implant" something like "considerations" in voters' minds. Furthermore, insofar as the electoral incentive entered as motive, what could conceivably be more autonomous as well as consequential than to implant a consideration and then profit from having implanted it?

At any rate, I do not see any need in this book to cling to the theoretical purism of the electoral incentive. Generally potent as that motivation may be, it does not illuminate such historical events as Congressman Muhlenberg's tie-breaking vote for the Jay Treaty (he evidently lost his next election as a result),[26] Senator Fulbright's anti–Vietnam War stance in 1966–68 (Arkansas was hardly a dovish state),[27] or Senator Mark Hatfield's (R-Oreg.) joining with thirty-three Democrats, the exact number of coalition partners needed, to defeat the proposed Balanced Budget Amendment to the Constitution in a showdown vote in 1995 (Hatfield was retiring and therefore not facing more elections; that happens in Congress, too). Also, is it really believable, even after entertaining the

25. In the United States or elsewhere, who ranks highest among twentieth-century politicians in autonomous consequentiality? Possibly Adolf Hitler. Among the notions that Hitler sought to "implant" in the minds of German voters as he aimed for power during the Weimar Republic, note the prominence of factual claims, causal claims, characterizations, pleasing scenarios, and moral claims.

26. Beyond that, he was (literally) stabbed by his fiercely Republican brother-in-law a few days after he broke the tie. See John C. Miller, *The Federalist Era, 1789–1801* (New York: Harper and Brothers, 1960), pp. 175–76.

27. In 1967, "a Little Rock television survey indicated that 54 percent of the viewers questioned indicated they opposed Fulbright's stand on the war whereas 46 percent approved." Randall Bennett Woods, *Fulbright: A Biography* (New York: Cambridge University Press, 1995), pp. 465–66. In the Arkansas Democratic senatorial primary a year later, Fulbright won only 53 percent of the vote "against candidates who consistently accused him of giving aid and comfort to the enemy" (p. 493). In general, southern Democratic senators used to enjoy much easier primaries than that. Fulbright finally did lose his seat six years later in a Democratic primary in 1974.

idea of potential right-wing primary challengers, that the Republicans' impeachment of Clinton in 1998 was driven by an electoral incentive? For evidence, shouldn't it count pretty heavily that both polls and election results (those of November 1998) were hostile to the enterprise?[28]

No matter, if MCs really do highlight or implant voter "considerations," then the politics involving members of Congress needs to be modeled not just as opinion *expression*—the custom in political science analysis—but also as opinion *formation*. I believe this is a warranted move. For one thing, in the historical dataset to be explored here, first-ranked statistically among the kinds of actions MCs engage in is "taking stands"—an activity that can serve a variety of ends but shaping public opinion, I will argue, is often one of them.[29] For another, compelling evidence surfaces now and then that shaping opinion is exactly what MCs sometimes try to do. How did members' offices proceed during the White House's 1993–94 health-care drive, for example? One answer is based on interviews with thirty-nine House and Senate staffers: "Instead of following public opinion, a plurality of respondents (36 percent) reported using public opinion information for the primary purpose of changing (and not responding to) public opinion. . . . Some stressed [that] rallying public opinion was necessary today to 'prove your own point' and win politi-

28. It was evidently not a political plus for Henry J. Hyde. See Rick Pearson and Ted Gregory, "Fallout Hits Hyde at Home," *Chicago Tribune,* January 31, 1999, pp. 1, 14. "Just three months after the DuPage Republican won re-election with 67 percent of the vote, only 53 percent of the poll respondents in Hyde's district said they had a favorable opinion of him." In DuPage County, 35 percent of respondents said they were less favorably disposed toward the congressman owing to his handling of the impeachment; 25 percent said they were more favorably disposed.

29. As a definitional matter, "taking stands" is meant to refer here to behavior, not to intent. Catering to an electorate might be the intent, but so might any number of other aims. In an earlier work I advanced the somewhat different term "position taking," where the intent is specifically reelection-oriented. Mayhew, *Congress: The Electoral Connection,* pp. 49, 61–73.

cal support. Others argued that legislators had a responsibility or duty
to 'educate people regarding the negative unintended consequences' of
policy choices. . . . About three of five staff looked to congressional leaders
to direct public opinion."[30]

If opinion is "formed" rather than fixed or given, that supports the
idea of a collective political consciousness or a "public sphere"—a kind
of realm where such "forming" can take place. Here is what often seems
to happen in a public, high-stakes U.S. policy process: Outcomes are uncertain. Public opinion is unclear and unstable. In the face of these circumstances, members of Congress and, of course, others make moves
(the "others" might include the president, cabinet members, out-of-office
politicians, interest groups, media personalities like Rush Limbaugh,
advocates like Ralph Nader—potentially, anybody). An MC's move might
be to make a speech, denounce the president, release a report, offer an
amendment, usher a bill through committee, issue a subpoena, or in-
terrogate a witness. Moves ordinarily occur one by one. Also, new events
may intrude (John Brown stages his raid on Harpers Ferry in 1859; the
Communists seize Czechoslovakia in 1948). Some moves and events like
these are noticed, considered, and adapted to by elite actors and much of
the mass public. The overall pattern is a narrative-like process in which
both elite actors and voters revise, to some degree, their policy preferences as they go along. There is nothing undemocratic or otherwise questionable about such voter plasticity; voters would have to be dense not to
consider updating their preferences in response to relevant moves and
events.

It might be objected that voters will reconsider their "surface" or
"contingent" views—as on whether Clinton's particular health-care plan

30. Lawrence R. Jacobs, Eric D. Lawrence, Robert Y. Shapiro, and Steven S. Smith,
"Congressional Leadership of Public Opinion," *Political Science Quarterly* 113 (1998), 21–
41, quotation at p. 27.

should be approved—but not their more "fundamental" or "fixed" ones —as on whether the government should guarantee everyone adequate medical care. Fixed constituent views, at some level, are needed to fuel certain theories of politics; as with the notion of "ether" in nineteenth-century physics, their existence needs to be assumed. But the distinction seems dubious. In real politics, any view, whether apparently contingent or fixed, seems to run the risk of being trumped in a voter's mind by competing "considerations." The option of "Yes, but" is always available. Learning can occur.[31] Nor are "values" necessarily a fixed standard. David Braybrooke and Charles E. Lindblom have written of the policy process: "Quite often we find that we simply do not know what our values are on some points because we have never had to face a concrete choice in which we could ask ourselves the question and test the answer."[32] As analysts of processes, we never know what is "basic" or "fixed"; all we know is that in extended, move-rich processes like Clinton's health-care drive of 1993–94 or Gingrich's budget-balancing drive of 1995–96, various "considerations" come to prevail for various people.[33] Policymaking is, among other things, a process of personal and national discovery.

Members of Congress, moreover, can occasionally shape the views of

31. "Political decision making is by its nature a choice under uncertainty. In the process of exchanging evidence related to proposed solutions, individuals discover information they did not previously have. They learn that a given choice will have a given consequence, and if these consequences contradict the original objective they may be led to alter that objective." Bernard Manin, "On Legitimacy and Political Deliberation," *Political Theory* 15 (1987), 349.

32. David Braybrooke and Charles E. Lindblom, *A Strategy of Decision: Policy Evaluation as a Social Process* (Glencoe, Ill.: Free Press, 1963), pp. 28–29.

33. There is a case for administering Occam's razor to the idea of fixed, fundamental voter views: like "ether," they are arguably a gratuitous, nonvisible entity that impedes understanding. For an older expression of doubt that stable individual "volitions" exist as a basis for public affairs, see Joseph A. Schumpeter, *Capitalism, Socialism, and Democracy* (New York: Harper and Brothers, 1950), pp. 252–64. See also Ilya Somin, "Voter Ignorance and the Democratic Ideal," *Critical Theory* 12 (1998), 413–58.

their colleagues. One classic instance is "a memorable speech by Senator Redfield Proctor of Vermont after a visit to Cuba [in 1898, just before the United States launched the Spanish-American War]. The account by this anti-imperialist senior Republican of the devastation in the Cuban countryside made a deep impression and led even the skeptical to the conclusion that Spain had lost its claim to rule Cuba."[34] Similarly, during the passage of the Federal Reserve Act in 1913, "the gold reserve behind the Federal Reserve notes was increased from thirty-three to forty per cent, as a result of a single speech by Senator Elihu Root [R] of New York."[35]

As opinion leaders but also in many other roles, such as simply legislators, the case goes here, members of Congress are capable of acting with a degree of autonomy.[36] Indeed, the idea that they do *not* enjoy autonomy

34. James A. Henretta et al., *America's History*, vol. 2, *Since 1865*, 2d ed. (New York: Worth Publishers, 1993). The speech resonated beyond Capitol Hill: "The inhuman ghastliness [witnessed in Cuba by Proctor], described utterly without emotion or affect, did more to inflame Americans than three years of Frederic Remington's atrocity art in the *New York Journal*. Intervention now assumed the noble repose of the Lincolnesque Proctor, summoning a crusade to eradicate evil. Though Proctor took no role in coercing the administration in its Cuba policy, his speech legitimized intervention for those groups hitherto opposed" (p. 678). Ivan Musicant, *Empire by Default: The Spanish-American War and the Dawn of the American Century* (New York: Henry Holt and Company, 1998), p. 165. Note than Senator Proctor did not need to appear on *Larry King Live* to make such a mark.

35. Arthur S. Link, *Woodrow Wilson and the Progressive Era, 1910–1917* (New York: Harper and Brothers, 1954), pp. 52–53.

36. To a certain extent this result is formally induced, according to Bernard Manin in his recent analysis of the national representative systems of France, Britain, and the United States: "Representative systems do not authorize (indeed explicitly prohibit) two practices that would deprive representatives of any kind of independence: imperative mandates and discretionary revocability of representatives (recall). None of the representative governments established since the end of the eighteenth century has authorized imperative mandates or granted a legally binding status to the instructions given by the electorate. Neither has any of them durably applied permanent revocability of representatives" *(Principles of Representative Government,* p. 163).

is no better grounded in theory or evidence than the idea that they do; it is just a latticework of assertions, assumptions, and sometimes plausible demonstrations.[37] Yes, background political environments do ordinarily channel, influence, or constrain moves by politicians — but they do not determine them.[38] Furthermore, the case goes, actions of MCs are often worth watching and reckoning with. That is, an attentive stratum of the public will key in on a certain range of member actions as being *consequential, potentially consequential,* or *otherwise significant.* By "otherwise significant," I refer here to scattered instances[39] where the public seems to dwell on the meaningfulness, somehow, of MC moves even if they lack current or potential consequentiality. An example is Congresswoman Jeannette Rankin's (R-Mont.) lonely stance against declaring war on the Axis powers in December 1941 even after Pearl Harbor — an often-told story. "Potentially consequential" is the largest category here; it includes such staple MC moves as introducing bills, delivering speeches on contested issues, assailing possibly changeable White House policies,

37. It is an oddity of social science that its practitioners routinely credit their own originality and autonomy for demonstrating that the people they study do not possess those same qualities — that those people's behavior and actions are otherwise explainable.

38. The late V. O. Key, Jr., wrote: "[A] wide range of discretion exists for whatever wisdom leadership echelons can muster in the public service. The generality of public preferences, the low intensity of the opinions of many people, the low level of political animosities of substantial sectors of the public, the tortuousness of the process of translation of disapproval of specific policies into electoral reprisal, and many other factors point to the existence of a wide latitude for the exercise of creative leadership. While the winning of consent for innovation may require skill in popular exposition and in political technique, those political leaders who shirk the task of popular education are misfits who do not understand the responsibilities of their jobs" (p. 555). Key, *Public Opinion and American Democracy* (New York: Knopf, 1961).

39. Probably less than 1 percent of this study's dataset. There is no need to allocate the dataset's 2,304 items into these categories of consequential, potentially consequential, and otherwise significant.

or launching their own candidacies for the presidency. Such moves as the introduction of the Wagner-Murray-Dingell bill calling for comprehensive national health insurance in the 1940s and Senator Phil Gramm (R-Tex.) announcing for the presidency in 1996 can exhibit major potential and be worth monitoring (although, in fact, both these moves failed).

Some MC moves stand out, however, for their direct, immediate consequentiality—as perceived at the time and, for the most part, since.[40] The case for consequentiality might seem obvious, but let me try to nail it down with some particularly apt historical instances: Without Senator Henry Clay, arguably no Compromise of 1850; without Stephen A. Douglas, no Kansas-Nebraska Act in 1854; absent Charles Sumner's opposition, President Grant might have gotten away with annexing Santo Domingo in 1870; in a Senate lacking Henry Cabot Lodge, who can say what would have happened to the League of Nations in 1919; without Senator George W. Norris, probably no Tennessee Valley Authority; without Congressman Richard M. Nixon (R-Calif.), no exposure of Alger Hiss by the House Un-American Activities Committee in 1948; without Congressman Adam Clayton Powell, Jr. (D-N.Y.), possibly no antisegregation moves of a "Powell amendment" sort in the 1950s; without Senator Lyndon B. Johnson (D-Tex.), possibly no Civil Rights Act of 1957; and lacking Senator Eugene McCarthy's (D-Minn.) challenge in the New Hampshire primary, President Johnson might have run for reelection in 1968.

40. A classic depiction of autonomous consequentiality in a politician—though not a member of Congress—is Robert A. Dahl's portrait of New Haven's Mayor Richard C. Lee in *Who Governs? Democracy and Power in an American City* (New Haven and London: Yale University Press, 1961), ch. 10. Without Lee, New Haven's pioneering steps in urban redevelopment during the 1950s would have been quite unlikely. For a recent appreciation of the autonomous consequentiality of House Speakers Henry Clay and Thomas B. Reed, see Randall Strahan, "Leadership in Institutional Time: The Nineteenth-Century House," paper delivered at History of Congress Conference, Stanford University, January 15–16, 1999.

Recent instances include the following: Without Bob Kerrey's affirmative vote (he nearly voted no),[41] Clinton's deficit-reduction plan might have failed in the Senate in 1993; without Newt Gingrich, no Contract with America; without Senator Edward M. Kennedy (D-MA), no minimum wage increase in 1996;[42] and without Henry J. Hyde, quite possibly no House impeachment of Clinton in 1998.[43]

To be sure, not every House or Senate member performs at the level of a Richard M. Nixon or an Edward M. Kennedy. Nothing more obviously leaps from the dataset assembled here than the immense *inequality*

41. See Bob Woodward, *The Agenda: Inside the Clinton White House* (New York: Simon and Schuster, 1994), pp. 303–9.

42. A comment on Kennedy's place in the Senate as of 1998: "But when it comes to legislative prowess, he's in the prime of his career. In this Republican-run Congress, the liberal Sen. Kennedy is arguably the most influential member on either side of either aisle. . . . In the 104th Congress, he crafted health care portability legislation with Nancy Kassebaum and spearheaded the first increase in the minimum wage in more than a decade. With Sen. Orrin Hatch (R., Utah), last year he pushed through a children's health care initiative. . . . A brilliant legislative pragmatist, he always makes short-term accommodations—if it advances his goals. . . . [Senate Majority Leader Trent Lott], according to associates, is driven crazy by Sen. Kennedy's restlessness and ability to cherry-pick Republicans on key issues" (p. A23). Albert R. Hunt, "The Liberal Lion Roars Louder Than Ever," *Wall Street Journal*, February 19, 1998.

43. "Mr. Hyde's reluctance gradually turned to resolve and his hesitation to absolute certainty. When Mr. Clinton was impeached . . . , it was in no small measure as a result of Mr. Hyde's determination to press forward. . . . Ralph Reed, the Republican strategist, who knows Mr. Hyde well, said: 'They mistook a teddy bear exterior for a soft core. If he feels strongly about something, he'll fight harder than anyone'" (p. 16). Melinda Henneberger, "How Henry Hyde's Resolve Was Shaped Against Clinton," *New York Times*, January 10, 1999, pp. 1, 16. From another detailed account: "But like much in politics, the drive to remove the president was kept in motion by a committed few who cared enough to push. Led by House Judiciary Committee Chairman Henry J. Hyde (R-Ill.) and Majority Whip Tom DeLay (R-Tex.), they dominated the process, even as their single-mindedness helped seal their [later Senate] defeat" (p. A1). Peter Baker et al., "The Train That Wouldn't Stop; Key Players Thwarted Attempts to Derail Process," *Washington Post*, February 14, 1999, pp. A1, A26–28.

among MCs in the conspicuousness of their performances. Some members prove to be vastly more significant than others—a result at odds with the formal roll-call voting equality that each house extends to all its members, and considerably beyond any pecking order associated with formal leadership posts or committee chairmanships. Talent and drive seem to make the chief difference.

This is more of a supply-side account of congressional politics than is to be found in most works on the subject. It is the equivalent of studying economics by examining what Bill Gates, George Soros, Michael Milken, and others do, not by dwelling on demand curves. One author I have consulted in thinking about MC "actions" is Joseph A. Schumpeter, who, in his 1911 work *The Theory of Economic Development*, isolated and discussed the role of capitalist "entrepreneurs."[44] Briefly, that role is "the carrying out of new combinations." Members of Congress arguably play a similar role as "political entrepreneurs"—at least, sometimes.[45] I have followed Schumpeter in highlighting the nature of a phenomenon rather than its causes. He zeroed in on what entrepreneurs do; he saw them as motivated by a variety of considerations, and that was a secondary matter.

Another author I have drawn from is Hannah Arendt, with her concept of "political action"—the unique exercise of freedom that she argues the ancient Greeks and, later, the French and American revolutionaries of

44. Joseph A. Schumpeter, *The Theory of Economic Development* (New York: Oxford University Press, 1961), pp. 74–94 (original edition, 1911). See also Manfred Prisching, "The Limited Rationality of Democracy: Schumpeter as the Founder of Irrational Choice Theory," *Critical Review* 9 (1995), 307–13; Jon Elster, *Explaining Technical Change: A Case Study in the Philosophy of Science* (New York: Cambridge University Press, 1983), ch. 5. For a historical account that emphasizes achievements by entrepreneurs, see Alfred D. Chandler, Jr., *The Visible Hand: The Managerial Revolution in American Business* (Cambridge: Harvard University Press, 1977).

45. For a portrait of MCs as entrepreneurs in policy realms, see David Price, *Who Makes the Laws? Creativity and Power in Senate Committees* (Cambridge, Mass.: Schenkman, 1972).

the late eighteenth century engaged in as they devised new constitutions or guarded established ones from eroding.[46] Any such Arendtian "political action" has fallen to near-zero levels in modern Western mass publics, though she allows that it may survive better in a certain kind of elected assembly: "[The U.S.] Constitution itself provided a public sphere only for the representatives of the people, and not for the people themselves."[47]

The U.S. Congress, it should be obvious, churns along ordinarily at a very sub-Arendtian level. Yet as I gathered my dataset I was struck by how often I came across MC actions that raised or provoked what looked like constitutional questions—ones about the geographic extent, organizational structure, autonomy from foreign intrusions or commitments, operating rules, citizenship rights, boundaries between state and society, or basic political economy of the U.S. regime.[48] Those questions have included: The right to oppose the government (as in the controversy surrounding the Sedition Act of 1798); U.S. autonomy from French or English intrusion during the European wars of 1793–1815; presidential veto and appointment powers (as during Andrew Jackson's presidency); free speech (as with the antislavery petitions in the 1830s and 1840s); territorial expansion through purchase and conquest; the spread, containment, or abolition of slavery; the defeat and reconstruction of the South in the 1860s; rights to equal protection and due process (as in

46. Hannah Arendt, *On Revolution* (New York: Viking, 1963), ch. 6. I have profited from the excellent analysis in George Kateb, *Hannah Arendt: Politics, Conscience, Evil* (Totowa, N.J.: Rowman and Allanheld, 1983), ch. 1 ("The Theory of Political Action").

47. Arendt, *On Revolution*, p. 241.

48. In addressing politics at a constitutional level, this work shares an emphasis with Bruce Ackerman's recent *We the People: Foundations* (Cambridge: Harvard University Press, 1991). My treatment differs from Ackerman's in two respects: I center on elected politicians rather than members of the mass public as constitutional actors, and I see constitutional action as being sprawled throughout U.S. history rather than concentrated at Ackerman's three key junctures (the Founding, the Civil War and Reconstruction, and the New Deal).

the adoption of the Fourteenth Amendment in the 1860s); the power and reach of patronage-based political parties (as in showdowns between the president and the Senate over appointments around 1880); U.S. imperialism in Asia and Latin America; the construction of a national welfare and regulatory state; whether to enter world organizations or foreign alliances (as with the League of Nations in 1919 and NATO in 1949); the autonomy of the courts (as in the controversy over Franklin Roosevelt's court-packing plan in 1937); loyalty to the regime (as during the McCarthy era); suffrage rights (as in the passage of the Voting Rights Act in 1965); and presidential warmaking powers (recurrently, though with particular intensity during the Vietnam War).

Not all MC actions, in short, notwithstanding the content of U.S. politics in much of the 1990s, are at the level of wrangling over the budget, expanding or shrinking this or that program, loosening or tightening this or that regulation, or raising the minimum wage. A common move in contemporary political science is to treat constitutions as exogenous—that is, to stipulate that they exist and then get on with the business of tracking the "normal politics" centering on economic policy that takes place under their rules.[49] In my view, this can be a historical and analytic mistake. Constitutions do not seem to march through time unattended by politicians. In the United States, it is impossible to comprehend the roles of House and Senate members without seeing them as, at least sometimes, performers at a constitutional level.

In two ways, this book offers a more "republican" picture of congressional politics than we are accustomed to. First, as the concept of "republican" faces off against that of "democratic," as in Madison's usage in *The Federalist*,[50] the emphasis here is on MC leeway from constitu-

49. As in Anthony Downs, *An Economic Theory of Democracy* (New York: Harper and Row, 1957), p. 12.

50. For a recent discussion of Madison's ideas, see Manin, *Principles of Representative*

ency influence. "Shirking," to use the current locution for lack of lockstep obedience to constituency wishes, is an important ingredient in the job description for MCs—and has been since 1787. To be sure, an accountability relation exists through future elections in which MC actions may need to be "explained" to constituencies.[51] Second, as "republican" faces off against classical "liberal," the emphasis here is on the endogeneity of politics.[52] This is the idea that preference formation, deliberation, and policymaking all tend to occur in a "public sphere" that engages both elected officials and at least an attentive sector of the public—as opposed to the idea that exogenously formed "interests" somehow simply penetrate into official processes to be registered. Methodologically speaking, these background considerations seem to call for a kind of exploration of the territory rather than a causal analysis, and that is the purpose of the chapters to come.

Government. "Madison did not see representation as an approximation of government by the people made technically necessary by the physical impossibility of gathering together the citizens of large states. On the contrary, he saw it as an essentially different and superior political system. The effect of representation, he observed, is 'to refine and enlarge the public views'" (p. 2). See also Gordon S. Wood, *The Creation of the American Republic, 1776–1787* (New York: Norton, 1969), ch. 15; Emery G. Lee III, "Representation, Virtue, and Political Jealousy in the Brutus-Publius Dialogue," *Journal of Politics* 59 (1997), 1073–95.

51. As in the traditional Burkean model, or in Fenno, *Home Style.*

52. See Sunstein, "Beyond the Republican Revival," pp. 1548–51.

Canvassing for Actions Through American History

The opening sketch of Chapter 1 grew from the following assignment I gave myself in 1995: Write a sketch of U.S. national politics and policymaking during 1993–94, centering on particularly conspicuous actions by members of the House and Senate. I wrote from memory as a close observer of public affairs during those years. If several close observers had each been asked to write a sketch like that, probably no two of them would have identified exactly the same events or participants. Unanimous mention of, for example, Senator Dole's opposition to the Clinton health-care plan would fade into spottier coverage of Senator Riegle's Whitewater hearings or Congressman Cooper's alternative health-care plan. Yet the results would be recognizable as a "family" of related accounts.

Now imagine a series of such sketches (or families of them) for each Congress from 1789 through the present, all written by contemporary observers. It would add up to a very long story. Looked at one way, the result would be a two-centuries-long extract from the U.S. collective political consciousness. As a story, such a series might dissatisfy us in at least one respect. It might cry out for "weighting." If the hundred-odd sketches each turned out to contain roughly the same number of conspicuous MC actions, which might happen if each two-year sketch were written in isolation from the rest of history, we would say that that makes little sense. In fact, according to any longer-term historical perspective, certain Congresses have generated many more conspicuous actions than others; somehow that consideration needs to be taken into account. Fortunately, that might be done using the same sources—by calling on contemporary observers to place their present Congresses in a context with past remembered ones and accordingly standardize the criteria for "conspicuous actions." It is a sure bet, for example, that if observers of the Second Congress of 1791–93 were asked to size it up in light of the event-packed First Congress of 1789–91—when the Bill of Rights was adopted, the federal courts and executive agencies were designed, and Secretary Hamilton's controversial blueprints for a national bank and federal assumption of state debts were approved—they would have listed many fewer conspicuous MC actions for 1791–93 than for 1789–91.

Of course, no such stock of contemporary sketches exists, and none is ever likely to exist. A fallback is required. As a practical matter, the closest available approximation to such sketches is a stock of existing writing by historians in a genre that might be called "public affairs history." Writers in this genre, such as Arthur S. Link, William E. Leuchtenburg, and John Morton Blum, serve up careful narrative accounts of U.S. national politics and policymaking. This is a familiar literary form, but note one key feature of it: In dealing with an era, whatever else their aims might be, such authors try to pick up and transmit to us a past collective understanding, at least among the politically aware back then, of what was going on. In doing this they transmit, among other things, past understandings about which politicians have recently and notably done what: "La Follette filibustered the bill for three hours" . . . "Mills and Byrnes struck a deal on Medicare" . . . "Then Goldwater went in and advised Nixon to resign" . . . "Clay put together the winning compromise" . . . "Eastland buried the bill in committee" . . . "McCarthy lashed back at the Tydings

Committee." When we come across statements like these in a public affairs history book, the odds are we are confronting events that were at least fairly widely known and taken into account during those politicians' times. Those of us who remember Congressman Wilbur Mills (D-Ark.), Senator James Eastland (D-Miss.), and Senator Joseph McCarthy can attest to that. Hence the utility of the public affairs genre as a window into past collective consciousness. Any future public affairs historian writing about the early Clinton years will very likely document many of the same items I did in my Chapter 1 sketch.

More needs to be said about approaching history books this way, but first I would like to discuss which works I used and how I used them. Briefly, my data strategy for this project was to ransack dozens of works on public affairs history for mentions of actions by members of the House and Senate, then shape those mentioned actions into a dataset.

I ended up using thirty-eight works in all, five of which may be described as "general histories" and thirty-three as "era histories." Each of the "general histories" is a one- or two-volume multiply authored college text that covers—in addition to the colonial era, which is irrelevant here—the full two centuries of U.S. national history from 1789 through the early 1990s. These are standard works. They are not just public affairs histories—they cover other topics and have other aims—but they are at least public affairs histories. To select them I first made a list of all the currently marketed U.S. history texts—there were thirteen—addressed in either of two discussions of the genre in the March 1993 issue of the *Journal of American History*. Next, I trimmed that number to six by zeroing in on those dated 1992 or later as of spring 1994 (I wanted up-to-date coverage) and then dropped one with a defective index (I needed to use the indexes) to arrive at the five works listed at the top of Table 2.1.[1]

1. The two discussions of the genre are: Dorothy Sue Cobble and Alice Kessler-Harris, "The New Labor History in American History Textbooks," *Journal of American History* 79

These general histories play two distinct roles in my design. First, they show which past MC actions, or kinds of actions, today's historians tend to reach for when space is precious and few items from any era can be accommodated. With so many topics and years to cover, the entry standards for items have to be high. Second, they function as overviews. Each "general history" results from a multicentury plan by a team of authors; they make collective decisions—at least rough ones—about which eras, junctures, or topics to cover and how much emphasis they should receive. This offers an overall design ingredient likely to be less present in any collection of "era histories" each written by a different author.

In order to obtain greater depth and detail, however, I needed to canvass "era histories"—that is, works of a scope suggested by such titles as *The Federalist Era* and *The Jacksonian Era*. Here my major step was to reach for the sixteen works of the respected New American Nation Series that address consecutive time spans between 1789 and 1945 as well as, in a recent volume, the 1960s. (See Table 2.1 for "era histories.") Eleven of these works were published between 1954 and 1968, one in the mid-1970s, four in the 1980s. Certain of the New American Nation Series volumes differ in focus from the rest—three dwell on wars, and Eric Foner's 1988 work gives detailed attention to social movements, state politics, and southern society in addressing Reconstruction—yet all sixteen of them, whatever else they do, cover U.S. national politics and policymaking. It seemed to me that if any large group of individually authored works on all (or almost all) of U.S. history could be said to exhibit a plan — about allocation of time spans, what to cover, and how deep to go—the New American Nation Series does that. An impressive level of design seems possible even when many independent authors are involved.

(1993), 1534–45; and Peter G. Filene, "Narrating Progressivism: Unitarians v. Pluralists v. Students," *Journal of American History* 79 (1993), 1546–62.

Next, using the New American Nation Series as a standard for type and depth of coverage, I added a second layer of "era histories" addressing the century and a half from 1789 through 1945. This was done to help iron out two kinds of wrinkles: Individual writers' idiosyncrasies, whatever they might be (for this purpose, two separately authored works on the same subject are probably better than one); and various analytic impulses that have figured in historians' writing at different times since World War II. To the latter end, I tried to balance works published in the 1950s or 1960s with ones published in the 1980s or later. Usually, though not always, this could be done. An instance of ideal pairing is John C. Miller's *Federalist Era*, published in 1960, with James Roger Sharp's *American Politics in the Early Republic*, published in 1993.[2] In Table 2.1, the time spans covered by the additional works are often longer than, and do not neatly match, those of the New American Nation Series works. As a consequence, once all sources are considered, certain stretches of time have received relatively shallow or in-depth coverage.[3] This effect is unavoidable and does not seem problematic; writers who address the same past juncture do, after all, tend to tell similar stories.

Finally, aiming for the same kind and scale of coverage, I chose post–World War II "era histories" (in addition to the New American Nation Series's Matusow volume on the 1960s). This was easy enough through Nixon's presidency, given the availability of works squarely in the public affairs tradition by Eric F. Goldman, Dewey W. Grantham, and John Mor-

2. For purposes here, the Sharp volume was more suitable than Stanley Elkins and Eric McKitrick, *The Age of Federalism* (New York: Oxford University Press, 1993), which has much more detail than either the Miller or the Sharp work.

3. Using the New American Nation Series definition of eras, and taking into account the number of non-NAN Series volumes used partly or wholly here for each era as well as the detail of coverage supplied by them, the era "most under-covered" by the non-NAN Series list is probably 1801–15. There is no obvious candidate for "most over-covered" era.

Table 2.1 Works of "Public Affairs History" Used

General history works

Bernard Bailyn, Robert Dallek, David Brion Davis, David Herbert Donald, John L. Thomas, and Gordon S. Wood, *The Great Republic,* 4th ed. (Lexington, Mass.: D.C. Heath, 1992), 2 vols.

Paul S. Boyer, Clifford E. Clark, Jr., Joseph F. Kett, Neal Salisbury, Harvard Sitkoff, and Nancy Woloch, *The Enduring Vision: A History of the American People,* 2d ed. (Lexington, Mass.: D.C. Heath, 1993), 2 vols.

James West Davidson, William E. Gienapp, Christine Leigh Heyrman, Mark H. Lytle, and Michael B. Stoff, *Nation of Nations: A Narrative History of the American Republic,* 2d ed. (New York: McGraw-Hill, 1994), 2 vols.

James A. Henretta, W. Elliot Brownlee, David Brody, and Susan Ware, *America's History,* 2d ed. (New York: Worth, 1993), 2 vols.

Winthrop D. Jordan and Leon F. Litwack, *The United States,* 4th ed. (Englewood Cliffs, N.J.: Prentice Hall, 1994).

Era history works

*John C. Miller, *The Federalist Era, 1789–1801* (New York: Harper and Row, 1960).

James Roger Sharp, *American Politics in the Early Republic: The New Nation in Crisis* (New Haven: Yale University Press, 1993).

*Marshall Smelser, *The Democratic Republic, 1801–1815* (New York: Harper and Row, 1968).

*George Dangerfield, *The Awakening of American Nationalism, 1815–1828* (New York: Harper and Row, 1965).

John Mayfield, *The New Nation: 1800–1845* (New York: Hill and Wang, 1982, revised ed. of 1961 work of the same title by Charles M. Wiltse).

*Glyndon G. Van Deusen, *The Jacksonian Era, 1828–1848* (New York: Harper and Bros., 1959).

Daniel Feller, *The Jacksonian Promise: America, 1815–1840* (Baltimore: Johns Hopkins University Press, 1995).

*David M. Potter, *The Impending Crisis, 1848–1861* (New York: Harper and Row, 1976).

J. G. Randall and David Donald, *The Civil War and Reconstruction,* 2d ed. (Lexington, Mass.: D.C. Heath, 1969).

*Phillip Shaw Paludan, *'A People's Contest': The Union and Civil War, 1861–1865* (New York: Harper and Row, 1988).

*Eric Foner, *Reconstruction: America's Unfinished Revolution, 1863–1877* (New York: Harper and Row, 1988).

*John A. Garraty, *The New Commonwealth, 1877–1890* (New York: Harper and Row, 1968).

Sean Dennis Cashman, *America in the Gilded Age: From the Death of Lincoln to the Rise of Theodore Roosevelt* (New York: New York University Press, 1984).

*Harold U. Faulkner, *Politics, Reform, and Expansion, 1890–1900* (New York: Harper and Bros., 1959).

Table 2.1 (*continued*)

R. Hal Williams, *Years of Decision: American Politics in the 1890s* (New York: Prospect Heights, Ill.: Waveland, 1978).

*George E. Mowry, *The Era of Theodore Roosevelt, 1900–1912* (New York: Harper and Row, 1958).

John Milton Cooper, Jr., *Pivotal Decades: The United States, 1900–1920* (New York: Norton, 1990).

*Arthur S. Link, *Woodrow Wilson and the Progressive Era, 1910–1917* (New York: Harper and Bros., 1954).

*Robert H. Ferrell, *Woodrow Wilson and World War I, 1917–1921* (New York: Harper and Row, 1985).

*John D. Hicks, *Republican Ascendancy, 1921–1933* (New York: Harper and Bros., 1960).

Geoffrey Perrett, *America in the Twenties: A History* (New York: Simon and Schuster, 1982).

Michael E. Parrish, *Anxious Decades: America in Prosperity and Depression, 1920–1941* (New York: Norton, 1992).

*William E. Leuchtenburg, *Franklin D. Roosevelt and the New Deal, 1932–1940* (New York: Harper and Row, 1963).

*A. Russell Buchanan, *The United States and World War II* (New York: Harper and Row, 1964), 2 vols.

John Morton Blum, *V Was for Victory: Politics and American Culture During World War II* (New York: Harcourt Brace Jovanovich, 1976).

Eric F. Goldman, *The Crucial Decade—And After: America, 1945–1960* (New York: Knopf, 1973).

Dewey W. Grantham, *Recent America: The United States Since 1945* (Arlington Heights, Ill.: Harlan Davidson, 1989).

*Allen J. Matusow, *The Unraveling of America: A History of Liberalism in the 1960s* (New York: Harper and Row, 1984).

John Morton Blum, *Years of Discord: American Politics and Society, 1961–1974* (New York: Norton, 1991).

Burton I. Kaufman, *The Presidency of James Earl Carter, Jr.* (Lawrence: University Press of Kansas, 1993).

Michael Schaller, *Reckoning with Reagan: America and Its President in the 1980s* (New York: Oxford University Press, 1992).

David Mervin, *Ronald Reagan and the American Presidency* (New York: Longman, 1990).

Michael Barone, *Our Country: The Shaping of America from Roosevelt to Reagan* (New York: Free Press, 1990).

* A work in the New American Nation series.

ton Blum.[4] But only Grantham's volume continues that line past 1974. I made do through 1988 by reaching for academic narratives treating the Carter and Reagan presidencies; these works are more presidency-centered than I would have liked, but they provide information about national politics in general. Also, I added coverage of the 1970s, 1980s, and several earlier decades by using Michael Barone's *Our Country: The Shaping of America from Roosevelt to Reagan.* This work, by a nonacademic, emphasizes elections more than do standard public affairs histories, but that is largely irrelevant here; the attraction is Barone's careful, event-rich coverage of Washington politics and policymaking. The late 1970s and 1980s are undeniably a problem for this analysis; the dataset for these years, compared with earlier entries, is too scanty and possibly skewed in some ways, though it seems acceptable for some purposes. Beyond 1988 I could not go. Usable histories do not yet exist.

Here is how I used each one of the five "general" and thirty-three "era" histories. In the first of two investigations of each volume, I scanned the index line by line, cross-checking in the *Biographical Directory of the American Congress* as I went along, to locate the names of all members of Congress and take certain steps when I found one. Let us say I came across Henry Clay's name in an index and identified him. My next move was to establish exactly when he served in the House or Senate. (I was interested in tracking what Clay did in, say, 1824 when he was a House member but *not* in, say, 1826 when he was Secretary of State.) Then I broke up Clay's index entry into its individual page references and, one by one, checked them out in the text. If a trail led to mention of an "action" by Clay—in principle, anything of any kind done by Clay—at a time when he was a member of Congress, I tagged that item for the dataset. In the second investigation, I read each volume from cover to cover to catch any

---

4. Also now available is James T. Patterson, *Grand Expectations: The United States, 1945–74* (New York: Oxford University Press, 1996).

"actions" I might have missed the first time (in some cases because they had not been indexed), and to spot prose passages that could be sorted more sensitively into "actions" given the availability of the extended narrative context. This served as a check on the first, intentionally mechanical, index-driven methodology. In effect, I used the second investigation of each volume to edit the yield of the first.

By an "action," I mean, in principle, "*doing* something." That designation was easy to make in instances where a member, for example, made a speech, introduced an amendment, filibustered a bill, conducted a hearing, ran for president, maneuvered somebody else's presidential nomination, advised the president, or, in the case of enraged southern Congressman Preston Brooks (States Right Dem-S.C.), caned Charles Sumner on the floor of the Senate in 1856, nearly killing him, as payback for the Massachusetts senator's "Crime against Kansas" speech. Those are all active verbs. But I aimed also for implied action, as in instances where a member "was appointed to the Cabinet" (that is ordinarily a career move), "was seriously considered for the presidency" (that was a nineteenth-century kind of career move), was accused of corruption or other misbehavior or censured (the alleged misdeed is the action),[5] or was said to be a "powerful" leader or committee chair or a state party "boss" (the powerfulness implies action).[6] At the outer fringe of "action" I included instances of what we call today "descriptive representation"—as in Hiram Revels's (R-Miss.) joining the Senate in 1870 as its first African-American mem-

5. Probably in all instances thus coded, a member had actually done *something* that drew the accusation or the censure, though in most cases whether the behavior deserved the opprobrium assigned to it was at least partly a disputed political or ethical question.

6. I take an attribution of "powerfulness" or "boss" status to imply in summary fashion that an MC had a record of performing political "actions" and was believed capable of performing more. Note that *blocking* something can be an "action," as when a "powerful" floor leader or state "boss" is said to take steps to ward off dissent, or a "powerful" committee chair bottles up a bill.

ber, which is customarily noted by historians. The point here is that a member like Revels arguably possesses the potential to act representatively in a distinctive way.[7] But in general I steered clear of instances of *being* as opposed to *doing*—as in reports that somebody "was" a member or "was" a formal leader (some formal leaders are ciphers, after all). I ignored reports that members were targets, as with Brown in "Smith lashed out at Brown," unless there was evidence that the victims did something notable to earn their target status. I ignored reports that members retired, died, or lost their seats in elections—and also, on the ground of triviality, routine reports that they won their seats in elections.

In Chapter 1 I argued that members of Congress can be autonomously consequential. In general, the "actions" being addressed here seem like good candidates for that designation, though not always. One soft spot came with a decision to count as "actions" all instances where MCs' names have been memorialized in eponymous labels such as "the Kassebaum-Kennedy Act of 1996"—the recent measure aiming to guarantee portability of health insurance across jobs. In fact, Senators Nancy Kassebaum (R-Kans.) and Edward Kennedy both did play significant roles in enacting that law; as a counterfactual speculation, it seems a good bet that a Senate otherwise true to history yet lacking either or both of these individuals in relevant committee posts in 1996 would not have passed it. Throughout U.S. history, major congressional entrepreneurs have left their names on such instruments as the McCarran Internal Security Act of 1950, the Wagner Act of 1935, the McKinley Tariff of 1890, the Crittenden Compromise of 1860–61, and the Wilmot Proviso of 1946.[8] Yet in an appreciable share of such measures named after members—I had no

7. Lest the reader worry that I am wandering too far from "action" with this category, I should say that fewer than 1 percent of the items in the dataset are coded as "descriptive representation."

8. Not all these cited measures became law, but a proposal can be significant without being successful.

way of telling which ones or how many—the named MC probably chaired a committee handling a bill and won the eponym for that reason without being very consequential. An example is Congressman Edward T. Taylor's (D-Colo.) slight role in the enactment of the Taylor Grazing Act of 1934.[9] Taylor and no doubt many others like him entered the dataset here anyway.

For the most part, spotting "actions" in the texts was a straightforward task, but there was no escape from making certain judgments about inclusion or exclusion. There arose a quotations problem. Often, MCs are quoted in histories because what they said was typical or representative—one senses that the *Congressional Record* was searched by the history book's author for illustrative material—rather than because it was influential or for some other reason particularly noted or noteworthy. For "actions" I was interested in the latter kind of statement but not the former, and I used as a test whether surrounding discussion in the histories pointed to the latter. There was a recurrent "such as" problem—as in a report that "senators such as Smith and Brown called for impeachment." I was interested if specifically Smith and Brown made or led that move; I was not if they just typified some larger set of performers. Again, I relied on surrounding text to supply the clues. A problem of list-making occasionally arose, as when, say, half a dozen senators were all said to "take the lead" on something. I trimmed several such lists to their evidently principal actors, though I stayed with full lists where the weight of a small group seemed to make a difference at a key policy juncture—

9. See William Voigt, Jr., *Public Grazing Lands: Use and Misuse by Industry and Government* (New Brunswick, N.J.: Rutgers University Press, 1976), p. 249. In coding, I did allow for a distinction between cases where MCs were named in a bill label and also discussed as playing a role in handling the measure, and cases where MCs were just named in a bill label. With the latter subset, however, there is no way to trace accurately what the MCs in question actually did without going beyond the "public affairs histories" to many specialized or primary sources.

as with six members of a Democratic "junto" who apparently committed President Pierce to signing the Kansas-Nebraska Act in 1854, four participants in the "Wormley House bargain" associated with settling the Hayes-Tilden election crisis of 1876–77, eight so-called irreconcilable Senate opponents of the League of Nations in 1919, and nine isolationist senators who went to the wall against U.S. involvement in European affairs as World War II broke out during 1939–40. Finally, I gave myself license, though I used it sparingly, to ignore text mentions that appeared fleeting or trivial by the authors' own standards—such as references to the lesser ranks of "favorite son" candidates at nineteenth-century nominating conventions.[10]

It also took judgment to harmonize differences in historians' accounts when they covered the same member of Congress playing a prominent, complicated role over a period of time—as did, for example, Senator Henry Clay in pressing his legislative program in 1841, or Congressman Thaddeus Stevens (R-Pa.) in promoting Reconstruction policies in 1865–67. In cases like this I had to resolve the varying narratives into a few discrete "actions." And sometimes, even if only one author was involved, I had to decide whether a member's performance over time amounted to just one "action" or more than one. I was guided by the way it was discussed in the histories. The McNary-Haugen bill, for example—the high-profile agricultural crop-support plan of the 1920s that never did become law—earned three "action" items for each of its cosponsors be-

10. In one burst of detail, J. G. Randall and David Donald discuss sixteen possible candidates, including three members of Congress, for the Democratic presidential nomination of 1868. One of the three, Senator Thomas A. Hendricks (D-Ind.), is listed among eight "leading Democratic contenders." The other two are among eight "less likely possibilities" (p. 639). Randall and Donald, *The Civil War and Reconstruction*, 2d ed. (Lexington, Mass.: D.C. Heath, 1969). I included Hendricks in my dataset but disregarded the other two.

cause it passed and was vetoed during three different Congresses and, in general, has been treated by historians as entailing three distinct events.

Each "member action" that made it into the dataset was coded for:

- The name, party, state, region, and legislative branch (Senate or House) of the MC who performed it, as well as his or her age and congressional tenure at the time it was performed.[11] Tenure was coded as number of Congresses served in consecutively by a member in the same house at the time of the action (this is the conventional measure of "seniority"), as well as, separately, total number of Congresses served in by the member at that time, regardless of whether in the House or Senate or whether the service was consecutive.[12]

- The Congress and year during which it occurred. Strictly speaking, some 15 percent of the actions had to be coded as extending across two

11. More specifically, "age" is the difference between the calendar year of the action and the calendar year of the actor's birth. "Party" is coded only for 1861 through 1988; before 1861, there is a problem of complicated data on party membership. "Region" refers only to South (the eleven secession states plus Kentucky and Oklahoma) versus non-South.

12. Whether a member "served in" a particular Congress might seem easy to code for, but messy problems did arise. How should one handle, for example, the instance where a newly elected senator assumes a seat immediately after a November election (the incumbent has died or resigned) rather than when the new Congress meets in January, thus technically joining briefly the "old" Congress even though that Congress may have adjourned forever back in September? Senator John Sherman Cooper (R-Ky.) pulled this off three times (in 1946, 1952, and 1956)! How about the nineteenth-century MC-elect who filled a seat on schedule in March of an odd year but resigned before the new Congress actually assembled for a first session in December? My decision rule was to count a Congress toward an MC's service record only if that member held a seat in it for at least one day *while it was in session*. There is one lightly populated class of exceptions: if an MC contributed an "action" to this dataset (such as running for president) during a Congress's off-session time, the Congress counts toward the member's service record even if the member never served a day while the Congress was in session.

or more years, and some 3.5 percent as extending across two or more Congresses. (An example of the latter is John Quincy Adams's campaign to win admittance of the antislavery petitions, which extended from 1835 through 1844.) Yet for analytic convenience here, all actions are treated in statistical calculations as if they took place during their first year and first Congress.[13]

- The prominence of its mention in the history books. An action earned a "C" if it was noted in only one work (whether a "general" or an "era" history); a "B" if it was noted in two or more works yet not more than one "general" history; an "A" if it met the stiffest requirement of being noted in at least two "general" histories.

- The kind of an action it was—such as legislating, taking a stand, conducting an investigation, or running for president. I coded for forty-three categories in all. They are listed and discussed at the close of this chapter. The coding is multiple—that is, an action could be assigned to more than one "kind," and many were. In one 1953 action, for example, Senator Joseph McCarthy is scored as conducting an investigation and also taking a stand.

At this point, it may help to exhibit some concrete results of these data manipulations. The accompanying tables do this for two selected slices of time. Table 2.2 presents the list of coded "actions" for the back-to-back Congresses of 1817–19 and 1819–21 under President Monroe, when slavery erupted as a national issue as Missouri sought statehood. A long series of legislative moves ended in the Missouri Compromise.[14] (Items within each Congress are listed alphabetically by member.) Table 2.3

13. The only exception to this guideline is Table 5.3, in Chapter 5 of this volume.

14. On the contemporary reporting of the Missouri controversy: "Historians have been impressed by the amount of coverage in local papers and the work of the new antislavery organizations to further popularize the arguments. Citizens in every state had an opportunity to share the mood of crisis in Washington." This is despite the fact that verbatim texts of congressional debates did not yet exist. Thomas C. Leonard, *The Power*

Table 2.2 Member Actions in the Fifteenth and Sixteenth Congresses

Year of Action	Actor	State	S or H	Text Sources[1]	Kind of Action	Content of Action
Fifteenth Congress						
1817	John C. Calhoun	S.C.	H	C	Take appointment	Appointed Secretary of War
1818	Henry Clay	Ky.	H	C	Take stand	Champions Lat. Am. republics
1819	Henry Clay	Ky.	H	C	Counsel pres.	Gives Monroe info. re Florida
1819	Henry Clay	Ky.	H	C	Censure	Presses censure of Gen. Jackson
1819	John Scott	Mo.	H[2]	C	Legislate Take stand	Argues vs. Tallmadge amdt.
1819	John W. Taylor	N.Y.	H	C	Legislate Take stand	Aids Tallmadge with his amdt.
1819	James Tallmadge, Jr.	N.Y.	H	A	Legislate Leg. eponym Take stand	Tallmadge amdt. to bar slavery in Missouri
Sixteenth Congress						
1821	James Barbour	Va.	S	C	Rules, pres. select.	Offers way to count Mo. votes
1819	Henry Clay	Ky.	H	C	Run for leader Leader	Elected Speaker
1820–21	Henry Clay	Ky.	H	A	Legislate, leader Take stand	Leader in Missouri Compromise
1821	Henry Clay	Ky.	H	C	Rules, pres. select.	Formula for counting elec. votes
1820	John H. Eaton	Tenn.	S	C	Legislate	Moves proviso re Mo. Comp.
1821	Samuel Foote	Conn.	S	C	Legislate	Amdt. re status of Missouri
1820	John Holmes	Mass.	H	C	Legislate Take stand	Says New Yorkers raise slavery to promote a new party
1820	Rufus King	N.Y.	S	B	Legislate Take stand	Antislavery stand re Missouri
1820	William Lowndes	S.C.	H	C	Legislate Take stand	Promotes proslavery view

Table 2.2 (*continued*)

Year of Action	Actor	State	S or H	Text Sources[1]	Kind of Action	Content of Action
1820	Nathaniel Macon	N.C.	S	B	Legislate, speech Take stand	Strong proslavery speech
1820	Charles Pinckney	S.C.	S	B	Legislate, speech Take stand	Eloquent reply to North re Missouri
1819–21	John Randolph	Va.	S	C	Legislate Take stand	Opposes admission of new states
1820	Jonathan Roberts	Pa.	S	B	Legislate Take stand	Antislavery move re Missouri
1820	William Smith	S.C.	S	C	Legislate Take stand	Presents proslavery arguments
1820	John W. Taylor	N.Y.	H	B	Run for leader	Elected Speaker on 22d ballot
1820	John W. Taylor	N.Y.	H	B	Legislate, speech Take stand	Antislavery amdt. re Missouri
1820	Jesse B. Thomas	Ill.	S	C	Legislate Leg. eponym	Thomas amdt. to bar slavery in northwest

[1] "C" if an action was noted in only one work (whether a general or era history); "B" if noted in two or more works but not more than one general history; "A" if noted in at least two general histories.

[2] Scott was a territorial delegate.

presents a list for the Congress of 1931–33 under President Hoover, when several New Deal policy ideas were rehearsed in legislative drives by Democrats and progressive Republicans. (In reading the tables, note that, before the mid-1930s, each Congress met for a final "lame duck" session extending into the early months of the odd year following the election that chose a successor Congress.)

With the addition of suitable plotlines, these "action" lists for 1817–21 and 1931–33 could flesh out the sorts of sketches I wrote to begin Chap-

of the Press: The Birth of American Political Reporting (New York: Oxford University Press, 1986), pp. 75–76.

Table 2.3 Member Actions in the Seventy-second Congress

Year of Action	Actor	Party	State	S/H	Text Sources[1]	Kind of Action	Content of Action
1932– 33	Hugo Black	D	Ala.	S	B	Legislate	Bill for 30-hour week
1931– 32	Edward Costigan	D	Colo.	S	B	Legislate Investigate	Hearings and bill re cities relief
1932	Edward Costigan	D	Colo.	S	C	Legislate	Bill for lower-income RFC
1932	Bronson Cutting	R	N.M.	S	C	Legislate	Promotes relief policy
1932– 33	Bronson Cutting	R	N.M.	S	C	Leg. eponym	Hawes-Cutting Act re Philippines independence
1932	Robert Doughton	D	N.C.	H	B	Legislate	Co-leads revolt vs. tax plan
1931	John N. Garner	D	Tex.	H	C	Run for leader	Elected Speaker
1932	John N. Garner	D	Tex.	H	A	Cand for P, VP Convention role Pres. select. role	Candidate for pres., vice pres.
1932	John N. Garner	D	Tex.	H	B	Legislate	Presses public works bill
1932	John N. Garner	D	Tex.	H	B	Legislate, leader Take stand	Presses tax hike to cut deficit
1932	Carter Glass	D	Va.	S	A	Leg., leg. eponym	Glass-Steagall Banking Act
1932– 33	Henry B. Hawes	D	Mo.	S	C	Leg. eponym	Hawes-Cutting Act re Philippines independence
1932	Cordell Hull	D	Tenn.	S	C	Take stand Convention role	Drys leader at Dem. convention

Table 2.3 (*continued*)

Year of Action	Actor	Party	State	S/H	Text Sources[1]	Kind of Action	Content of Action
1933	Cordell Hull	D	Tenn.	S	C	Take appointment	Appointed Secretary of State
1931–32	Robert La Follette, Jr.	R	Wis.	S	B	Legislate Investigate	Hearings and bill re cities relief
1932	Fiorello La Guardia	R	N.Y.	H	C	Legislate	Bill for lower-income RFC
1932	Fiorello La Guardia	R	N.Y.	H	B	Legislate	Co-leads revolt vs. tax plan
1932	Fiorello La Guardia	R	N.Y.	H	B	Legislate Leg. eponym	Norris–La Guardia labor management relations act
1931–32	David J. Lewis	D	Md.	H	C	Legislate	Presses relief bill
1932	Huey Long	D	La.	S	B	Convention role Pres. select. role	Backs FDR at Dem. convention
1932–33	Huey Long	D	La.	S	C	Take stand Filibuster	Ties up lame duck session with filibuster
1931	George H. Moses	R	N.H.	S	C	Run for leader	Reelected pres. pro tem of Senate
1932	George Norris	R	Nebr.	S	B	Legislate Leg. eponym	Norris–La Guardia labor management relations act
1932	George Norris	R	Nebr.	S	B	Legislate	Gets 20th (anti–lame duck) amdt.
1932	George Norris	R	Nebr.	S	C	Legislate	Promotes relief policy

Table 2.3 (*continued*)

Year of Action	Actor	Party	State	S/H	Text Sources[1]	Kind of Action	Content of Action
1931– 32	Wright Patman	D	Tex.	H	B	Leg., leg. eponym	Patman veterans bonus bill
1932	Henry T. Rainey	D	Ill.	H	C	Legislate, leader	Bill to use RFC $ for relief
1932	Samuel Rayburn	D	Tex.	H	B	Pres. select. role Convention role	Moves Texas to FDR at Dem. convention
1931	Bertrand Snell	R	N.Y.	H	C	Run for leader	Loses race for Speaker
1932	Henry Steagall	D	Ala.	H	A	Leg., leg. eponym	Glass-Steagall Banking Act
1932	J. W. Elmer Thomas	D	Okla.	S	C	Legislate	Bill to reduce farm acreage
1931	Robert F. Wagner	D	N.Y.	S	C	Legislate	Bill for state employmt. agencies
1932	Robert F. Wagner	D	N.Y.	S	B	Legislate	Presses public works bill

[1] "C" if an action was noted in only one work (whether a general or era history), "B" if noted in two or more works but not more than one general history; "A" if noted in at least two general histories.

ter 1. But the question of using historians' works this way still needs to be addressed. At issue is whether they can serve as windows to past "collective consciousness," at least among the politically aware, about public affairs. I organize a discussion here around three objections that might be posed.[15]

15. Beyond these three objections, another lesser one might be that historians occasionally make factual mistakes, and that I have faithfully carried forth any such mistakes into this project. Very likely, these mistakes do appear. I did not verify all the material

First, isn't it true that no two historians ever tell the same story? If so, how can any precise list of "actions" be compiled? The argument is apt, as it was regarding my Chapter 1 sketches. On any subject we are likely to see a "family" of overlapping treatments. As I see it, to draw an analogy, historians who write "public affairs" accounts of the same past era are likely to agree on what to cover about as closely as do ABC, CBS, and NBC in preparing the news for the same evening. Convergence will occur on certain items that are thought to be major, but divergence grows and comes to dominate as items are seen to be more peripheral—although the same *kinds* of items may be identified even in the peripheral range. Here, my chief remedy for this divergence problem is plural sources— the two layers of "era" history and the five "general" histories covering all Congresses during the two centuries. In addition, for what it is worth, public affairs historians seem to home in on the same *actors* even if they diverge on those actors' portfolios of actions. Still, the present work needs

---

presented in the thirty-eight history books used here. Still, in a hundred or so instances I did choose to dig deeper into primary or more detailed secondary sources. That was when any of four conditions obtained: an "action" item was vaguely or incompletely reported in the one or more works that reported it (the date may have been missing, for example); two or more works supplied conflicting relevant information about an "action"; an "action" occurring before 1935 was identified with an odd year but not a specified Congress (instances like this sent me to the library because before the Twentieth "lame duck" Amendment kicked in in the mid-1930s, two separate Congresses met early and late within every odd year after 1789, and I needed to know *which Congress* accommodated each "action"); a reported "action" conflicted with my memory, which (though flawed, like everyone else's) extends back directly through a surprising one-quarter of American national history. Through the resulting digging, I cleaned up the dataset a bit. For example, I attributed the Johnson Immigration Act of 1924 to the correct Johnson (one of the thirty-eight history books listed an incorrect Johnson). I moved the Reed-Bulwinkle Act to the year in which it belongs: 1948. I gave up on counting Thomas Hart Benton (D-Mo.) as a leading opponent to building the Smithsonian Institution when I couldn't find any detailed secondary historical documentation to support that at any rate skimpily reported item. Several other such corrections were made.

to be approached with a tolerance for erratic evidence; please read all the numerical results as if they were bracketed by confidence intervals.[16]

Out of curiosity, I coded two public affairs histories not used for my dataset to see how their "actions" lists jibed with mine. From William E. Leuchtenburg's *The Perils of Prosperity, 1914–1932*, a work of standard scale for the genre, I extracted fifty-seven "action" items, of which forty-seven appear in my dataset, and, again, for what it is worth, eight others were performed by MCs already otherwise represented there.[17] From James T. Patterson's recent *Grand Expectations: The United States, 1945–1974*, a detailed 790-page work, I extracted 179 items, of which 121 appear in my dataset and fifty others were performed by MCs already otherwise represented there.[18] That gives a sense of the "family" relations among similar works.[19] (An opposite sort of objection to the data use here, let it be said,

16. One implication is that there are surprising omissions from the 2,304-item dataset. That is, certain MC moves that were probably prominent at the time of performance and that would ring a bell today with anyone broadly familiar with U.S. history may *not* have made an appearance in any of this study's thirty-eight history texts and hence not have entered the dataset. Here are five items that seem to me to qualify as thus "left out": in 1841, Congressman John Quincy Adams argued the case of the *Amistad* slave ship's mutineers before the Supreme Court. During the Civil War, Senator Sumner argued the Union cause to his many friends and admirers in England. In 1912, Senator William Alden Smith (R-Mich.) conducted an immediate, highly publicized hearing in New York City into the causes of the sinking of the *Titanic*. In the mid-1940s, Senator Fulbright ushered into existence the fellowships that still bear his name. In 1950, Senator Margaret Chase Smith (R-Maine) issued her well-known "Declaration of Conscience" decrying the tactics of Senator Joseph McCarthy.

17. William E. Leuchtenburg, *The Perils of Prosperity, 1914–1932* (Chicago: University of Chicago Press, 1958).

18. Patterson refers to Margaret Chase Smith's "Declaration of Conscience," at p. 203.

19. When Patterson's 179 items are sorted into categories (often, into more than one; see my discussion at the close of Chapter 2 of this volume), his nine most heavily populated ones are, in order: take stand, 57 percent of the 179 items; foreign policy, 36 percent; legislate, 28 percent; opposition, 20 percent; committee role, 13 percent; leader, 13 percent; presidential or vice-presidential candidate, 13 percent; counsel president, 7 per-

is that historians sometimes *copy* each other, thereby generating a tighter "family" of accounts of the past than one might like. No doubt this often happens; all I can do is to note the point and go on.)

Second, what do I really have here in this dataset? Isn't it just a post–World War II construction of the past? Well, it is at least that. The history books it draws on were all published between 1954 and 1995. They are bound to reflect the intellectual tendencies and research methodologies of those decades. Even so, in the case of the raw material for "public affairs" history, I do not think it is necessary to surrender to skepticism about the ability of current texts to apprehend the past. Remember that it is *past stories,* insofar as they figured in the collective consciousness of contemporaries, that I am in principle trying to consult for primary data. The stories we find familiar about Madison, Clay, Sumner, Lodge, and many of the rest have been around for a long time.

But how long? Possibly the test case is the earliest stretch of U.S. history under George Washington in 1789–97, when national consciousness was new, communication through newspapers was slow and sparse, public records were close to nonexistent (the House lacked an equivalent of the later *Congressional Record,* and the Senate conducted its sessions in secret until 1795), and the craft of writing general histories of American national politics had yet to be developed.[20] Is it really true that

---

cent; investigate, 7 percent. My own top nine categories (all those containing more than 30 items) drawn from the twelve "general" and "era" histories addressing those years (including the two works on World War II) are, in order: take stand, 46 percent of the total of 448 dataset items; legislate, 35 percent; foreign policy, 28 percent; opposition, 28 percent; committee role, 24 percent; leader, 19 percent; investigate, 10 percent; presidential or vice-presidential candidate, 8 percent; party convention role, 7 percent. Compared with Patterson, the twelve-volume blend is, for one thing, relatively heavy on basic Capitol Hill process activities such as "legislate" and "committee role."

20. On U.S. national consciousness: Joseph M. Torsella, "American National Identity, 1750–1790: Samples from the Popular Press," *Pennsylvania Magazine of History and Biography* 112 (1988), 167–87. On early- to mid-nineteenth-century media coverage of Con-

a story about public affairs developed in people's minds way back then that has passed down to us today? So far as I can tell, the answer is yes. I invite anyone who is curious about this matter to search through five works: The Sharp (1993) and Miller (1960) works on the Federalist era that I used for my dataset; John Spencer Bassett's *The Federalist System, 1789–1801*, published in 1906 in the American Nation Series;[21] Richard Hildreth's *Administration of Washington, 1789–1797*, issued in 1851 and now regarded as a pioneering professional achievement;[22] and volume five of John Marshall's *Life of George Washington*, issued by the chief justice in 1807 as a biography (although it can just as well be seen as a public affairs history of the years 1789–99).[23] Marshall, a witness of and

---

gress: Leonard, *Power of the Press,* ch. 3. On the state of historical writing: David D. Van Tassel, *Recording America's Past: An Interpretation of the Development of Historical Studies in America, 1607–1884* (Chicago: University of Chicago Press, 1960), chaps. 7, 8; Richard Hofstadter, *The Progressive Historians* (New York: Knopf, 1968), ch. 1 ("Historical Writing Before Turner").

21. John Spencer Bassett, *The Federalist System, 1789–1801* (New York: Harper and Brothers, 1906). The twenty-seven volumes of the American Nation Series were published in 1904–8, a half century before the first volumes of the New American Nation Series. On the earlier series, see Michael Kraus, *The Writing of American History* (Norman: University of Oklahoma Press, 1953), pp. 229–32; John Higham (with Leonard Krieger and Felix Gilbert), *History* (Englewood Cliffs, N.J.: Prentice-Hall, 1965), p. 20. I spent a good deal of time in the Yale and Stanford libraries examining these largely forgotten ninety-year-old volumes. Working from a baseline of later scholarship, I found especially illuminating the detailed and coherent accounts of public affairs in Edward Channing, *The Jeffersonian System, 1801–1811* (New York: Harper and Brothers, 1906), and George Pierce Garrison, *Westward Extension, 1841–1850* (New York: Harper and Brothers, 1906).

22. Richard Hildreth, *History of the United States of America,* vol. 1, *Administration of Washington, 1789–1797* (New York: Harper and Brothers, 1851). On Hildreth as historian: Van Tassel, *Recording America's Past,* pp. 139–40; Hofstadter, *The Progressive Historians,* pp. 20–23.

23. John Marshall, *The Life of George Washington* (London: printed for Richard Phillips, No. 6, New Bridge-street, 1807), vol. 5. Biography was the accepted literary form at the time. On Marshall's work: Kraus, *Writing of American History,* ch. 4; Van Tassel, *Recording America's Past,* p. 70.

major politician during the Federalist era, stepped forth as in effect that era's contemporary sketcher; it seems a plausible inference that he wrote down a broadly shared memory of what had just happened. Once past his stilted prose, page-long quotations, and concentration on official behavior, readers today would have no trouble situating Marshall's volume in a family of narrative accounts of the Federalist era alongside Hildreth's through Sharp's. If page counts can be taken to index importance, Marshall's coverage of Congress emphasizes the legislative program of 1789 (the country's first revenue measure, the Bill of Rights, the structuring of the executive departments); the debate about assuming state debts that culminated in the well-known deal in 1790 to locate the capital in the District of Columbia; the trade debate centering on Madison's commercial resolutions in 1794; and the handling of the Jay Treaty in 1796.[24] Along the way he takes up, among other things, Hamilton's national bank plan, the emergence of an opposition Republican party, and the debate over the new democratic societies in 1794. Madison stands out as the leading congressional actor. It is a familiar story.

It is true that Marshall wrote with a decidedly pro-Federalist spin,[25] and that raises the question of historians' "interpretations"—in the sense of either differing evaluations of the past or differing explanations of it. Of course, interpretations do vary among historians and across time. But they do not seem to impinge a great deal on the kind of data at issue here. Much as Marshall disagreed with the Republican Madison, he had to portray him as the leading figure in Congress and tell the reader what he did. Elsewhere in U.S. history, to cite perhaps the extreme case of historiographical dissonance, evaluations of the Reconstruction era have gone

24. Marshall's page counts for these four items are, respectively, 21, 21, 43, and 18.

25. Thomas Jefferson cast about for someone to write a competing pro-Republican account, but he had little luck. See Van Tassel, *Recording America's Past*, pp. 80–86; Joseph J. Ellis, *American Sphinx: The Character of Thomas Jefferson* (New York: Knopf, 1996), pp. 252–56.

down and up among historians during the twentieth century—Thaddeus Stevens, the Radical Republican leader, has ranged all the way from a villain to a hero—but writers on the subject, regardless of their orientations, have routinely seen fit to document actions by Stevens, Senator Benjamin Wade (R-Ohio), Senator Lyman Trumbull (R-Ill.), Congressman John A. Bingham (R-Ohio), Congressman George W. Julian (R-Ind.), and other principal congressional figures. To cite an extreme of explanatory dissonance, the historian Gabriel Kolko advanced in the 1960s a new interpretation of the Progressive era—that business corporations, not good-government reformers, were largely responsible for its regulatory reforms—but that did not deter him from writing about Congressman Carter Glass (D-Va.) as manager of the Federal Reserve Act of 1913, or Senators Nelson W. Aldrich (R-R.I.), Joseph W. Bailey (D-Tex.), and Benjamin Tillman (D-S.C.) as figures in the consideration of the Hepburn Act of 1906.[26] (Although, to be sure, members of Congress do recede from being autonomous or consequential if corporations are said to be pulling the strings.) The important point here is that standard facts about MCs are likely to turn up in histories regardless of their authors' interpretations; such facts may serve as grist for interpretations, but I am interested here in the grist, not the interpretations.

All this having been said, it remains true that I did rely entirely on works published since 1950 for my "action" data. This means, at the least, that the authors of those works may have used *sources* or exhibited *tastes* foreign to the past generations they wrote about. At stake may be *which* actions or *which kinds* of action they took cognizance of—I make this distinction because much of my later analysis hinges on kinds of action. Through better sources, for example, modern historians know more

26. On the Federal Reserve Act: Gabriel Kolko, *The Triumph of Conservatism: A Re-Interpretation of American History, 1900–1916* (Chicago: Quadrangle, 1967), ch. 9. On the Hepburn Act: Kolko, *Railroads and Regulation, 1877–1916* (Princeton, N.J.: Princeton University Press, 1965), ch. 7.

about the Senate's proceedings under George Washington than did informed citizens of that time; this obviously bears on which actions can be written about now.[27] As for kinds of action, better sources (like newly discovered personal letters) can impinge in the following way: Behind-the-scenes moves, such as advising the president, scheming to get somebody nominated for president, accepting a bribe from a nineteenth-century railroad, or even spying for the Soviet Union, as did Congressman Samuel Dickstein (D-N.Y.) in the late 1930s,[28] may be written about today even if they were not public knowledge back then.[29] Certain "action" categories no doubt are thus augmented in the dataset. Under the rubric of shifts in authors' tastes, I probably owe a few "action" items to the surge of labor, race, and women's history during recent decades. The Sheppard-Towner Maternity Aid Act of 1921, for example, is covered in the newer era histories by Perrett (1982) and Parrish (1992) but not in the older one by Hicks (1960). The Indian Removal Act of 1830 draws two "action" mentions in Feller (1995) though none in Van Deusen (1959). I kept a particular lookout for any changes in historians' tastes during the past half cen-

27. Writing in 1807, Marshall refers only in passing to the now-familiar moves in the Senate of the First Congress bearing on the use of executive titles and the practical application of the "advice and consent" clause of the Constitution. He does not seem to know much about what went on. See *Life of George Washington*, vol. 5, pp. 256–59.

28. Dickstein makes an appearance in this work's dataset for his successful 1934 resolution setting up a special House committee to investigate Nazi and other subversive activities (a precedent, as it turned out, for the establishment of Martin Dies's special committee to investigate un-American activities four years later), but not for his espionage, which has recently been documented in Allen Weinstein and Alexander Vassiliev, *The Haunted Wood: Soviet Espionage in America—The Stalin Era* (New York: Random House, 1999), ch. 7.

29. My impression is that not more than 1 or 2 percent of the 2,304 items in the dataset are in this "not public at the time" category. The title of this book is thus off target by that 1 or 2 percent. For some instances of nineteenth-century bribery, or at least conflict of interest, involving members of Congress, see Eric Foner, *Reconstruction: America's Unfinished Revolution, 1863–1877* (New York: Harper and Row, 1988), pp. 466–68.

tury involving *kinds* of actions (as opposed to their issue content alone). I came up with possibly one. References to what I have coded as "descriptive representation" are hardly novel—Hiram Revels has been cited for generations as the first African-American senator[30]—but the volume of them in very recent years is new. Highlighted by Foner (1988) are six new African-American members of the House in the 1870s, and by Henretta et al. (1993) five new women members of the House in the 1970s.[31] In general, however, in the dataset, new sources and tastes seem to intrude rather lightly into a continuous U.S. civic history where public performances in familiar roles extend back two centuries. Note the publicness and orthodoxy of the roles shown for 1817–21 and 1931–33 in Tables 2.2 and 2.3. This is not Russian history, where past events are in dispute and the kinds of moves keep changing, and it is not diplomatic or intelligence history (Congressman Dickstein aside), where a release of government documents decades later can give a decisive new cast to old events.

The third objection is: But what about "weighting"? Whatever else they do, historians have to decide how much attention to spend on various time segments of the past. This can immediately affect MC "action" counts for past eras. In history books published since 1950, won't those weighting judgments be accordingly post-1950 ones?

For a beginning of an answer to this question, see Figure 2.1, which presents counts of MC actions (of all kinds) by decade through the two centuries. I should comment on this form of display because I use it in many graphs. A "decade" is the span of time occupied by five consecutive Congresses elected in years ending with a 0, 2, 4, 6, and 8—hence, for

30. See James Schouler, *History of the Reconstruction Period, 1865–1877* (New York: Dodd, Mead and Company, 1913), p. 170; James G. Blaine, *Twenty Years of Congress: From Lincoln to Garfield* (Norwich, Conn.: Henry Bill, 1886), vol. 2, p. 448.

31. Foner, *Reconstruction*, pp. 533–34; Henretta et al., *America's History*, vol. 2, p. 971. One of Foner's six delivered a speech that won national attention; the other five I have classified simply as "descriptive representation."

example, 1951 through 1960 on the modern calendar but March 4, 1861, through March 3, 1871, back when long lame duck postelection sessions were held.[32] Thus "the 1850s" includes the secession crisis of the winter of 1860–61.[33] Although, summing data by decade makes for great convenience in exposition (I can write about "the 1840s" or "the 1960s"), it does carry a small practical penalty at both ends: "The 1790s" must expand backward to include the First Congress, elected in 1788, thus embracing six Congresses rather than five, and "the 1980s" has to end in 1988, thus embracing four Congresses rather than five. These anomalies need to be kept in mind whenever frequencies per decade appear in graphs.

In Figure 2.1, the vertical bars enumerate "actions" per decade according to the most permissive standard—that is, they were mentioned in at least one historical work and thus satisfied the "A," the "B," *or* the "C" coding criterion. This is the full dataset. Item counts range from 37 in the 1800s to 236 in the 1930s (see the scale in the left margin). The bullets connected by straight lines in Figure 2.1 show actions per decade according to the strict "A" criterion—that is, they were mentioned in at least two "general" histories. Readings range from 5 in the 1800s and 1810s to 21 in the 1930s (see the scale in the right margin). Broadly speaking, the two time series move up and down together.[34] This is a satisfying result.[35] It suggests that "era" historians (overwhelmingly the source of the

32. Under the old calendar, a new Congress could begin as early as March 4 of an odd year if a special session was called for that date, which occasionally happened. Ordinarily, though, December of an odd year was the starting time.

33. For a recent account of that crisis, see Maury Klein, *Days of Defiance: Sumter, Secession, and the Coming of the Civil War* (New York: Knopf, 1997).

34. One reason that they do that, of course, is because the A+B+C series includes the A series. But because the former has over ten times as many items as the latter, it is not basically driven by it. In another kind of calculation, the A readings per decade correlate with the B+C readings per decade at 0.69.

35. For many readers, the chief anomaly in Figure 2.1 will be the high reading on the "A" series for the 1920s. Here is the explanation. In the "general" historians' coverage

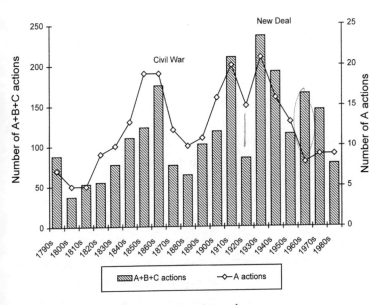

Figure 2.1. All data set actions versus A actions only

many "B" and "C" items in the dataset) do not head off every which way to pursue their own enthusiasms as they decide how much material to document; instead, they exhibit a shared set of standards with the "general" historians. This enhances the credibility of the full dataset.

The past is certainly "weighted" in Figure 2.1—probably not surprising to anyone historically informed. In general, MC "actions" accumulate in decades when the federal government has been active.[36] In particu-

of the twentieth century, a higher share of MC name mentions than one would like is from eponymous bill titles. In small, decade-specific datasets, this propensity can make a difference, and it does in the 1920s where the multiply coded McNary-Haugen Bill and other such items inflate the total quite a bit. In the "B" and "C" series, eponymous bill titles do not pose such a problem.

36. For an account of bursts of legislative activism at the federal level since th see David R. Mayhew, "Presidential Elections and Policy Change: How Much o

lar, the surges on the graph bear out what might be thought of as three fundamental scripts that have, in sequence, dominated the writing and understanding of American history—plus one additional theme.[37] During 1789 through 1801, performances by Madison and others, which result in a relatively high "action" reading for that decade, help complete a "founding" script that begins in the 1760s, weaves through the American Revolution and the writing of the Constitution, then ends with the launching of the new nation during the Federalist era.[38] Starting in the 1830s, what might be called a "testing the nation through civil war" script gains volume and intensity with U.S. expansion into Texas and Mexico in the 1840s, the Compromise of 1850, and the struggle over Kansas in the mid-1850s, then culminates in the secession crisis of 1860–61 and the Civil War and Reconstruction. And a "building the regulatory and welfare state" script, which rises to peak moments with Woodrow Wilson's New Freedom, Franklin D. Roosevelt's New Deal, and Lyndon B. Johnson's Great Society (though it is worth emphasizing that all those were congressional as well as presidential enterprises) runs intermittently from the late 1880s through, on current evidence, the mid-1970s. This last script, by far the chief preoccupation of twentieth-century public affairs historians, has been told by Richard Hofstadter, Arthur M.

---

nection Is There?" ch. 5 in Harvey L. Schantz (ed.), *American Presidential Elections: Process, Policy, and Political Change* (Albany, N.Y.: State University of New York Press, 1996).

37. I found the following sources useful in thinking about a sequence of scripts: Gordon S. Wood, "A Century of Writing Early American History: Then and Now Compared; Or How Henry Adams Got It Wrong," *American Historical Review* 100 (1995), 679–82; Hofstadter, *The Progressive Historians*, pp. 25–26; Arthur Mann, "The Progressive Tradition," ch. 9 in John Higham (ed.), *The Reconstruction of American History* (New York: Harper and Brothers, 1962); Bruce Ackerman, *We the People: Foundations* (Cambridge: Harvard University Press, 1991).

38. The "action" count for the Federalist era appears relatively high, even after taking into account the six-Congress span of the 1790s in the data presented here.

Schlesinger, Jr., James L. Sundquist, and many others. The additional historical theme is wars—particularly the Civil War, World War I, World War II, and the Vietnam War, which figure prominently in MC actions in the 1860s, 1910s, 1940s, and 1960s–70s—but also the Mexican War, the Spanish-American War, and the Korean War, which contributed rather heavily to MC "actions" in one way or another during the 1840s and 1890s and around 1950.

Earlier, I discussed the limitations of the dataset for the years since the mid-1970s. Closeness to the present is one obvious cause of those limitations: History books are not written immediately. Another reason may be that because the century-long "building the regulatory and welfare state" project has fallen on hard times or possibly come to an end, none of the familiar scripts applies anymore. It is no longer clear how to construct "public affairs history." Older liberal historians such as John Morton Blum tend to view events since 1968 with distaste or alarm; younger historians studying the United States tend to steer clear of public affairs in favor of other subjects. One achievement of Barone's *Our Country*, a statement from outside the academic history profession, is to show that recent U.S. public affairs history can be organized without reliance on a liberal welfare-state teleology.

Are the "weightings" by decade shown in Figure 2.1 a post–World War II imposition? For the most part, the answer must surely be no. To an appreciable degree, they no doubt trace back to American experience as it was originally lived. Can it have been a secret in 1933, for example, that something special was going on with the launching of the New Deal? Or in 1861, with the secession of the South? I cannot prove this claim through any evidence at hand, but at least I can show that the judgments by post–World War II historians exhibited here echo ones made by their professional predecessors. Figure 2.2 draws data from three earlier multivolume histories, each spanning several decades, writ-

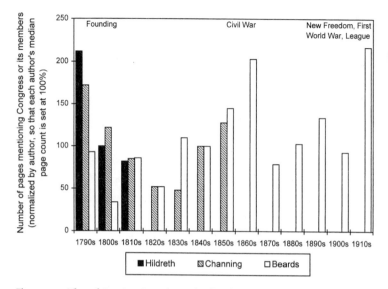

Figure 2.2. Three historians' emphasis, by decade

ten by Richard Hildreth (issued in 1851), Edward Channing (published in 1917–25), and Charles and Mary Beard (published in 1927).[39] My objective here was to find out how these earlier writers balanced their coverage of congressional politics over time. To that end, I counted in each work, for each decade, the number of *pages* that mention activity by Congress or its members.[40] The method used to organize the results appear-

39. I used the following editions: Richard Hildreth, *The History of the United States* (New York: Harper and Brothers, 1879), vols. 4–6; Edward Channing, *A History of the United States* (New York: Macmillan, 1905–25), vols. 4–6 dated 1917, 1921, and 1925; Charles A. Beard and Mary R. Beard, *The Rise of American Civilization* (New York: Macmillan, 1930). For a discussion of Channing's work, see Higham, *History*, pp. 168–69. On Charles Beard's scholarship: Hofstadter, *The Progressive Historians*, pp. 298–304.

40. This is a simpler, more easily executed methodology than the one I used to gather the main dataset. Here, I should say that in tracking activity engaged in by individual members outside sessions of Congress, I focused only on members prominent enough to make an appearance in the main dataset. Otherwise, I would have had to delve some-

ing in Figure 2.2 can perhaps be best explained by example. Hildreth's work, which covers the three decades from 1789 through 1821, yielded Congress-related page counts of 478 for the 1790s (that is, for 1789–1801), 226 for the 1800s, and 185 for the 1810s. The median of these three values, 226, is scored as 100 percent on the left vertical axis of the figure. The 478 value is scored as 212 percent on that axis (that is, itself as a percentage of the median value); the 185 value is scored as 82 percent (also itself as a percentage of the median value). Page counts per decade for the Channing and Beard works are also wrapped around their medians this way. (These normalizing steps were taken because Hildreth's page counts are much higher than those for the other works.)

On this evidence, modern emphases do reassuringly have roots further in the past. For Hildreth, writing at the middle of the nineteenth century, the activities of the founding generation are the main story. Channing adds a second statistical peak for the coming of the Civil War. (His account ends during Lincoln's presidency, so I could not code it for the full decade of the 1860s, but his three highest-scoring *Congresses* are, respectively, those of 1789–91, 1859–61, and 1861–63.) The Beards, writing from the perspective of the 1920s, skimp on the 1790s, yet they do highlight the 1860s and the just-finished decade of 1911–21—the latter both for its New Freedom domestic reforms and for World War I and its aftermath.

All three familiar scripts (plus wars) make an appearance in Figure 2.2, yet the graph does show, when juxtaposed to Figure 2.1, that the Beards prefigured later writers in downgrading the first two or three generations of American public affairs history. Old, once eye-catching events and participants are not so interesting anymore. Congressman Thomas FitzSimons of Pennsylvania, for example, who promoted the Federalist

times into detailed accounts of local politics to identify a member of Congress. Any resulting oversights are minor.

cause in Marshall's account in 1807, Hildreth's in 1851, and Channing's in 1917 (though not Bassett's in 1906), vanishes from Miller's work in 1960 and Sharp's in 1993.[41] My data accumulations for these early decades are accordingly rather small, and for many comparative purposes it makes sense to focus on percentage distributions within them (they are not too small for that) rather than on their absolute numbers.

To round this methodological discussion toward a close, see Tables 2.4 and 2.5, which highlight one value of the 2,304-item dataset: Records of individual MCs can be teased out. The nineteenth-century "action career" of the versatile John Sherman (R-Ohio), which spans forty-two years and twenty-three data items, includes roles as legislator, investigator, party potentate, cabinet appointee, and would-be presidential nominee. His record sprawls across thirteen works of history—all five "general" and all eight relevant "era" histories. This omnipresence validates, to a certain extent, the methodology. If I had used a different set of history works, no doubt some of these twenty-three Sherman items would have disappeared, alternative ones would have appeared, and the list would have ended up somewhat shorter or longer, but the overall impression would probably be about the same. Table 2.5 exhibits "action careers" for two mid-twentieth-century figures, Senators J. William Fulbright and Joseph McCarthy, who had virtually nothing in common but did share one characteristic relevant here: They were both largely *nonlegislative* performers. Their careers point to the importance of congressional actions other than trying to enact or block bills.

Finally, Table 2.6 provides the list of forty-three categories into which the 2,304 "action" items have been sorted, and the data totals per category. Note that the frequencies in the left-hand column of the table add

41. Yet he does resurface in Elkins and McKitrick's comprehensive work, *The Age of Federalism* (1993).

Table 2.4 Action Career of John Sherman (R-Ohio)

Year	S/H	Age	Cong/Tenure[1] Consec.	All	Action	ABC Sources[2]	Sources
1856	H	33	1	1	Member of Howard Committee to investigate conditions in Kansas	C	Potter
1859–60	H	36	3	3	Republican candidate for Speaker	C	Potter
1860	H	37	3	3	Plan to admit all territories to solve sectional crisis	C	Potter
1863	S	40	1	4	Powerful speech for a banking bill	C	Paludan
1864	S	41	2	5	Sends out circular favoring Chase over Lincoln, then backs down	C	Paludan
1865–66	S	42	3	6	A leader of Republican moderates	B	Davidson, Foner
1867	S	44	3	6	Chairs committee to prepare Reconstruction bill	B	Foner, Randall/Donald
1867	S	44	3	6	Construes Tenure of Office Act as it passes	C	Randall/Donald
1868	S	45	4	7	Argues for conviction of Pres. Johnson	C	Randall/Donald
1868	S	45	4	7	Proposal to cut wages if federal workweek shortened	C	Foner
1869	S	46	5	8	Promotes Public Credit Act of 1869	C	Boyer
1874	S	51	7	10	Bill to stabilize currency	C	Foner
1875	S	52	7	10	Author of Specie Resumption Act	A	Bailyn, Boyer, Cashman, Randall/Donald
1876–77	S	53	8	11	In on Wormley House Bargain to settle disputed 1876 election	B	Bailyn, Cashman
1877	S	54	8	11	Appointed Secretary of the Treasury	C	Cashman

Table 2.4 (*continued*)

Year	S/H	Age	Cong/Tenure[1] Consec.	All	Action	ABC Sources[2]	Sources
1884	S	61	2	13	Candidate for GOP pres. nomination	C	Garraty
1888	S	65	4	15	Helps block Democratic tariff reform	C	Cashman
1888	S	65	4	15	Candidate for GOP pres. nomination	C	Garraty
1889–91	S	66	5	16	Informal dinners with Pres. Harrison	C	Williams
1890	S	67	5	16	Role in Sherman Antitrust Act	A	Bailyn, Boyer, Cashman, Davidson, Faulkner, Garraty, Henretta, Jordan, Williams
1890	S	67	5	16	Role (in fact, possibly a passive one) in Sherman Silver Purchase Act	A	Bailyn, Boyer, Cashman, Davidson, Faulkner, Garraty, Henretta, Jordan, Williams
1890–91	S	67	5	16	A leader in advancing Lodge's Force Bill to enfranchise southern blacks	C	Faulkner
1897	S	74	8	19	Appointed Secretary of State	B	Faulkner, Williams

[1] "Consec." means number of Congresses served in consecutively in the same house; "all" means total number of Congresses served in at that time, regardless of which house or whether consecutively.

[2] "C" means mentioned in only one history work; "B" means mentioned in at least two works though not more than one "general" work; "A" means mentioned in at least two "general" works.

Table 2.5 Action Careers of J. W. Fulbright (D-Ark.) and Joseph McCarthy (R-Wis.)

Year	S/H	Age	Cong/ Tenure[1] Consec.	All	Action	ABC Sources[2]	Sources
Fulbright							
1943–44	H	38	1	1	Fulbright Reso to commit U.S. to a United Nations	C	Buchanan
1945	S	40	1	2	Strong support of U.N.	B	Blum I, Goldman
1951	S	46	4	5	Investigates RFC corruption	B	Barone, Goldman
1961	S	56	9	10	Advises JFK on Bay of Pigs	B	Bailyn, Blum II, Grantham
1962	S	57	9	10	Advises JFK on Cuban Missile Crisis	C	Blum II
1964	S	59	10	11	Pilots Gulf of Tonkin Res. through the Senate	B	Blum II, Matusow
1964	S	59	10	11	Wide-ranging speech re Cold War mythology	C	Matusow
1965	S	60	10	11	Breaks with LBJ on policy in Dominican Republic	B	Barone, Matusow
1965	S	60	11	12	Publicly criticizes Vietnam policy	B	Barone, Blum II
1966	S	61	11	12	Writes *The Arrogance of Power*	C	Matusow
1966–67	S	61	11	12	Holds televised hearings vs. Vietnam War	A	Blum II, Boyer, Davidson, Grantham, Matusow
1967–68	S	62	12	13	Keeps criticizing Vietnam policy	B	Blum II, Matusow
McCarthy							
1950	S	42	2	2	His Wheeling and other speeches launch "McCarthyism"	A	Bailyn, Barone, Boyer, Davidson, Goldman, Grantham, Henretta, Jordan
1950	S	42	2	2	Makes disloyalty accusations before Tydings Committee	A	Barone, Boyer, Davidson, Goldman, Grantham

Table 2.5 (*continued*)

Year	S/H	Age	Cong/Tenure[1] Consec.	All	Action	ABC Sources[2]	Sources
1950	S	42	2	2	Butts into Conn. and Md. elections	A	Boyer, Davidson, Grantham
1951–52	S	43	3	3	Attacks Acheson, Marshall, et al.	A	Barone, Boyer, Goldman, Jordan
1953	S	45	4	4	Opposes Bohlen appointment as ambassador to USSR	B	Davidson, Grantham
1953	S	45	4	4	Gets Greek shipowners to stop China trade	B	Goldman, Grantham
1953	S	45	4	4	Hunts Communists in State Department	A	Boyer, Davidson Goldman, Grantham
1954	S	46	4	4	Army-McCarthy hearings	A	Bailyn, Barone, Boyer, Davidson, Goldman, Grantham, Henretta, Jordan
1954	S	46	4	4	Censured by Senate	A	Bailyn, Barone, Boyer, Davidson, Goldman, Grantham, Henretta, Jordan

[1] "Consec." means number of Congresses served in consecutively in the same house; "all" means total number of Congresses served in at that time, regardless of which house or whether consecutively.

[2] "C" means mentioned in only one history work; "B" means mentioned in at least two works though not more than one "general" work; "A" means mentioned in at least two "general" works.

up to well over 2,304—in fact, they reach about twice that total—a tipoff that many "actions" have been multiply coded. A 1964 entry for Senator Richard Russell (D-Ga.), for example, who led the South's last-ditch opposition to that year's historic Civil Rights Act,[42] is scored for that role as "legislate," "take stand," "filibuster," "leader" (he was the acknowledged

42. Also known as the Public Accommodations Act.

Table 2.6 Numbers of Each Kind of MC Action

Parliamentary moves

977 Legislate—tries to pass, block, or amend a bill, resolution, treaty, or constitutional amendment through arguments or motions or other means

239 Leg. Eponym—name becomes attached to a measure, as in the Wagner Act (In 137 cases, where activity by an MC was specifically mentioned, these are also coded as Legislate)

45 Make Appointment—takes part in consideration of a presidential appointment

37 Impeach/Censure—takes part in (or calls for) a process to impeach, convict, or censure a member or the executive or judicial branch

8 Censure/Expel—takes part in (or calls for or opposes) a process to censure, expel, or not seat another member of Congress

36 Rules—takes part in (or calls for or opposes) some process regarding House or Senate rules, as in the introduction of the House's "Reed rules" in 1890

23 Exec.-Legis. Procedure—takes part in (or calls for or opposes) some action regarding procedural relations between executive and legislative branches

114 Investigate—calls for, takes part in, or otherwise is associated with a congressional hearing or investigation

Stances

1,081 Take Stand—takes a stand on some matter, through any of a variety of means, on or away from Capitol Hill (NB: In 428 cases, where a source specifically reported that a member took a stand in the course of legislating, these items are also coded as Legislate)

71 Big Speech—makes an influential or otherwise remarkable speech, as in the Webster-Hayne debate in 1830

15 Filibuster—threatens or takes part in a filibuster

32 Singular Stand—stands out against a majority, as did Senators Wayne Morse and Ernest Gruening against the Tonkin Gulf Resolution authorizing the Vietnam War in 1964

8 Tipping Vote—casts the decisive vote, as did F. Muhlenberg for the Jay Treaty in 1796

7 Disclose—discloses something, as did S. T. Mason in leaking the Jay Treaty text in 1795

20 Write—writes a politically relevant book or article, such as J. W. Fulbright's *The Arrogance of Power* in 1966 or Barry Goldwater's *The Conscience of a Conservative* in 1960

Congressional roles

346 Leader—is a significant formal or informal leader of a congressional party or bloc *or* is mentioned as a leader in a report of some other action

35 Run for Leader—runs for a party leadership post (including the House Speakership)

Table 2.6 (*continued*)

232	Committee Chair—is a significant committee chair *or* is mentioned as a chair in a report of some other action
103	Committee Member—is a significant committee member (though not chair) *or* is mentioned as a committee member in a report of some other action
75	Special Committee—in either of the two preceding categories, the committee was *not* a House or Senate standing committee (it was a joint, special, select, or conference unit)

Target or subject

511	Opposition—tries to thwart the aims or impair the standing of a presidential administration, through any of a variety of techniques including rhetoric, investigations, or moves to impeach officials, block appointments, or pass or block important legislation
539	Foreign Policy—the action in question pertains to U.S. foreign or defense policy; includes being appointed Secretary of State, Defense, War, or the Navy, or as an emissary abroad

Executive connections

141	Counsel admin.—meets with, advises, or otherwise counsels the president or some other high executive official
15	Speak for admin.—speaks for a presidential administration
74	Take appointment—is appointed (or considered for appointment) by the president to a judgeship, cabinet post, or other high diplomatic or administrative position (this includes nominations that were blocked or withdrawn)
36	Big four cabinet—is appointed Secretary of State, Treasury, or War (Defense after 1947), or attorney general

Extraconstitutional roles

34	Noncongress. role—takes on a judicial, administrative, diplomatic, executive, or subnational governmental role not envisioned by the Constitution as congressional
7	Commission—serves on joint leg./exec. commission at least partly appointed by president

Parties and elections

152	Pres. or vice pres.—runs (or is seriously considered) for the presidency or vice presidency, or for a party nomination for one of those offices
116	Pres. selection—tries to help decide who becomes president or vice president, as through convention processes *or* (in a few cases) works to revise rules for presidential selection
152	Party convention—participates in a party convention, for whatever reasons
46	State/local organization—is a powerful state or local party organization leader, such as Senators Matthew Quay and Tom Platt in the late nineteenth century

Table 2.6 *(continued)*

---

32 Other party—takes part in extracongressional party activity not included in the four categories above, as did Hugh Scott in serving as GOP national chairman in 1948

23 Mobilization—tries (outside election campaigning) to mobilize the public for some cause, as did Senator Huey Long with his Share Our Wealth program

28 Cong. elections—does something connected with congressional elections, as did Tony Coelho and Jesse Helms in devising new techniques to raise campaign money around 1980

Rare kind of member

3 Rare party/ideology—rare party or ideology, e.g., the Socialist Victor Berger in 1919

20 Rare race/ethnic/gender—"descriptive representation," as with Jeannette Rankin appearing as the first woman member of the House in 1917

Questioned behavior

51 Dubiousness—is accused of illegal or unethical behavior, as was Edward Kennedy in the Chappaquiddick incident of 1969

12 Is censured/expelled—is censured, expelled, or not seated by the House or Senate; or at least such a move is proposed

Various

9 Resigns—resigns from Congress or a leadership position, for whatever reasons

18 Other eponym—name becomes attached to something other than a legislative measure, as in "McCarthyism," or "the Nye Committee"

17 Distributive politics—engages in particularistic distributive politics, as did Russell Long with tax breaks on the Senate Finance Committee

25 Unusual—not easily classifiable, as when Preston Brooks caned Charles Sumner in 1856

---

leader of the Senate's southern bloc), and "opposition" (the measure was a Johnson administration priority). One virtue of multiple coding is that with the aim of enriching the dataset, it allows the use of auxiliary categories that deviate from the strict idea of "action." Thirty-seven of the forty-three categories in Table 2.6 always incorporate "actions" as that concept was defined earlier in this chapter. But typically, four categories ("leader," "committee chair," "other committee," and "special committee") simply track attributes of members performing otherwise recorded "actions." Therefore, Congressman Wilbur Mills, who is nearly always identified as chairman of the House Ways and Means Committee in reports of his role in enacting Medicare in 1965 (coded as "legislate"), earns an auxiliary tick as "committee chair" for that move. Furthermore, two highly populated categories in Table 2.6, "opposition" (to a presidential administration) and "foreign policy," always track only these characteristics, where relevant, of "actions" otherwise coded; their entries never stand on their own. Thus, a self-standing action such as "impeach/censure" or "investigate" might carry a side connotation of "opposition," and any of a variety of actions might be coded as "foreign policy" because they involve that policy territory. "Foreign policy" is the only policy area I have coded for here, although the dataset could be reworked to explore other such areas.

That is the dataset. In the chapters to come, unless otherwise specified, all displays and calculations are based on the full deck of 2,304 items—that is, actions satisfying the strict "A, the middling "B," *or* the loose "C" criterion for inclusion.

T H R E E

A Basic Profile of Member Roles

Congress is a lawmaking establishment, but it is a good deal more than that. In terms of political influence and legitimacy, it is a successful rival to its companion executive branch—not an easy achievement for a legislature in any regime. In filling this niche during the past two centuries, Congress has exhibited a distinctive blend of offensive and defensive capabilities, and it has vied rather effectively with the presidency to represent, and at times to shape and mobilize, the American public.

This ample place of Congress in the American regime, I hope to show in this chapter, can be illuminated by profiling a particular mix of kinds of MC "action"—a selection from the categories listed in Table 2.6. *Legislate* is given due attention here, but it shares the spotlight with the often devastating activity of *investigate* (a glance is also taken at *impeach/censure* and *make appointment*) and the busy activity of *take stand*. One result of this "action" juxtaposition is that MCs are portrayed more as shapers or mobilizers, and less as passive representers, than is the case in most scholarly treatments of Congress. Another result is that an appreciation of Congress's major roles in *foreign policy* and in staging *oppositions* to presidential administrations is fostered. Looking only at *legislate* would not elicit that appreciation; in both these kinds of endeavors, investigating and stand-taking are key "action" ingredients. ⟩

That, after a preliminary framing move, is the plan of the chapter. The relevant kinds of "action" are taken up one by one with data displays—chiefly time series—as centerpieces of discussion. Unpatterned "episodicness" is the record across the two centuries in most of the time series. That record points to certain more or less stable qualities of the American regime rather than to any evolution of practices during it, though in at least one kind of "action"—investigating—evolution does come to light.

The chapter closes with a consideration of Stuart England—a setting several generations earlier than the founding of the American republic, where a strong legislature also classically competed and coexisted with a strong executive, and in so doing, as it happens, exhibited an "action" profile similar to the later American congressional one. Similar profiles worked, at least in a Darwinian sense of institutional survival, for Parliament back then and for Congress more recently. I argue that the analogy is instructive.

Extraconstitutional Roles

But first the preliminary framing move. There are certain kinds of activity that members of Congress have not engaged in much or at all during the past two centuries. In general, they have steered clear of constitutional roles assigned elsewhere in the 1780s. This is a "dog that doesn't bark" story worth presenting at the start, especially if it is placed in comparative perspective. In the long history of Western representative assemblies, members have won prominence for a wide variety of activities. Judicial functions used to be intermingled with legislative ones. In parliamentary regimes, ministerial roles have tended to displace legislative ones; for example, Tony Blair, the prime minister, is the leading member of the British Parliament today. Local versus national involvements have played out in various ways; for example, it surprises some Americans that many members of the French national assembly (former prime minister Alain Juppé and the late Gaston Defferre are cases in point) have served simultaneously as city mayors.[1] And change occurs: For any parliamentary body in any country during any two-century period, "role drift" among its members has been a good hypothesis.

The framers of the U.S. Constitution made two general moves relevant to this discussion as they addressed governmental roles in 1787.[2] First, they *specified* roles: Federal officials in the different branches were given explicit duties and powers. Second, to an appreciable degree they *segregated* roles. Notwithstanding the well-known U.S. pattern of separated branches sharing power, there were to be limits.[3] Most important, in a replay of an English reform a century earlier that had targeted the power of the crown by barring executive "placemen" (paid officials) from the House of Commons, members of the U.S. Congress were to be barred from serving simultaneously as federal administrators. In fact, the English themselves had given up on that idea of segregation as new arrangements of cabinet government took shape during the eighteenth century, but the Americans referred back to it.[4] "Placemen" were ruled out by the "incompatibility clause" of the Constitution: "No person holding any

1. Bordeaux and Marseille are the cities in these two instances. In 1996, over half the members of the French parliament were also city mayors. See "Mayors' nests," *The Economist*, November 16, 1996, p. 55.

2. For this paragraph I have relied on the excellent account in Steven G. Calabresi and Joan L. Larsen, "One Person, One Office: Separation of Powers or Separation of Personnel?" *Cornell Law Review* 79 (1994), 1047–78, 1146–53.

3. See the discussion in Jeffrey K. Tulis, "The Two Constitutional Presidencies," in Michael Nelson (ed.), *The Presidency and the Political System*, 4th ed. (Washington, D.C.: Congressional Quarterly, 1995), pp. 100–104.

4. See Gordon S. Wood, *The Creation of the American Republic, 1776–1787* (New York: Norton, 1969), pp. 143–50, 156–59.

office under the United States shall be a member of either house during his continuance in office." Cabinet members, among others, were
to be non-MCs. Also, at the interface between federal and state levels,
the new MCs' salaries were to be paid by the federal government rather
than, as earlier under the Articles of Confederation, by the states. This
was a segregating move (on the logic that he who pays the piper may pick
the tune). It is true that simultaneous officeholding at state and federal
levels was not formally ruled out by the Constitution. This comes as a
surprise today, given our decisive norm against such practices as U.S.
House members doubling as state legislators.[5] It is not clear how strong
this norm was two centuries ago, but for analytic purposes here I treat as
anomalies or "violations" anything that looks like state or local governing
activity (this might mean joint officeholding, but not only that) engaged
in by sitting MCs at any time since 1789.

That is the formal constitutional background plus a norm. In gathering
the dataset for this study I watched for both lateral and vertical "violations"—that is, for any "actions" during the past two centuries in which
MCs, at the same time they held their congressional seats, can be said to
have figured in executive, administrative, or judicial roles not prescribed
by the Constitution at the federal level,[6] or in governmental roles of any
kind at the state or local level. Leaving aside instances of MCs doubling as
state and local party "bosses" (which may belong here but are discussed
in Chapter 4), the full results are presented in Table 3.1. They are mea-
ger, even after generous coding. The items in the top half of the table
are probably better thought of as practical accommodations between the

5. In the 1990s, forty-seven *state* constitutions banned simultaneous service in legislatures at the two levels.

6. *Not* included here as "violations" are instances in which MCs have provided informal advice to members of the executive branch, as did, for example, Senator Fulbright in
advising President Kennedy on U.S. policy toward Cuba or Senate Majority Leader Mike
Mansfield (D-Mont.) in advising President Johnson on Vietnam.

Table 3.1 Nonconventional MC Roles

Member of a joint executive-judicial commission appointed at least partly by the president

—1897	Sen. Edward O. Wolcott (R-Colo.)	Named to currency commission to work with Europeans
—1908	Sen. Nelson W. Aldrich (R-R.I.)	Made head of U.S. currency commission
—1907–10	Sen. William Dillingham (R-Vt.)	Head of Dillingham Commission on immigration
—1938	Sen. Joseph O'Mahoney (D-Wyo.)	Chairs TNEC investigation of corporate monopoly
—1983	Rep. Barber Conable (R-N.Y.)	Member of Social Security Commission
—1983	Sen. Robert Dole (R-Kans.)	Member of Social Security Commission
—1983	Sen. Daniel P. Moynihan (D-N.Y.)	Member of Social Security Commission

Delegate to a foreign project appointable by the president

—1898	Sen. Cushman K. Davis (R-Minn.)	Appointed to Spanish peace treaty delegation
—1898	Sen. William P. Frye (R-Maine)	Appointed to Spanish peace treaty delegation
—1898	Sen. George Gray (D-Del.)	Appointed to Spanish peace treaty delegation
—1903	Sen. Henry Cabot Lodge (R-Mass.)	Member of Alaska boundary claims delegation
—1921	Sen. Henry Cabot Lodge (R-Mass.)	Delegate to D.C. naval conference
—1921	Sen. Oscar Underwood (D-Ala.)	Delegate to D.C. naval conference
—1933	Sen. Key Pittman (D-Nev.)	Promotes silver at London Economic Conference
—1944	Sen. Charles Tobey (R-N.H.)	Delegate to Bretton Woods economic conference
—1945	Rep. Sol Bloom (D-N.Y.)	Delegate to UN conference in San Francisco
—1945	Sen. Thomas Connally (D-Tex.)	Delegate to UN conference in San Francisco
—1945	Rep. Charles Eaton (R-N.J.)	Delegate to UN conference in San Francisco
—1945	Sen. Arthur Vandenberg (R-Mich.)	Delegate to UN conference in San Francisco

Freelance foreign policy enterprises

—1789–90	Rep. Thomas Scott (Pa.)	Schemes with British about western territory

Table 3.1 (*continued*)

—1797	Sen. William Blount (DR-Tenn.)	Is expelled for conspiring to invade Spanish territory
—1804–5	Sen. Jonathan Dayton (F-N.J.)	In on Burr conspiracy with foreign powers re western lands
—1808	Sen. John Smith (DR-Ohio)	Almost expelled for role in Burr conspiracy
—1918	Sen. Henry Cabot Lodge (R-Mass.)	Tells UK and French leaders Wilson doesn't speak for U.S.
—1953	Sen. Joseph McCarthy (R-Wis.)	Gets Greek shipowners to stop trading with Red China
—1978	Rep. Leo Ryan (D-Calif.)	Is murdered in visit to Jonestown Guyana cult

Judicial activities

—1794	Sen. John Taylor (DR-Va.)	Pleads case against U.S. tax in federal court
—1807	Rep. John Randolph (DR-Va.)	Grand jury foreman in Burr treason trial
—1837	Sen. Daniel Webster (W-Mass.)	Argues *Charles River Bridge* case at Supreme Court
—1856	Sen. Henry S. Geyer (D-Mo.)	Argues *Dred Scott* case at Supreme Court
—1864	Sen. Charles Sumner (R-Mass.)	Sponsors a black lawyer to practice at Supreme Court

Various

—1813	Richard M. Johnson (DR-Ky.)	Leads a Kentucky regiment in War of 1812
—1814	Samuel Smith (DR-Md.)	Heads militia defending Baltimore against the British
—1849	Thomas Butler King (W-Ga.)	Sent to California by Pres. Taylor to prod statehood bid
—1900	Mark Hanna (R-Ohio)	Helps settle miners strike
—1902	Matthew Quay (R-Pa.)	Role in settling another miners strike
—1933–34	Robert F. Wagner (D-N.Y.)	Leads National Labor Board in implementing NRA
—1961	James O. Eastland (D-Miss.)	Guarantees safety of civil rights protesters in Mississippi
—1964	Adam Clayton Powell (D-N.Y.)	Takes over local Harlem antipoverty project
—1981–82	Phillip Burton (D-Calif.)	Engineers pro-Dem. districting plan in Calif. legislature
—1986	Paul Laxalt (R-Nev.)	Bears Reagan message to Philippines' Marcos: Quit

branches than as violations. That is, MCs have sometimes served as (unpaid) members of joint executive-legislative commissions, such as the one that brokered an overhaul of Social Security financing in 1983, or as (unpaid) delegates appointed by the White House to represent this country at international bodies or meetings, as in the case of a Capitol Hill quartet including Senator Arthur Vandenberg (R-Mich.) that helped launch the United Nations in San Francisco in 1945. This role of delegate was prominent between 1898, when the peace conference ending the Spanish-American War included members of Congress, and 1945 at the close of World War II—a pattern that says something about the political risk Woodrow Wilson took in *not* sending any MCs to the Versailles conference at the close of World War I.

A variety of one-person "designer" enterprises appears in the bottom half of Table 3.1. In actions during the past half century, for example, Senator Joseph McCarthy, wielding his new powers as chairman of the Government Operations Committee in 1953, upstaged the State Department by making a deal with Greek shipowners to stop them from trading with Communist China. Senator James Eastland (D-Miss.) performed something like a territorial feudal baron in guaranteeing the Kennedy White House that civil rights protesters would be safe during a trip through Mississippi in 1961—he seemed to have the local authority to make that promise stick. Congressman Leo Ryan (D-Calif.) was murdered in Guyana while trying to help some Bay Area constituents caught up in the Jonestown cult colony there in 1978. Senator Paul Laxalt (R-Nev.) carried a Reagan administration message to Philippines President Ferdinand Marcos in 1986 that it was time to resign.

All these are extraconstitutional roles in one way or another, but the list does not add up to a great deal. Given the ways legislatures often actually operate and evolve, Table 3.1 presents close to a null result. In general, MCs have drawn notice for doing the kinds of things they were programmed to do two centuries ago.

Legislating

Congress was certainly programmed to legislate, and that role among the institution's actually important ones is taken up here first. In brief, approximately half of all the "actions" presented in this dataset have been associated with legislating. That outcome can be seen as a cup half full, but also as a cup half empty.

For purposes here, "legislating" means any kind of rhetorical, coalition-building, or formal parliamentary move by an MC aimed at enacting, amending, or blocking a bill, a resolution, a treaty, or a constitutional amendment (this definition yields 977 "action" items); *or* it can mean, even absent any other evidence, the memorialization of a member in an eponymous bill title such as the Kerr-Smith Tobacco Control Act of 1934 or the Erdman Act of 1898 (this definition yields another 102 items).[7] This category of actions, then, totals 1,079 legislative items, or 47 percent of the 2,304 items in the dataset.[8]

MC legislative moves measured this way have been distributed across U.S. history radically unevenly, as is shown in Figure 3.1. For the total legislative items for any particular decade, see the relevant vertical bar and the calibration on the left axis. For a relative measure—the percentage of all "actions" of all kinds during a decade that were legislative—see the line-connected bullets and the calibration on the right axis. Accord-

7. This joint usage blends the first two categories of Table 2.6.

8. If this study centered on the state of California rather than the whole country, it would be hard to ignore a class of policymaking events that have taken place outside that state's regular legislative process—that is, ballot initiatives. "Actions" could be documented for, to cite examples, Howard Jarvis, Ward Connerly, and Ron Unz, the promoters of, respectively, Proposition 13 cutting property taxes in 1978, Proposition 209 rolling back affirmative action in 1996, and Proposition 227 rolling back bilingual education in 1998. No doubt a theory could be spun out that California public opinion was open to these particular enterprises at these times, and that it was therefore inevitable that entrepreneurs would appear to conduct them. As with comparable theorizing about lawmaking within legislatures, the case is dubious.

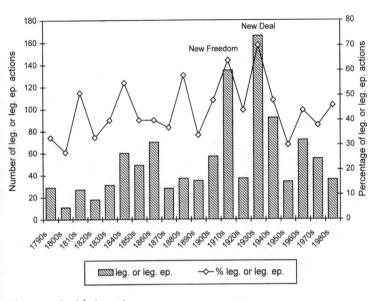

Figure 3.1. Legislative actions

ing to both these measures, the classic U.S. legislative eras have been, not surprisingly, those of Wilson's domestic New Freedom program (and the processing of the Versailles treaty with its League of Nations provision) in the 1910s, and the New Deal in the 1930s. Recent decades appear historically normal by comparison.

To give a sense of particulars, twice since World War II have legislative drives generated ten or more "action" items—those associated with the era-defining Civil Rights Act of 1964 (fifteen items) and the no less era-defining Reagan budget of 1981 (ten items). Great drama infused both campaigns. In 1964, which can serve as an example, CBS's Roger Mudd became a household name by reporting the Senate proceedings live every night for several weeks from the Capitol steps.[9] Here are some of the

9. William Small, "Equality of Access for Broadcast Journalism," in Robert O. Blanchard (ed.), *Congress and the News Media* (New York: Hastings House, 1974), pp. 67–69.

key moves made by MCs on both sides during that civil rights drive: Senate Judiciary Committee Chairman Eastland did his best to stonewall the enterprise; segregationist Congressman Howard Smith (D-Va.) added a gender-equality clause to the House bill (he hoped this action would derail the whole effort by overloading it, but the clause remained and became law); Congressman William McCulloch (R-Ohio), an influential regular in his party, supplied key backing for the civil rights cause; House Judiciary Committee Chairman Emanuel Celler (D-N.Y.) took a puristic liberal stance that the White House and its allies thought was endangering the cause's prospects; Hubert Humphrey (D-Minn.) did a skillful job of managing the ultimate bill on the Senate floor; Senator Russell led a classic, seemingly endless southern filibuster; Senate Republican Minority Leader Everett Dirksen (Ill.) contributed some characteristic crafty maneuvering that helped bring the needed sixty-seven votes for cloture.[10]

Events like this show Congress at peak energy, and passing laws is no doubt the institution's chief constitutional task. Still, to me it is a noteworthy result that legislative items make up only 47 percent of this study's dataset. As with representative assemblies elsewhere,[11] members of Congress really do spend a great deal of time and energy doing things

10. For a comprehensive account of the enactment of the Civil Rights Act of 1964, see Robert Mann, *The Walls of Jericho: Lyndon Johnson, Hubert Humphrey, Richard Russell, and the Struggle for Civil Rights* (New York: Harcourt Brace and Co., 1996), chs. 18–20.

11. Classic treatments of parliamentary bodies written before the twentieth century tended to downplay legislating in favor of such roles as checking the executive and expressing public opinion. See, for example, John Stuart Mill, *Considerations on Representative Government* (London: Parker, Son, and Bourn, 1861), ch. 5; Walter Bagehot, *The English Constitution* (Boston: Little, Brown, 1873), ch. 5. See also K. C. Wheare, *Legislatures* (New York: Oxford University Press, 1963), pp. 1–4. In the twentieth century, executive roles absorbed the time and energy of leading members of parliamentary bodies in nonpresidential systems.

besides legislating. One can read much of today's political science and not become aware of that.

Investigating

One additional hat often ostentatiously worn by members of Congress is that of investigator. The members patrol the executive branch in an "oversight" role,[12] and, beyond that, they probe anything else that strikes their fancy. This can be one of the most eye-catching kinds of pursuit in American public life.

Here, the label "investigate" applies when an MC calls for, takes part in, or is otherwise associated with a congressional investigation or hearing on any subject for any purpose. Within this category of 114 items, or 5 percent of the full dataset, a surprising time skew emerges: Six-sevenths of these investigative actions took place during the twentieth century. Figure 3.2 shows this decisive twentieth-century emphasis in both absolute and relative terms. What accounts for the skew? Could the full 2,304-item dataset somehow be basically underreporting the nineteenth century? Probably not, as is suggested by time series for two additional MC roles that are similar to investigating in some respects. In Figure 3.3, the open bars track MC actions associated with attempts to impeach or censure officials in the executive or judicial branch ($N = 37$ items); the patterned bars track actions associated with approval of presidential appointees to those branches ($N = 45$ items). (These categories are defined in Table 2.6.) This graph offers a kind of cross-century reality check. In the case of impeachment and censure, the data spikes for the eras embracing Andrew Johnson's and Richard Nixon's presidencies jut

12. See, for example, Mathew D. McCubbins and Thomas Schwartz, "Congressional Oversight Overlooked: Police Patrols versus Fire Alarms," *American Journal of Political Science* 28 (1984), 165–79.

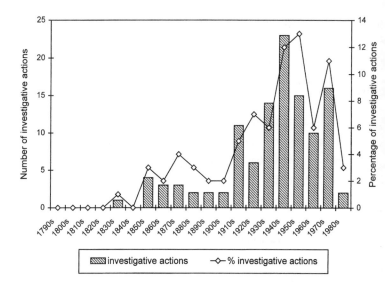

Figure 3.2. Investigative actions

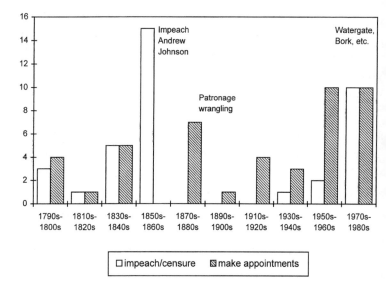

Figure 3.3. Impeach/censure and making appointments actions

up as one would hope and expect. (A graph updated to include the 1990s would show a Clinton spike, also.) In the case of appointments, the late twentieth century does stand out, but for an understandable reason: the high-intensity conflict during that era over Supreme Court nominations sent up by Presidents Johnson, Nixon, and Reagan. The showdown over conservative Robert Bork's failed nomination in 1987 brought five "actions" all by itself. (The third highest spike in the appointments series, for the 1870s and 1880s, reflects wrangling over federal patronage jobs at that time.)

To return to investigations, it is not that those conducted in the nine-teenth-century do not register at all. To cite three instances, "actions" materialize for Congressman John Covode's (R-Pa.) probe of lax money handling in the Buchanan administration, Senator Benjamin Wade's investigation of the North's military disaster at Ball's Bluff during the Civil War, and Senator John Scott's (R-Pa.) hearings on conditions in the South during Reconstruction.

Yet Capitol Hill probes, as the standard of highly publicized affairs we have become familiar with, do not seem to have come of age until around 1910. This is a pattern that demands explanation, and an interesting one is offered by Telford Taylor in his 1955 work, *Grand Inquest*.[13] During the Progressive era, a time when journalists developed the related genre of "muckraking," a cohort of innovative politicians found they could grab the public's attention and generate pressure for social and economic reforms by conducting what amounted to social exposés—that is, they could stage official hearings backed up by the congressional subpoena power to dramatize dubious practices by business corporations or by government officials said to be doing the bidding of corporations. This was a kind of "unmasking," to use Marxist terminology, of the capital-

---

13. Telford Taylor, *Grand Inquest: The Story of Congressional Investigations* (New York: Simon and Schuster, 1955), ch. 4.

ism of that era and its lackeys. It took a certain kind of style and temperament to do this work. A recent book addresses the rhetorical style of Progressive Republican Senator Robert La Follette, Sr., which is said to have featured a "propensity for reducing a complex phenomenon . . . into a simple melodramatic scenario where good and evil are clearly contrasted. . . . The major thrust of this pattern is to condemn the character of the evil villain."[14] La Follette figures in two investigative actions in this study's dataset, as does (a generation later) his son, Senator Robert La Follette, Jr. (R, then IND-Wis.), who exhibited a similar aggressiveness and ideological inclination. One characteristic move (though not an investigation-related one) by the elder of these Wisconsin senators, in a speech accusing Standard Oil and the J. P. Morgan interests of plotting the panic of 1907, was reported by the *New York Times* as follows: "'I have here a list of about 100 men,' he said, waving a paper at the Senate, 'who control the industrial, financial, and commercial life of the American people.'" The *Times* printed the full list on page one.[15]

With exposure as their motif, MCs of the Progressive left spurred and dominated high-publicity congressional investigations from 1913 through 1937—even during the 1920s when the Republicans formally

14. Carl R. Burgchardt, *Robert M. La Follette, Sr.: The Voice of Conscience* (Westport, Conn.: Greenwood, 1992), p. 20.

15. *New York Times*, March 18, 1908, p. 1. From a continuation of this "Money Power" speech a few days later: "Sir, I have named certain individuals from time to time in the course of my argument upon the pending bill. If I am understood as making war upon these men, I disavow it here and now, I do not direct my attack against a Rockefeller, a Morgan, a Harriman. They are but types. They but embody an evil. Back of these men is the THING which we must destroy if we would preserve our free institutions. Men are as nothing; the System which we have built up by privileges, which we have allowed to take possession of Government and control legislation, is the real object of my unceasing warfare." *Congressional Record*, March 24, 1908, p. 3795. The list of names, along with related information, appears in the *Congressional Record* of March 17, 1908, at pp. 3436–47.

controlled Congress. An early model was the "money trust investigation" of 1913—also named the "Pujo hearings," after Congressman Arsène Pujo (D-La.)—a public grilling of Wall Street financiers described by Taylor as "the first congressional investigation conducted in the 'grand manner' of modern times."[16] (Actually, special committee counsel Samuel Untermyer, not Pujo, played the leading role.) In probes in the mid-1920s, Senator Thomas J. Walsh (D-Mont.) exposed government mishandling of the Teapot Dome oil reserves (oil companies as well as federal officials were involved, making for a classic Progressive target), and Democratic Senator Burton K. Wheeler delved into Attorney General Harry M. Daugherty's related dubious activities.[17] The Depression era brought a regrilling of Wall Street in the dramatic, villain-rich "stock exchange investigation" of 1932–33 (also called the "Pecora hearings," after Ferdinand Pecora, a committee staffer rather than a member of Congress);[18] Senator Gerald P.

16. Taylor, *Grand Inquest,* pp. 62–63.

17. These Democrats led the two probes, in line with the reality that Democrats and Progressive Republicans dominated the Senate floor on the subject of Teapot Dome, although a Republican did formally chair each investigative unit. It was a busy season. In his history of the Senate, George H. Haynes wrote in 1938: "At no other period in its history had the Senate been so engrossed with investigations as during the six months [of the] first session of the 68th Congress (December 3, 1923–June 7, 1924)." At least fifty senators went at it as eleven committees held public hearings. *The Senate of the United States: Its History and Procedures* (Boston: Houghton Mifflin, 1938), vol. 1, p. 565.

18. As a sideline in gathering the dataset (though without entering anything into it as a result), I kept a record of "actions" by congressional staffers. They, too, turn up in history books occasionally. I came up with twenty-four actions involving eighteen individuals, of whom twelve were performers in twentieth-century investigations—an emphasis worth noting. These include the following committee counsels: Ferdinand Pecora in the stock exchange investigation, Samuel Untermyer in the Pujo investigation in 1913, Roy Cohn (along with "consultant" G. David Schine) in Senator McCarthy's loyalty probes of 1953–54, Robert F. Kennedy in Senator John McClellan's (D-Ark.) probe of union corruption in 1957–58, Samuel Dash with Senator Ervin's Watergate committee in 1973, and John Doar with the House Judiciary Committee as it considered impeaching President Nixon in 1974.

Nye's spirited probe of World War I munitions makers in 1934–35; Senator Hugo Black's (D-Ala.) probe of business lobbying in 1935; and Senator Robert La Follette, Jr.'s locale-by-locale exposé of often violent or illegal antiunion practices of business firms during the CIO's major organizing drive in those locales in 1936–37.[19]

Then, in an irony noted by Taylor, the left's well-developed exposure technology passed into conservative hands in 1938 with Congressman Martin Dies's (D-Tex.) spectacular probe that year of Communist influence in labor unions and government agencies.[20] Members of the special Dies Committee and its standing-committee successor, the House Un-American Activities Committee (HUAC), generated eleven action items for this dataset between 1938 and the mid-1950s. Senator Joseph McCarthy, who rose to national attention on a claim in a 1950 speech in West Virginia that "I have here in my hand a list of 205 [Communists in the State Department],"[21] went on to investigative fame as a committee chairman in 1953–54. Adding to the high investigative readings for the 1940s and 1950s shown in Figure 3.2 are hostile probes of federal agencies or labor unions by southern conservatives such as Congressman Howard

19. "The La Follette Committee became a mighty organ of publicity, pumping out exposés of the criminal underside of corporate labor relations policies—including espionage, naked intimidation, and armed thuggery" (p. 304). David M. Kennedy, *Freedom from Fear: The American People in Depression and War, 1929–1945* (New York: Oxford University Press, 1999).

20. It turns out that the transition from La Follette's corporation-bashing in 1937 to Dies's Communist-bashing in 1938 was, among other things, a shift from investigation *by* members of the Communist party to investigation *of* members of that party. Unknown at the time to La Follette, his committee's chief counsel and several other staffers were closeted Communists earlier associated with the now well-known "Ware group," which had operated in Washington during the early New Deal. See Harvey Klehr, John Earl Haynes, and Fridrikh Igorevich Firsov, *The Secret World of American Communism* (New Haven and London: Yale University Press, 1995), pp. 96–106.

21. The wording of this quotation is disputed; see David M. Oshinsky, *A Conspiracy So Immense: The World of Joe McCarthy* (New York: Free Press, 1983), pp. 108–112.

Smith and Senators Harry F. Byrd (D-Va.), Kenneth McKellar (D-Tenn.), and John McClellan (D-Ark.).

Beginning in the mid-1960s, the locus of investigative energy and enthusiasm switched back to the left, albeit with a fresh set of targets. Officials associated with the Cold War "imperial presidency" rather than, as earlier, business corporations, came under fire in Senator Fulbright's anti–Vietnam War hearings in 1966, Senator Ervin's Watergate investigation in 1973, the Nixon impeachment inquiry chaired by Congressman Peter Rodino (D-N.J.) in 1974,[22] and Senator Frank Church's (D-Idaho) exposé of foreign assassination attempts, domestic surveillance, and other practices by the Central Intelligence Agency in 1975.

Of the impact, or at least the reach, of some of these twentieth-century investigations there can be little doubt. Senator Wheeler "rocketed from relative obscurity to national prominence" on the strength of his Daugherty probe in 1924.[23] During the Nye hearings in 1934, "newspapermen from all over the United States and from other countries gave them detailed coverage, providing for readers throughout the world a daily round of headlines and sensations," and "the committee, its hearings and reports, and the speeches and legislative activities of its members undoubtedly strengthened isolationist or noninterventionist sentiment in the United States before World War II."[24] For, in effect, running interference for the CIO in 1936–37, the La Follette committee "elicited a torrent of congratulatory messages from leftist individuals and organizations. . . .

22. From 1972 through 1974, the Watergate affair and its resulting impeachment inquiry generated a total of twelve investigative "actions."

23. Richard Ruetten, "Senator Burton K. Wheeler and Insurgency in the 1920's," *University of Wyoming Publications* 32 (1966), 118. Later in 1924, Wheeler was selected as Senator La Follette's vice presidential running mate on the Progressive Party's national ticket.

24. Wayne S. Cole, *Senator Gerald P. Nye and American Foreign Relations* (Minneapolis: University of Minnesota Press, 1962), pp. 73, 96.

Very early in its life the committee became a source of inspiration to pro-letarian novelists, writers of nonfiction, film producers, and playwrights. Even before its most dramatic hearings, its preliminary findings pro-vided raw material for left-wing artists."[25] In 1938, the Dies Committee won from the *New York Times* "more than five hundred column-inches of space in its first month and a half of life, and other newspapers were even more accommodating." In a December 1938 Gallup poll, among the roughly three-fifths of voters who had heard of the Dies unit—note that this was well before television—74 percent favored keeping the investi-gation going.[26] Senator Estes Kefauver's (D-Tenn.) investigation of orga-nized crime in 1950 drew an estimated twenty to thirty million television watchers and a quarter of a million letters.[27] In 1966, Senator Fulbright's Vietnam hearings are said to have "impinged on the lives of virtually all Americans. Those that did not watch directly caught excerpts on the six and ten o'clock news." In late February of that year, after Secretary of State Dean Rusk had testified, "[Johnson aide] Bill Moyers reported to the president that the approval rating for his handling of the war had in one month—from January 26 to February 26—dropped from 63 per-cent to 49 percent."[28] In 1973, Senator Ervin became "a neo-folk idol. . . .

25. Jerrold S. Auerbach, *Labor and Liberty: The La Follette Committee and the New Deal* (Indianapolis: Bobbs-Merrill, 1966), p. 155. Also, on the committee's hearings: "These revelations further fostered a climate of opinion favorable to labor and, at least for a sea-son, restrained management from its customary reliance on the mailed fist." Kennedy, *Freedom from Fear,* p. 304.

26. Walter Goodman, *The Committee: The Extraordinary Career of the House Committee on Un-American Activities* (New York: Farrar, Straus and Giroux, 1968), pp. 27, 53.

27. William Howard Moore, *The Kefauver Committee and the Politics of Crime, 1950–1952* (Columbia: University of Missouri Press, 1974), pp. 184, 200.

28. Randall Bennett Woods, *Fulbright: A Biography* (New York: Cambridge University Press, 1995), pp. 405, 410. Another assessment: "These hearings would have the revolu-tionary effect of rendering legitimate—even patriotic—what would have seemed almost treasonous just a few months before: raising fundamental questions about the entire

His uniquely Southern, cadenced English, and his use of homespun, Shakespearean, and Biblical allusions, made him an instantly popular television personality." In September of that year, "57 percent of those questioned believed that the [Ervin] committee was more interested in gaining facts than in discrediting the Nixon Administration, while only 28 percent criticized it."[29] In July 1974, the Nixon impeachment hearings drew thirty-five to forty million viewers, and sentiment favoring impeachment rose 13 percent during the week after the House Judiciary Committee's members each voiced their own positive or negative (mostly negative) judgments publicly.[30] If any realm exists in which MCs can be autonomous and consequential, it is the realm of investigation.

Since the 1970s, Figure 3.2 suggests, MC investigative "action" has taken a nosedive.[31] The most recent probe in the "grand manner," with daily headline-catching revelations and a generous supply of villains, was arguably Senator Church's investigation of the CIA in 1975. The Iran-Contra inquiry of 1987 was rather flat by comparison.[32] The House Judiciary Committee's impeachment inquiry of 1998 drew attention, but that was flat in a sense, too. There were few revelations—those had already been ferreted out by aggressive journalists and Independent Counsel Kenneth Starr. We may see a clue here to the slump shown in Figure 3.2. Since the mid-1970s, the congressional exposé role, or at least much of it, seems to have shifted to Watergate-style investigative journalists and a

---

policy of containing communism." Richard Gid Powers, *Not Without Honor: The History of American Anticommunism* (New Haven and London: Yale University Press, 1998), p. 321.

29. Stanley I. Kutler, *The Wars of Watergate: The Last Crisis of Richard Nixon* (New York: Norton, 1990), pp. 258, 381.

30. Kutler, *Wars of Watergate*, p. 531.

31. For a discussion of congressional investigations of the executive branch since World War II, see David R. Mayhew, *Divided We Govern: Party Control, Lawmaking, and Investigations, 1946–1990* (New Haven and London: Yale University Press, 1991), ch. 2.

32. It generated only two items for this dataset.

Role of independent counsels [handwritten marginal note]

long line of independent counsels. In the case of the counsels, at least, it is a fair question whether that displacement has been a good thing. Charges of dereliction by officials have come to be tested through legal processes, in which the players have autonomous jurisdictions and veiled modes of operating, rather than through political processes, in which elected MCs make their distinctive kinds of moves splashily day by day, with one eye on public reaction. This is a complicated matter. Should Kenneth Starr and Lawrence E. Walsh (the independent counsel who indicted Republican former Defense Secretary Caspar W. Weinberger just four days before the 1992 election; Walsh, like Starr, seems to have had his own agenda) be traded in for Tom Walsh (in his Teapot Dome role), Richard Nixon (in his HUAC role), Joseph McCarthy, J. W. Fulbright, and Sam Ervin? For a suitable comparison, the net needs to be cast that wide, and a strange collection of fish appears.

Notwithstanding the apparent recent decline in congressional investigative actions, the potential for such actions remains. Society as well as public officials can be spotlighted. A latter-day Samuel Untermyer or Ferdinand Pecora, for example, might have found a way to parade before television cameras the CEOs of the 1990s who pocketed tens of millions of dollars for themselves at the same time they downsized their employee ranks. That sort of activity is a natural for Capitol Hill dramatization, although it is true that successful probes, like successful lawmaking enterprises, do not just happen; they require an exercise of initiative and ingenuity.

Taking Stands

While gathering this study's dataset, I came to believe that a great deal of MC behavior warrants, whatever else, the commonsense label "take stand"—that is, registering a position on some matter before some audience. In practice, that audience has almost always been the American public or some part of it, although certain MC stands have been aimed at, for example, presidents—as when the six Democratic members met with President Pierce to lobby him to back the Kansas-Nebraska Act[33] in 1854—or even occasionally at foreign countries, as when three congressional leaders spoke out to assure Germany of America's good intentions in February 1917, when the United States was still a bystander to World War I.[34]

As coded, "take stand" could share an "action" with such behavior as legislating or investigating, but it could also constitute an action by itself —as when Senator "Pitchfork Ben" Tillman (D-S.C.) lashed out at Theodore Roosevelt for inviting black guests to the White House in 1901. In practice, considerable overlap occurs with the "legislate" category in particular: 427 of the 977 actions coded as "legislate" are also coded as "take stand." In principle, an item was coded jointly if a member exhibited "legislate" activity that included "taking a stand" such as making a speech that stated a position (purely parliamentary moves, as in "Congressman Jones offered an amendment," were not sufficient). Senator Seward, for example, won joint coding for delivering his provocative "Higher Law" speech against slavery during the debate over the Compromise of 1850.

"Take stand" was a lot more slippery to code for than such relatively concrete actions as "legislate," "investigate," or "censure/expel." In practice, I searched for instances where a history text said, or strongly implied, that a member had registered a position before an audience. This designation encompasses a wide range of items. For example, "stand-taking" in the course of legislating includes Seward's speech in 1850, Senator Russell's filibuster in 1964, and Fisher Ames's pro–Jay Treaty

33. David M. Potter, *The Impending Crisis, 1848–1861* (New York: Harper and Row, 1976), pp. 161–62. According to Potter, this lobbying was reported in the press at the time.

34. Arthur S. Link, *Woodrow Wilson and the Progressive Era, 1910–1917* (New York: Harper and Bros., 1954), p. 206.

speech in 1796—or, to go beyond speeches, Jeannette Rankin's solo vote against declaring war notwithstanding Pearl Harbor, which is ordinarily written about as a kind of stand.

Table 3.2 presents a list of stands taken outside the realm of legislating, a category that constitutes a sizable 60 percent (653 of 1,081) of all "take stand" actions during the two centuries under study. Its entries include: Speaker Theodore Sedgwick's (F-Mass.) boycott of Jefferson's inauguration as a hostile Federalist gesture in 1801; Southern spokesman Robert Toombs's (D-Ga.) issuance of a secession manifesto in 1860; right-wing Senator William Jenner's (R-Ind.) denunciation of General George Marshall as a front man for traitors in an extraordinary speech in 1950; Republican Senate Minority Leader Hugh Scott's (R-Pa.) reaction to the just-disclosed Nixon tapes in 1974, in which he publicly labeled them "disgusting." Among other things, the table shows—this was the chief selection criterion—the great variety of (nonlegislative) ways in which stands can be taken. Among the operative verbs are spit, cane, wave, boycott, walk out, lead fight, resign, defect, found, call for, back, stage, dare, write, draft, author, deliver, sign, celebrate, eulogize, promote, endorse, introduce, suggest, charge, attack, denounce, issue, and fume. The sites of action include Congress itself, the Washington setting generally, news conferences, television sound bites, party conventions, speeches delivered virtually anywhere, a book, a newspaper, a journal, even two church services. The subjects range across the spectrum of U.S. politics and policymaking; anything is fair game.

"Take stand" thus defined takes on particular significance—it becomes a basic substance of politics—if the idea of public affairs laid out in Chapter 1 has merit. From this perspective, public affairs largely *consists of* the cut and thrust of politicians' (and others') moves like those shown in Table 3.2, lined up through time, generating notice and reaction, sometimes leading to deliberation and opinion formation. It can make a difference if Senate Republican leader Hugh Scott denounces the Nixon tapes

Table 3.2 Selected Instances of Nonlegislative MC Stand-Taking

1798	Matthew Lyon (DR-Vt.)	H	Spits in the eye of ideological foe Roger Griswold (F-Conn.)
1801	Theodore Sedgwick (F-Mass.)	H	Boycotts Jefferson's inauguration as Federalist gesture
1814	Timothy Pickering (F-Mass.)	S	Promotes secessionist Northern Confederacy
1825	George Kremer (D-Pa.)	H	Charges (in newspaper) corrupt deal between Clay and J. Q. Adams
1831	John Quincy Adams (NR-Mass.)	H	Introduces his first antislavery petition to House
1856	Preston Brooks (D-S.C.)	H	Canes Charles Sumner on Senate floor after Kansas speech
1858	Stephen A. Douglas (D-Ill.)	S	Engages Lincoln in Lincoln-Douglas debates
1858	William Seward (R-N.Y.)	S	Delivers his "irrepressible conflict" speech in Rochester, N.Y.
1860	Robert Toombs (D-Ga.)	S	Issues a secession manifesto
1861	Clement Vallandigham (D-Ohio)	H	As "Copperhead," backs obstruction of northern war effort
1867	William D. Kelley (R-Pa.)	H	Tours South to carry GOP doctrine to freedmen audiences
1868	Benjamin Butler (R-Mass.)	H	Waves a bloody shirt (literally) as Johnson impeachment manager
1872	Charles Sumner (R-Mass.)	S	Backs Democrat Greeley over Republican Grant for president
1874	Lucius Q. C. Lamar (D-Miss.)	H	Eulogizes deceased Sumner in North-South reconciliation speech
1881	Roscoe Conkling (R-N.Y.)	S	Resigns Senate seat in a huff over Garfield's patronage turndowns
1889	Henry Cabot Lodge (R-Mass.)	H	Writes *North American Review* piece backing House rules reform
1892	William B. Cockran (D-N.Y.)	H	Delivers anti-Cleveland oration at Dem. national convention
1896	David B. Hill (D-N.Y.)	S	Boycotts New York City speech of pres. candidate W. J. Bryan
1901	Benjamin Tillman (D-S.C.)	S	Assails Theodore Roosevelt for inviting blacks to the White House
1910	Nelson W. Aldrich (R-R.I.)	S	Moves to fund orthodox GOP congressional candidates
1910	Jonathan Dolliver (R-Iowa)	S	Dares Taft to try to expel Progressives from GOP
1917	Henry Cabot Lodge (R-Mass.)	S	Runs to shake Wilson's hand after presidential speech proposing war

Table 3.2 *(continued)*

1920	Andrew W. Volstead (R-Minn.)	H	Co-leads a church service to celebrate Prohibition
1922	Robert La Follette, Sr. (R-Wis.)	S	Calls national conference of Progressives
1926	Fiorello La Guardia (R-N.Y.)	H	Stages news conference to mix an (anti-Prohibition) illegal drink
1934–35	Huey Long (D-La.)	S	Promotes his Share Our Wealth program nationwide
1936	Ellison D. Smith (D-S.C.)	S	Walks out of Dem. convention as black preacher speaks
1937	Josiah Bailey (D-N.C.)	S	Co-drafts anti-FDR Conservative Manifesto
1940	Gerald P. Nye (R-N.Dak.)	S	Helps found America First movement
1943	Arthur Vandenberg (R-Mich.)	S	Presses anti-isolationist resolution at GOP Mackinac Island meeting
1944	Alben Barkley (D-Ky.)	S	Resigns Democratic leadership post in tiff with FDR over taxes
1950	William Jenner (R-Ind.)	S	Denounces General Marshall as a front man for traitors
1951	Joseph Martin (R-Mass.)	H	Assails Truman administration after General MacArthur firing
1952	Henry C. Lodge, Jr. (R-Mass.)	S	Promotes pro-Ike "fair play" reso. at GOP national convention
1952	Wayne Morse (R-Oreg.)	S	Defects from GOP over McCarthyism
1956	Albert Gore (D-Tenn.)	S	Won't sign segregationist Southern Manifesto
1956	Adam Clayton Powell (D-N.Y.)	H	Endorses Republican Eisenhower for reelection
1957	Eugene McCarthy (D-Minn.)	H	Takes lead in founding liberal Democratic Study Group
1962	Barry Goldwater (R-Ariz.)	S	Authors foreign policy book *Why Not Victory?*
1962	Kenneth Keating (R-N.Y.)	S	Charges JFK administration tolerates Soviet missiles in Cuba
1964	Kenneth Keating (R-N.Y.)	S	Leads walkout of moderates from GOP national convention
1968	Robert F. Kennedy (D-N.Y.)	S	Celebrates Easter mass with labor organizer Cesar Chavez
1968	Eugene McCarthy (D-Minn.)	S	Won't back Humphrey after Democratic convention in Chicago
1970	Gaylord Nelson (D-Wis.)	S	Suggests celebration of Earth Day (and it happens)
1973	Lowell Weicker (R-Conn.)	S	Assails Nixon administration in Watergate hearings

Table 3.2 (*continued*)

1974	Hugh Scott (R-Pa.)	S	As leader of Senate GOP, calls Nixon tapes disgusting
1975	Bob Carr (D-Mich.)	H	Puts Vietnam $ cutoff res. through House Democratic Caucus
1978	Edward Kennedy (D-Mass.)	S	Attacks Carter admin. from the left at midterm Dem. conference
1983	Phil Gramm (D-Tex.)	H	Switches to GOP, resigns House seat, and is reelected
1984	Barry Goldwater (R-Ariz.)	S	Fumes at CIA mining of Nicaragua harbors
1984	Jesse Helms (R-N.C.)	S	Backs right-wing El Salvadoran leader D'Aubuisson
1987	Edward Kennedy (D-Mass.)	S	Leads fight against Bork nomination to Supreme Court

as disgusting. A great value of holding a congressional seat is that one's stands may be noticed by an attentive public. A few MCs I have referred to in this work—James Madison in the 1790s, for example, or Robert F. Kennedy (D) as a New York senator in the 1960s—could no doubt have reached the public anyway, but those are rare cases. For almost all the MCs listed in Table 3.2, holding a House or Senate seat was probably a necessary condition to drawing notice.

Why do politicians take stands? To help win reelection (or higher office) is an obvious answer, but I would like to steer clear of any simple explanation. For one thing, as Daniel Walker Howe has written, one major strain of American political rhetoric, that of the nineteenth-century Whigs, had roots in a tradition of Protestant sermonizing and also the early American idea of republicanism: "Rhetorical ability, everyone agreed, was crucial in a republic, for free men who could not be coerced had to be persuaded." [35] Anybody who has listened to, say, Senators George McGovern

35. Daniel Walker Howe, *The Political Culture of the American Whigs* (Chicago: University of Chicago Press, 1979), ch. 2, quotation at p. 27.

or Orrin Hatch (R-Utah), will not be sure that those old roots have entirely shriveled up. Also, many MCs are no doubt committed activists trying to "make history" on their own.[36] It is a complicated question. Ducks quack; politicians take stands. For purposes here, the propensity can be treated as a primitive.

Whatever it is that motivates MCs to take stands, sometimes they really do try to change the content of public opinion. This is a significant point, because in contemporary political science, MCs are so dominantly seen as passive receivers of opinion. It is true that most members are not crusaders. As Richard F. Fenno, Jr., has demonstrated, the typical House member does not put much effort into "educating" a home constituency.[37] This is one of those areas, however, where it is useful to examine the total as well as the typical. On the extreme end of the scale, *some* House and Senate members during the past two centuries have spent a great deal of energy trying to "educate" not just their home constituencies but the entire country—and, so far as one can tell, often with effect. That they have done this—and that no doubt countless other MCs have aimed lower in more modest attempts to persuade—constitutes a major

36. See Nathan Teske, *Political Activists in America: The Identity Construction Model of Political Participation* (New York: Cambridge University Press, 1997).

37. Richard F. Fenno, Jr., *Home Style: House Members in Their Districts* (Boston: Little, Brown, 1978), pp. 162–68. Of the senators Fenno has addressed in monographic works in recent years, one is coded in this dataset as "taking a stand"—Pete Domenici (R-N.Mex.) for his role as a deficit hawk in 1981–82, which Fenno discusses as "policy leadership." Other "actions" by Fenno's senators: John Glenn (D-Ohio) ran for president in 1984, Dan Quayle (R-Ind.) ran for vice president in 1988, and Arlen Specter (R-Pa.) aggressively interrogated Anita Hill in the Clarence Thomas confirmation hearings televised in 1989. This last item is not included in the 1789–1988 dataset, but I picked it up in consulting the thin historical sources that cover the years since 1988. The relevant works by Fenno, all published by Congressional Quarterly Press in Washington, D.C.: *The Making of a Senator, Dan Quayle* (1989), *The Presidential Odyssey of John Glenn* (1990), *The Emergence of a Senate Leader: Pete Domenici and the Reagan Budget* (1991), and *Learning to Legislate: The Senate Education of Arlen Specter* (1991).

property of Congress as an institution, and it should not be ignored. I
will try to nail down the point by example. Listed below are ten instances
in which MCs unquestionably intended to change public opinion, took
steps to do so, and were acknowledged by historians for their attempts.[38]
Sometimes the effort involved use of formal congressional processes,
sometimes not. In a few of these cases the actors were party leaders, but
in most cases not.[39] It is not necessary to be a party leader in order to set
up shop on Capitol Hill as a public persuader.

- Congressman James Madison (DR-Va.), in the early 1790s, worked with
  Thomas Jefferson to launch a newspaper in Philadelphia (then the temporary national capital) that could serve as the new Republican party's
  house organ. That was the *National Gazette*, edited by Philip Freneau.
  Then, Madison wrote a year-long series of eighteen *Gazette* essays that
  are said to have been "a very full index to the ideology, the system of
  prejudices and beliefs, of the emerging Republican party."[40]
- Senator Robert J. Walker (D-Miss.), in 1844, "wrote a public letter on
  the annexation of Texas. It had a circulation of millions; no letter in the
  entire antebellum era had greater significance." In it, Walker crafted a
  bizarre argument, evidently convincing to many northern Democrats
  of the time, that annexation of Texas would help rid the country of
  slavery *and* serve the cause of whites-only democracy. The U.S. slave

38. These are examples of "coalition leaders," not simply ordinary members of Congress, in the language of R. Douglas Arnold, *The Logic of Congressional Action* (New Haven
and London: Yale University Press, 1990), p. 7.

39. In Jacobs's account of health-care politics during 1993–94, Republican Party leaders were the MCs who tried to change or crystallize public opinion. Jacobs et al., "Congressional Leadership of Public Opinion."

40. Stanley Elkins and Eric McKitrick, *The Age of Federalism: The Early American Republic, 1788–1800* (New York: Oxford University Press, 1993), pp. 263–70, quotation at
p. 269. This was in 1791–92. Madison's earlier-mentioned "Helvidius" essays came later,
in 1793. Elkins and McKitrick, p. 362.

population would trickle southwest into Texas and then possibly, when the land ran out there, down into Mexico.[41]

- Senator Charles Sumner (D-Free Soil, then R-Mass.), in the 1850s, delivered several long, impassioned antislavery speeches to his fellow senators, but, according to his biographer David Donald, he came to believe that " 'no senator is reached by any argument,' and that his orations could have an effect only if 'addressed somewhat as harangues to the whole country.' " Sumner's "Freedom National" speech of 1852 was issued in a pamphlet that went through five editions. His "Crime Against Kansas" speech of 1856 had a circulation of around a million copies. Following his "Barbarism of Slavery" speech of 1860: "Long after Congress adjourned, he remained in sweltering Washington franking thousands of copies for distribution all over the country."[42]

- Senator Henry Cabot Lodge (R-Mass.), in 1919, staved off U.S. membership in the League of Nations by, among other things, consciously appealing to public opinion. According to one account: "He early came to the conclusion that once they understood, the American people

41. John Ashworth, *Slavery, Capitalism, and Politics in the Antebellum Republic* (New York: Cambridge University Press, 1995), vol. 1, pp. 424–26, quotation at p. 424.

42. David Donald, *Charles Sumner and the Coming of the Civil War* (New York: Knopf, 1967), pp. 227–39, 254–56, ch. 11, and pp. 352–63; quotations and other particulars at pp. 354, 238–39, 302, 361. See also Thomas C. Leonard, *The Power of the Press: The Birth of American Political Reporting* (New York: Oxford University Press, 1986), pp. 83–86. On public reaction to Sumner's hard-hitting 1860 speech: "After a few weeks, Sumner's exertions to circulate and publicize his speech began to pay off. Though the more sophisticated Republican Eastern cities had repudiated it, the rural areas of the North and West welcomed it. . . . Practically every small-town newspaper in Massachusetts, most of those throughout the rest of New England, and a great many others stretching out to the western frontier—in fact, wherever New Englanders had settled—enthusiastically praised both the speech and the senator. . . . So great was the reaction in Sumner's favor that the same party managers who treated him coolly in June warmly solicited his aid in August. The congressional Republican committee decided to circulate 'The Barbarism of Slavery' as a campaign document at two dollars a hundred." Donald, pp. 362–63.

would not be willing to give such a guarantee [as the collective security one specified in the Versailles treaty's Article X] and that therefore, as he told [Albert] Beveridge, 'the second thought is going to be with us.' But meanwhile the first thought, Lodge concluded, was 'probably against us,' and this called for special tactics. . . . 'I think what is necessary for us to do is to begin to discuss it, and try to get what it involves and what it means before the American people. That will be done.'" The result was six months of delaying tactics including two of public hearings laden with controversy. The strategy seems to have worked: "It is difficult to deny that the more the public learned about the League the more they became disenchanted with it."[43] When President Wilson conducted a cross-country speaking tour promoting the League, Lodge helped stage-manage a tour by Republican senators rebutting him.[44] Senators, like presidents, can sometimes "go public."

- Senator Robert M. La Follette, Jr. (R-Wis.), as the Depression set in around 1930, ran something of a reform industry. Owner of a weekly journal, *The Progressive,* which was "a major source of information on progressivism's fight for change in America's domestic and foreign policies," he also wrote for *The Nation,* delivered radio addresses, "took

43. William C. Widenor, *Henry Cabot Lodge and the Search for an American Foreign Policy* (Berkeley: University of California Press, 1980), pp. 314–15. See also John A. Garraty, *Henry Cabot Lodge: A Biography* (New York: Knopf, 1953), pp. 353–70. Why did Lodge do it? In Widenor's account: "The lesson of Lodge's experience was that in matters pertaining to the country's foreign policy it was wise 'to commit the Government only so far as the Government could redeem its pledges. . . .' To his way of thinking the sanctity of treaties was so basic to peaceful international relations that if the United States ever gave a guarantee such as that envisaged under Article X, then it would have to be sustained. Consequently, it was of signal importance to have the American people understand the road they were traveling, that they be prepared for and deliberately undertake such obligations" (pp. 312–13).

44. James Oliver Robertson, *No Third Choice: Progressives in Republican Politics, 1916–1921* (New York: Garland, 1983), pp. 206–12.

Sen. Tillman

his campaign for federal relief for the unemployed to the public during January 1931 [in New York City]," co-sponsored a Progressive conference in Washington, D.C., and then released on Capitol Hill the report of that conference's Unemployment and Industrial Stabilization Committee.[45]

- Senator Gerald P. Nye (R-N.Dak.), starting in 1934, conducted an eight-year isolationist crusade by way of his munitions hearings but also, for example, through speeches in New York, Chicago, Philadelphia, and other major cities in late 1934, and a thirty-eight-state speaking tour in 1936. In 1941, with America First paying the expenses, "he and his wife traveled many thousands of miles and he addressed approximately one hundred and sixty America First meetings and made numerous radio broadcasts. . . . Thousands upon thousands heard him, and millions more read the newspaper reports of his speeches and interviews."[46]

- Congressman Martin Dies (D-Tex.), starting in 1938, not only ran his un-American activities probes but also wrote a book (*The Trojan Horse in America — A Report to the Nation*), kept a "busy schedule of appearances around the country (160 speeches between August 1938 and February 1941), [and produced] his magazine articles (*Liberty* was his favored outlet) and [gave] newspaper interviews about menaces internal and external."[47]

- Senator J. William Fulbright (D-Ark.), in his 1966 Vietnam hearings,

45. Ronald L. Feinman, *Twilight of Progressivism: The Western Republican Senators and the New Deal* (Baltimore: Johns Hopkins University Press, 1981), ch. 2, quotations at pp. 13, 20.

46. Matthew W. Coulter, "The Franklin D. Roosevelt Administration and the Special Committee on Investigation of the Munitions Industry," *Mid-America* 67 (1985), 28; Cole, *Senator Gerald P. Nye*, pp. 75–76, 111, 115, 124, 176–82, quotations at p. 182.

47. William Gellermann, *Martin Dies* (New York: John Day Co., 1944), pp. 93, 208; Goodman, *The Committee*, quotation at pp. 121–22. Dies's book was evidently ghostwritten by committee staffer J. B. Matthews. See Powers, *Not Without Honor*, p. 172.

consciously angled for media attention. In the view of Fulbright and his chief aide, Carl Marcy, "It was now more than ever necessary to generate a congressional and public debate over Vietnam, to start a controversy over a very controversial subject." At stake was "control of the television airways and, through them, American public opinion." The two men "had long recognized that their struggle with the [Johnson] administration was essentially a competition for the attention of the press—that to change American foreign policy, they would have to have massive exposure."[48]

- House Speaker Thomas P. O'Neill (D-Mass.), in the early 1980s, "assumed the major responsibility for defining the position of his party with respect to the challenge to Democratic liberalism posed by Ronald Reagan. He entered into a symbolic struggle with the president." This was a novel role for a Speaker. "In the election year of 1984, O'Neill issued forty-three prepared statements during 101 daily press conferences. Almost all were harsh attacks on Reagan."[49]

- Congressman Newt Gingrich (R-Ga.), as a sophomore backbencher in 1982, began a decade-long drive to energize the country's conservatives and pave the way for a Republican takeover of the House. This involved, among other things, using c-span inventively to reach out to a small but engaged national audience, and stirring up media exposure of Speaker Jim Wright's (D-Tex.) finances—with the result of dethroning him in 1989. Gingrich turned himself into "a multimedia Whirling Dervish of books, writings, lectures, tapes, and television, spewing out ideas. . . . He believed in the power of ideas, particularly his own, and he looked to spread them through every medium possible. . . .

48. Woods, *Fulbright,* pp. 402, 404, 432.

49. Ronald M. Peters, Jr., *The American Speakership: The Office in Historical Perspective* (Baltimore: Johns Hopkins University Press, 1990), pp. 210–64, quotations at pp. 233, 255.

There was a think tank called the American Opportunity Foundation, and a book, *Windows of Opportunity*. . . . There was a political action committee called GOPAC. There was the National Republican Congressional Committee. Later came a lecture series beamed by satellite to sites around the country and a weekly television program on the conservative National Empowerment Television network." In 1994 came the culmination, the Contract with America, marketed through an ad in *TV Guide* and a staged ceremony on the steps of the Capitol as a platform for the 1994 election.[50]

Note that in all ten cases, it would be very difficult to write a history of U.S. public affairs without recounting the above-mentioned ventures of Madison through Gingrich to mobilize or persuade the public. Note also that most of these figures—perhaps all except Fulbright—pursued causes that were probably more popular in their home constituencies than in the nation as a whole. That is, in these cases, MCs who represented home bases located off the national median viewpoint, insofar as one existed, could undertake to build "designer" nationwide followings also located off the national median, or to try to alter the national median—or at least to alter the balance of opinion intensities around it. This is a distinctive aspect of the system that, looked at cross-sectionally, produces a flavor of far-left to far-right proportional representation in a Congress like the 106th, which included members with national followings like, say, Congresswoman Maxine Waters (D-Calif.) and Congressman Barney Frank (D-Mass.) on the left through Senator Jesse Helms on the right.

50. Dan Balz and Ronald Brownstein, *Storming the Gates: Protest Politics and the Republican Revival* (Boston: Little, Brown, 1996), pp. 37–43, 118–26, 143–46, quotation at p. 143.

Foreign Policy

Nearly a quarter of MC actions during the past two centuries have involved foreign or defense policy (539 actions, or 23 percent of the full dataset). Included here, in principle, are all items pertaining in any way to the conduct of U.S. policy in those realms.[51] Some two-fifths of these items are coded also as "legislate"; three-fifths are coded also as "take stand."[52] As discussed in Table 2.6, about a tenth of these items involve MCs being named to foreign policy or defense posts, chiefly in the cabinet but also as ambassadors, emissaries, and special delegates.

At certain junctures in U.S. history, the share of MC actions relating to foreign policy or defense has risen to a third or a half. Figure 3.4 shows high proportionate readings like that for the 1790s, 1800s, and 1810s, when relations with Britain or France brought chronic trouble, and the world war decades of the 1910s and 1940s. The readings for the two world war decades are also obviously the highest ones in absolute terms.

Are 539 items a little or a lot? To political scientists (though not historians), this number may seem high; a plausible lesson here is that congressional specialists in political science tend to underplay foreign and defense policy. This happens for possibly two reasons. First, congressional politics, like American politics generally, is ordinarily modeled as

51. This category includes moves to provision the U.S. economy for defense or war against foreign countries. It includes moves related to the Louisiana Purchase, the annexation of Texas (an independent nation at that time), the war with Mexico in the 1840s, and independence for the Philippines. It excludes moves related to the U.S. Civil War; immigration and foreign trade policies (unless relations with particular other nations were at stake—as they were with, for example, the Jay Treaty in 1795–96 and Jefferson's embargo in 1807–8—in effect, items like these were included but conventional tariff policy was excluded, as in, say, the Underwood-Simmons tariff act of 1913); and the governing or admission to statehood of U.S.-owned territories.

52. The overlap here between "legislate" and "take stand" is 118, or just over one-fifth of the 539. In this context, the "legislate" total includes legislative "eponym" items.

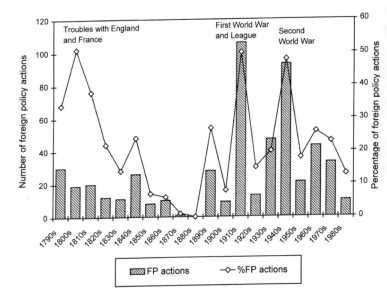

Figure 3.4. Foreign policy actions

a "who gets what, when, and how" game involving only domestic players; anything else is a distraction. Second, the profession tends to restrict its attention to the act of legislating. True, if treaties are included, legislating is a large part of the story in the foreign policy realm, as is shown in this dataset's many items associated with, for example, the Jay Treaty, the nonjoining of the League of Nations, the Truman Doctrine and Marshall Plan in the 1940s, and SALT II in the 1970s—not to mention such eponymous enterprises as the Ludlow amendment of 1937–38, which would have required a national referendum for the United States to go to war; the Bricker amendment of 1953–54, which would have curbed presidential treaty-making powers; and the Boland amendments of 1982 and 1984, which curbed U.S. aid to the Central American Contras.[53]

---

53. The Ludlow and Bricker amendments would have amended the Constitution; they failed. The Boland amendments were statutory; they passed.

Other large parts of the foreign policy realm, however, involve investigating and "taking stands." During the twentieth century, relevant high-intensity investigations have included those led by Senators Nye on World War I munitions makers, McCarthy on alleged subversion in the State Department and the Army, Fulbright on Vietnam, and Church on the CIA. And for any stretch of American history, no one could write an adequate account of foreign policy without reckoning with MCs who took notable stands. Examples abound. Congressman James Madison wrote his "Helvidius" essays in 1793. Congressmen Henry Clay, John C. Calhoun (DR-S.C.), Langdon Cheves (DR-S.C.), and other "war hawks" agitated for war against England in 1811–12.[54] Speaker Clay took up the cause of the newly independent Latin American republics around 1820. Senators Henry Cabot Lodge and Albert Beveridge (R-Ind.) took the lead in promoting American expansionism around 1900. Senator William E. Borah (R-Idaho) pressed a variety of causes—including recognition of the Soviet Union—as head of the Senate Foreign Relations Committee in the 1920s.[55] The Senate's various isolationists made their mark in the middle and late 1930s. Senators William Knowland (R-Calif.), Karl Mundt (R-S.Dak.), and others promoted an aggressive "Asia First" policy in the late 1940s. Senator Robert A. Taft assailed the Truman administration in 1950 for not asking Congress's approval of U.S. military action in Korea. Senators Frank Church, George McGovern, Robert F. Kennedy, Eugene McCarthy, and others came out against the Vietnam War in 1965–67.[56] Senator Christopher Dodd (D-Conn.) sparred with the Rea-

54. For a detailed account, see Henry Adams, *History of the United States of America*, vol. 6 (New York: Scribner's, 1890), pp. 122–236.

55. On Borah during Coolidge's presidency: "He had become the chairman of the Foreign Relations Committee and was to use that position to set up a second Department of State as well as to expand his influence on all party and Senate matters" (p. 268). Donald R. McCoy, *Calvin Coolidge: The Quiet President* (New York: Macmillan, 1967).

56. On McGovern, see Daryl Webb, "Crusade: George McGovern's Opposition to the Vietnam War," *South Dakota History* 28 (1998), 161–90.

gan administration over Central America policy in the early 1980s. Recently, Senator John McCain (R-Ariz.) shaped the case for all-out military intervention in Yugoslavia.[57] All these items except the last appear in the dataset.

Locke wrote that a government's executive branch exercises the "federative" power—that is, "the power of war and peace, leagues and alliances, and all the transactions with all persons and communities without the commonwealth."[58] Yet in practice, the American presidency's "federative" power has been exercised against a background of congressional authority and commentary—and sometimes initiative. In this dataset, beyond the 23 percent of all MC items classified as "foreign policy," also arguably federative in nature are the 6 percent deriving from secession, Civil War, and Reconstruction during the 1860s and 1870s (that was a matter of "war and peace" plus military occupation of the South), and another 4 percent for tariffs and other foreign trade policies—rounding up to 34 percent of the dataset.

Oppositions

In the American governmental context, what and where is the "opposition"? In a British-style parliamentary system, both "the government" and "the opposition" are easy to locate: They are the majority party in power (or, at least, the cabinet arising from that party) and the minority party out of power. Things are much more complicated in the constitutional environment of the United States,[59] but, as a first approxima-

57. See James Carney, "The McCain Moment," *Time,* May 3, 1999: "His blunt talk was in such demand that his staff lost track of the number of Kosovo-related TV appearances the Senator had made after the first week of the conflict" (p. 55).

58. John Locke, *Second Treatise of Government,* ed. C. B. Macpherson (Indianapolis: Hackett Publishing Co., 1980), p. 76.

59. See Robert A. Dahl, "The American Oppositions: Affirmation and Denial," in

tion, a presidential administration is something like a "government. White House commands the federal bureaucracy, and it is ordinarily the country's center of power, energy, initiative, and public attention. Significant "opposition" to presidential administrations, however, has traveled around. It has resided in a number of institutional locations—in the Supreme Court, for example, as Franklin Roosevelt experienced in 1935 when his New Deal statutes were struck down; in the state governments, as when South Carolina brought on the nullification crisis of 1832 or when Alabama and Mississippi challenged the Kennedy administration's civil rights moves in the early 1960s; in the cabinet, as during the presidencies of Washington (when Jefferson did his best to undermine Treasury Secretary Hamilton's economic policies and helped found an opposition party *while* he was a cabinet member during 1790–93), Madison, Monroe, and Andrew Johnson;[60] and even in the Office of Independent Counsel: Ask President Clinton.

The main site of "opposition" to presidential administrations, however, is unquestionably Congress, and playing that role is unquestionably one of the main things Congress does. What, in principle, is "opposition"? Here, it means *any effort by a member of Congress to thwart the aims or impair the standing of a presidential administration*. Note that this effort goes beyond policy disagreements, to include attacks on personnel. In the world of real politics, it can be a winning move—often productive of policy consequences—to show that a president or his top officials are crooked, unethical, incompetent, traitorous, or otherwise questionable. Thus, in an early instance of what we now call opposition research, Senator James Monroe (DR-Va.) gathered information in 1792 on Alexander

Dahl (ed.), *Political Oppositions in Western Democracies* (New Haven: Yale University Press, 1966); Nelson W. Polsby, "Political Opposition in the United States," *Government and Opposition* 32 (1997), 511–21.

60. On this pattern through Monroe, see James Sterling Young, *The Washington Community, 1800–1828* (New York: Columbia University Press, 1966), chs. 10, 11.

Hamilton's personal associates and sex life.[61] In the 1860s, congressional Republicans moved smoothly from disagreeing with President Andrew Johnson to impeaching him. For Capitol Hill Republicans in 1994, it was health care one day, the Whitewater scandal the next.[62] For purposes here, the effect of this definition of "opposition" is to make, say, Senator Ervin as much of an "opposition" for exposing Watergate as was Senator Lodge for blocking the League of Nations. Not least given the dynamic of Clinton's recent impeachment, this seems to be a realistic way to approach the American presidential system.[63]

As for tactics, congressional opposition can be waged in any of a variety of ways. A member of Congress might conduct an investigation, call for an impeachment, take a hostile stand, oppose a presidential appointment, oppose legislation the White House strongly wants, promote legislation the White House strongly does not want, or even challenge an incumbent president in an election.[64] For this dataset, any such move,

61. Elkins and McKitrick, *The Age of Federalism,* pp. 293–95. The information was not used immediately. A Republican operative went public with it in 1797.

62. "I think Whitewater is about health care," Rush Limbaugh posited. "Most people think that health care is a good idea, but they haven't read the plan. They're taking the President's word for it. Now . . . if people are going to base their support for the plan on whether they can take his word, I think it's fair to examine whether or not he keeps his word" (p. 276). Haynes Johnson and David S. Broder, *The System: The American Way of Politics at the Breaking Point* (Boston: Little, Brown, 1996).

63. This elastic opposition style also suggests a resemblance between the U.S. presidency and the English monarchy, of which it is (in certain respects) a descendant. For the Tudors and Stuarts, opposition was opposition, period, regardless of whether it had a policy focus. On the English roots of the American presidency, see Samuel P. Huntington, *Political Order in Changing Societies* (New Haven and London: Yale University Press, 1968), ch. 2.

64. Typically, works of history do not discuss presidential candidacies by members of Congress as opposition moves (as "opposition" is defined here), and I have not coded most of them that way. But in some cases an "opposition" label is obviously warranted— for example, Senator Henry Clay's pro-Bank challenge to Andrew Jackson in the general election of 1832, Senator Eugene McCarthy's antiwar challenge to Lyndon Johnson in

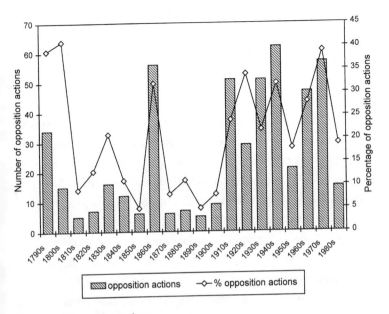

Figure 3.5. Opposition actions

beyond its basic coding, was coded additionally as "opposition" if, as discussed by historians, it was directed toward thwarting the aims or impairing the standing of a presidential administration.

The yield of this exercise is 511 "opposition actions," or 22 percent of the dataset, as exhibited by decade in Figure 3.5. Scoring highest in absolute terms are the 1860s, when Congress engineered its own Reconstruction policy over the objections of the presidency; the 1940s, which featured loyalty probes and incessant harsh criticism of federal agencies and the Truman administration; and the 1970s, which brought anti–Vietnam War moves, Watergate, and after that continual carping at the Carter administration. Interestingly, the decade of the 1970s, from which

the Democratic primaries in 1968, and Senator Edward Kennedy's liberal challenge to Jimmy Carter in the Democratic primaries in 1980.

a negative image of U.S. political processes still seems to resonate, registered the highest *proportion* of MC actions labeled "opposition" (at least until the 1990s) since the far-distant 1790s and 1800s with their anti-Hamilton maneuvers and episodic convulsions over, particularly, foreign policy.

Table 3.3 presents a different organization of the data (more specifically, from just over half of the 511 "opposition" items). Here, with the aim of locating occasions when congressional opposition might have packed a special punch, I scanned for *clusters* of "opposition actions." The criterion was whether historians have in fact treated items as parts of a cluster—that is, discussed them as parts of a single interrelated effort, as they typically do, for example, the various moves made by individual "isolationist" senators around 1940. Given such a historians' judgment of interrelatedness, I stipulated a threshold size that a group of MC actions had to exhibit in order to qualify as an opposition cluster for Table 3.3: at least fifteen actions in all; *or* at least five actions that reached the overall dataset through the moderately rigorous "B" criterion (that is, mention in at least two history works);[65] *or* at least three actions including one or more that reached the dataset through the stiff "A" criterion (that is, mention in two "general" history works).[66] This formula may seem more complicated than necessary, but there is a reason. I wanted to let opposition clusters include both shotgun-style and rifle-style manifestations. In the former case, many interrelated items documented possibly only by "era historians" may add up to a formidable opposition assault. In the latter case, as I think Table 3.3 bears out, just a few interrelated items that peak to high ("A"-level) historical prominence can be formidable also.

Eighteen opposition clusters appear in Table 3.3. They are well scat-

65. Though not more than one "general" history.

66. I made certain exclusions here. The third standard could *not* be satisfied by an "A"-level opposition item that was also coded as "legislative eponym" or that had "run for president" as its leading content.

Table 3.3 Clusters of Opposition Actions

Years	Leading Actors	Cause	A	B	C	Total
1790–93	James Madison (DR-Va.)	Vs. Hamilton's Treasury program	3	3	3	9
1793–96	James Madison (DR-Va.)	Vs. Washington admin.'s pro-UK foreign policy	0	6	9	15
1803–8	John Randolph (DR-Va.) Nathaniel Macon (DR-N.C.)	"Quid" opposition to Jefferson administration's policies	2	1	2	5
1832–36	Henry Clay (W-Ky.) Daniel Webster (W-Mass.) John C. Calhoun (W-S.C.)	Whig opposition to Jackson administration	6	1	1	8
1857–60	Stephen A. Douglas (D-Ill.)	Vs. Buchanan admin.'s pro-South slavery policies	2	1	3	6
1864–68	Thaddeus Stevens (R-Pa.) Charles Sumner (R-Mass.) Benjamin F. Wade (R-Ohio)	Congressional vs. presidential Reconstruction policy; impeachment of Andrew Johnson	10	10	26	46
1869–72	Charles Sumner (R-Mass.) Carl Schurz (R-Mo.) Lyman Trumbull (R-Ill.)	Liberal Republican opposition to Grant administration	3	2	2	7
1877–81	Roscoe Conkling (R-N.Y.)	Patronage showdowns with Hayes and Garfield admins.	3	0	1	4
1906–12	Robert La Follette, Sr. (R-Wis.) Jonathan Dolliver (R-Iowa)	Progressive insurgency	2	1	2	5
1917–20	Robert La Follette, Sr. (R-Wis.) Henry Cabot Lodge (R-Mass.) William E. Borah (R-Idaho)	Antiwar opposition in 1917 blends into anti-League opposition led by Lodge in 1919	6	5	17	28
1922–24	Robert La Follette, Sr. (R-Wis.) George Norris (R-Nebr.) Thomas J. Walsh (D-Mont.)	Progressive oppo. to Harding and Coolidge admins.; Teapot Dome probe	2	4	6	12
1934–35	Huey Long (D-La.)	Populist "Share Our Wealth" challenge to FDR	1	0	2	3
1937–38	Josiah Bailey (D-N.C.) Burton K. Wheeler (D-Mont.) John J. O'Connor (D-N.Y.)	Break with FDR over court-packing, executive reorganization, unions, minimum wage; the "Conservative Manifesto"	0	8	10	18

Number of Actions

Table 3.3 *(continued)*

Years	Leading Actors	Cause	A	B	C	Total
			\multicolumn{4}{c}{Number of Actions}			

Years	Leading Actors	Cause	A	B	C	Total
1939–41	Gerald P. Nye (R-N.D.) Arthur Vandenberg (R-Mich.) Burton K. Wheeler (D-Mont.)	Isolationist opposition to involvement in Europe	0	6	8	14
1938–44	Martin Dies (D-Tex.) Howard Smith (D-Va.) Harry F. Byrd (D-Va.) Kenneth McKellar (D-Tenn.)	Conservative assault on New Deal and war agencies; many investigations	0	2	16	18
1947–54	Joseph McCarthy (R-Wis.) William Knowland (R-Calif.) William Jenner (R-Ind.) Patrick McCarran (D-Nev.)	Anti-Communist loyalty probes blended with Asia First policy critique; "Who lost China?" "Who promoted Peress?"	11	10	8	29
1964–72	J. William Fulbright (D-Ark.) Eugene McCarthy (D-Minn.) George McGovern (D-S.D.)	Vs. Vietnam War and national security establishment; the government's "credibility gap"	6	8	14	28
1972–74	Samuel Ervin (D-N.C.)	Watergate	2	7	9	18

tered across American history. (None of them comes after the mid-1970s, though this may be partially the result of the shakiness of the data base after that time.) Many kinds of causes and issues are represented here, although it is interesting that foreign policy dominates five clusters and enters into another four—including, during the twentieth century, every entry from isolationism in the late 1930s through Watergate in the 1970s.[67] Half of the twentieth-century clusters have involved investiga-

67. The five: 1793–96, 1917–20, 1939–41, 1947–54, and 1964–72. The four: 1803–08, 1869–72, 1938–1944, 1972–74. In the last case, the Nixon administration's so-called secret Cambodian bombing of 1969 figured for awhile in the Watergate proceedings, and, in general, it is not easy to abstract the colossal Watergate showdown of 1973–74

tions. An instance of a "shotgun" data profile is the largely investigative assault waged by congressional conservatives against FDR's New Deal and World War II agencies from 1938 through 1944. "Rifle" profiles are exemplified by Senator Stephen A. Douglas's party-splitting challenge to President Buchanan over slavery in Kansas and other matters in 1857–60, and Senator Huey Long's populist challenge to FDR, cut short by Long's assassination, in 1934–35. In terms of sheer volume, according to the standard here, the leading exercises of congressional opposition in American history have been those staged by the Radical Republicans pursuing Reconstruction in the 1860s, the anti–World War I and then anti-League coalition in 1917–20,[68] the mix of Asia First advocates and disloyalty hunters during 1947–54, and the anti–Vietnam War critics of the Johnson and Nixon administrations during 1964–72. Anyone who lived through these last two clusters—"Who lost China?," "I have in my hand a list of 205 [Communists]," the Vietnam "credibility gap," and the rest—will probably agree that, except for (no doubt) Watergate, we have not seen anything of quite the same intensity level since.

What can be learned from this list of opposition clusters? Especially notable is the way they map onto the American party system. Three points are worth making. First, exercises of MC opposition like this used to be, though they do not seem to be any longer, powerful *producers of political parties.* The opposition led by Madison (along with Jefferson) around 1790 evolved into the Democratic Republican Party, as did the one led by Clay in the 1830s into the Whig Party. Senator Douglas's break with fel-

---

from the Vietnam War background of the surrounding 1970s. No Vietnam, very likely no Watergate.

68. This seems to be a plausible, if awkward, way to group the events of those years. In terms from a later era, Progressive doves like Robert La Follette, Sr., who had opposed the war from the start, drifted into a postwar alliance in 1919 with conservative, realpolitik hawks like Henry Cabot Lodge.

low Democrat Buchanan carried through to 1860 when their party itself fragmented into northern and southern factions during that crisis election year. The Liberal Republicans' challenge to Grant over Santo Domingo and other questions, the Progressive insurgency during William Howard Taft's administration, and yet another Progressive uprising led by La Follette, Sr., during Harding's administration all carried over into breakaway third-party moves in the following presidential elections of 1872, 1912, and 1924, respectively. If he had lived, Huey Long might have added another major instance in 1936.[69]

Since the 1930s, however, no third party worth mentioning has emerged from a Congress-based opposition. One reason for this may be changes in the rules for nominating presidential candidates. Consider the options available to Senate Democrats opposing the Vietnam War—Fulbright, Church, McGovern, Eugene McCarthy, Robert F. Kennedy, and the rest—in, specifically, 1967–68. In previous eras, a dissident faction like that might have generated a third party, but this 1960s faction could target the Johnson administration in the Democratic Party's presidential primaries—which is exactly what McCarthy and Kennedy did. It is true that presidential primaries were not as universal, wide-open, or determinative at that time as they became in the 1970s, but they were there in the 1960s as an option—a legacy of earlier twentieth-century reforms in many states.[70] Senator Estes Kefauver, in his challenge to President

69. Without Long as a candidate, the Union party challenge led by Congressman William Lemke (R-N.Dak.) in 1936 did not amount to much.

70. Former President Theodore Roosevelt waged a spirited, though losing, challenge against President Taft in the then new Republican primaries in 1912 (twelve states held primaries that year). Senator La Follette also entered the Republican primaries in 1912, though he did poorly. But the 1912 nominating contest (which spilled over into Roosevelt's third-party candidacy on the Progressive ticket) failed to set a new style. Between 1912 and 1952, no incumbent president aiming for reelection suffered a serious challenge in his party's primaries—not even the otherwise beleaguered Hoover in 1932. See

Truman in the 1952 primaries, had shown what kind of damage could be done to an incumbent administration.[71]

The second point regarding the opposition clusters presented in Table 3.3 is that the congressional oppositions *have centered as often as not in the president's own party.* The clearest such cases of same-party challenges are the ultra-Republican "Quids," who tangled with the Jefferson administration in 1803–8; Senator Douglas in 1857–60; the Liberal Republicans in 1869–72; Senator Roscoe Conkling (R-N.Y.), whose struggle for Senate control of federal patronage jobs in 1877–81 gave major headaches to fellow Republican Presidents Hayes and Garfield and more or less preempted the policy agenda of those years; the Progressives in 1906–12; Huey Long in 1934–35; and the Democrats who clashed with FDR over his court-packing plan, executive reorganization, and other issues in 1937–38. Possibly codable as "same-party" is the Radical Republican opposition of the 1860s; that judgment needs to be accompanied by an asterisk, however, because the Radicals' target, President Andrew Johnson, although Lincoln's running mate and the inheritor of the assassinated president's ruling team, was a long way from being an orthodox Republican. Dominantly same-party, although more of a mixed case, are the Progressives in 1922–24 (they included some Democrats), the conservative investigators in 1938–44 (they included some Republicans), and the anti–Vietnam War coalition in 1964–72 (this is a mixed case chiefly because the congressional assault led by Democrats continued against Nixon's Republican administration after it had arguably already enjoyed its maximum impact against Johnson's Democratic administration).

James W. Davis, *Presidential Primaries: Road to the White House* (New York: Thomas Y. Crowell, 1967), chs. 1–8.

71. Thus earning an "action" in this study's dataset.

Dominantly of the party *not* holding the presidency are the anti-Communists and Asia First advocates of 1947–54 (this group consisted primarily of Republicans who attacked Truman administration Democrats, although it is true that Democratic Senator Patrick McCarran of Nevada was a formidable disloyalty hunter all by himself during the Truman years, and that Senator Joseph McCarthy, once he obtained a committee chair in 1953–54, targeted his own party's administration), and the Watergate probers in 1972–74 (this was chiefly a Democratic enterprise, though Republicans such as Senator Lowell Weicker of Connecticut gave the Nixon administration trouble, too). Close to purely other-party challenges are the Republican-led opposition to the Wilson administration in 1917–20 and the isolationist challenge to FDR in 1939–41 (this was chiefly Republican, although Democratic Senator Burton K. Wheeler ranked high in the cause). Because the antipresidency parties in question originated in issue-based congressional oppositions at exactly those times, it is no surprise that the instances of purely other-party enterprises, or something like that, are the Madison-led oppositions of 1790–93 and 1793–96 and the anti-Jackson Whigs of 1832–36. That is a complete rundown. It demonstrates an approximately fifty-fifty distribution between same-party and other-party challenges—if anything, the spread tilts toward same-party opposition. In other words, during the past two centuries it has been close to a coin flip whether a major, eye-catching congressional opposition to a presidential administration would emerge in the president's own party or in the other—ordinarily, we would say the "opposition"—party.

The third point about these clusters is that the oppositions under scrutiny here *have nearly always centered in a party that controlled Congress (or a relevant house of Congress)—whether or not that controlling party was the president's party.* This is a decisive conclusion, not a fifty-fifty result. Note the instances in Table 3.3: the Madison Republicans against Washington's foreign policy,[72] the Quids against Jefferson, the Senate Whigs against Jackson, the Radical Republicans against Andrew Johnson, La Follette against President Taft, Lodge against Wilson, those against FDR's court-packing, Fulbright against Lyndon Johnson, the Ervin committee against Nixon. These and many other examples, however else they may differ, share at least that one property: A presidential administration was countered by an opposition centered in a congressional majority party. Of the eighteen opposition clusters, only one is an ambiguous case and only two are clear exceptions—that is, instances where members of a party not controlling *either* the presidency or a relevant house of Congress managed to stage a telling opposition. The ambiguous case is the Madison Republicans against Hamilton in 1790–93, when too many House members were still identifying themselves as nonpartisans for the idea of "party control" to mean much.[73] The clear exceptions are the largely Republican isolationist faction in 1939–41, and the McCarthy-Jenner-Knowland Republicans in 1949–52.[74] These cases bring to mind the Dole-Gingrich Re-

72. Party lines were not yet crystal clear during the Third Congress of 1793–95, but the Madison Republicans rose to unambiguous majority status in the House elected in 1794, which took up the Jay Treaty in 1795–96.

73. Although, note that this absence of order did not just mask an underlying House reality in which a Hamilton faction dominated a Madison faction. Treasury Secretary Hamilton lacked a House majority on the question of assuming state debts in 1790; he had to get what he wanted through the famous deal locating the capital on the Potomac. Hamilton won his bank plan rather easily in early 1791, but after that, during the Second Congress of 1791–93, he had a difficult time prevailing on the House floor and had to abandon his remaining economic program. In short, the nascent Madison Republicans sporadically resembled a House "majority party" in 1790–93, at least in policy terms.

74. I coded the latter opposition more comprehensively to embrace 1947 through 1954, which I think is appropriate. But if it were stripped back to include just the completely out-of-power Republicans during Truman's second administration in 1949–52, it would still qualify statistically as an opposition cluster, given especially the prominence of Senator McCarthy around 1950.

publicans of 1993–94, who caused such a disturbance regarding health-care reform and other matters while completely out of power.[75] But in Table 3.3 the wholly out-of-power profile is rare.

In the British parliamentary model—or at least the stylized version of it familiar to most people[76]—an "opposition" is supposed to be out of power. Greatly off key by that standard is the American record shown here, in which almost all the telling congressional oppositions, some sharing the president's party affiliation, some not, have been *in* power— at least in the sense of being centered in a party controlling a relevant house of Congress.[77]

What explains this American pattern? In terms of this study's data-set, one clue is that, in general, members of a House or Senate majority party enjoy what might be called an "action bonus." If you are an MC,

75. My guess is that historians will discuss the Republican domestic policy opposition to Clinton during 1993–96 as one continuous phenomenon with a beginning and an end. It spanned the three successive showdowns over Clinton's budget in 1993, Clinton's health-care plan in 1993–94, and the Gingrich-Dole "shut down the government" budget drive of 1995–96. After that, things settled down as it became obvious that neither side could get what it wanted. Interbranch conflict, though it did not disappear, dropped from the headlines. Legislative compromises were struck relatively harmoniously during mid-1996 (welfare reform, portability of health insurance, a minimum wage hike) and in 1997 (the deal to balance the budget). But in the summer of 1998 a *second* serious anti-Clinton opposition materialized on Capitol Hill—the Republican impeachment drive triggered by Kenneth Starr's report about Clinton and Monica Lewinsky. This idea of two possible "opposition clusters"—in 1993–96 and 1998–99—tracks the content of public affairs reasonably accurately during Clinton's presidency through early 1999.

76. British history, if suitably analyzed to look past party labels, offers exceptions to the stylized model. Consider, for example, Winston Churchill's opposition to Prime Minister Neville Chamberlain's appeasement policy vis-à-vis Germany in the late 1930s. This took place among Tories. Has any other opposition based in the House of Commons been more prominent or important during the twentieth century?

77. In this respect, the American regime resembles Britain's less than it does those like Italy's where coalition governments typically contain party or factional leaders who engage in ostentatious oppositional behavior.

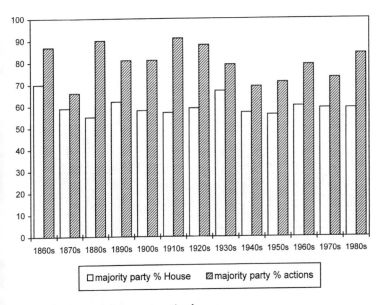

Figure 3.6. House majority party action bonus

you are likelier to score "actions" if you belong to your house's majority party. This seems to be a basic fact of congressional existence. For exhibits here, I prepared time-series statistics on this subject covering *all* the dataset's 2,304 actions, not just the ones coded "opposition," because I wanted to address the House and Senate separately, and, unfortunately, an "opposition" series calculated decade by decade for either of the two houses taken by itself runs into hazards of too few data points and resulting eccentricity. At any rate, a pattern emerges for the full dataset that is both interesting in its own right and broadly valid for the "opposition" subcategory.

Figures 3.6 and 3.7 illustrate relevant House and Senate data, respectively, since 1860. (Before that time, given the often nuanced party affiliations attributed to MCs by standard reference sources, it is not easy to sort members into majority and minority parties.) For each decade in

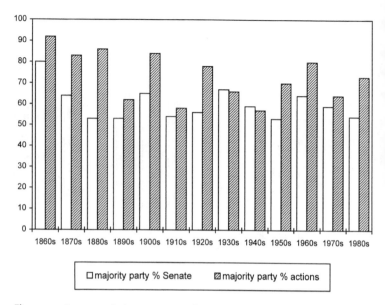

Figure 3.7. Senate majority party action bonus

each of the two graphs, the open bars on the left show the average size of a house's party majorities across the five Congresses within a decade; the peak decades are the 1860s (the Civil War and Reconstruction era) and the 1930s (the New Deal era), with their respectively immense Republican and Democratic membership edges.[78] Correspondingly in each case, the patterned bars on the right show the proportion of a decade's MC "actions" performed by members who, at the time they performed

78. The average for a decade is across *different parties'* majority sizes in cases where party control switched hands during the decade. In the 1950s, for example, a mean for either house picks up a Republican percentage of total membership for 1953–54 (when the GOP controlled Congress) along with a Democratic percentage of total membership for 1951–52, 1955–56, 1957–58, and 1959–60 (when the Democrats controlled Congress). In all calculations, independent and third-party members are scored as "minority party," except for Unionists in the 1860s and the Readjuster (an independent from Virginia) who helped the Republicans organize the Senate in 1881, who are scored as "majority party."

them, belonged to the majority party of the house they were serving in.[79] For any decade, the difference between the heights of the two bars offers a rough measure of "action bias," and it is substantial: a mean pro–majority party bias of 20 percent in the House and 13 percent in the Senate across the thirteen relevant decades. In the "action" arena, majority members tend to be favored beyond their numbers; minority members tend to get crowded out. As for the "opposition" subcategory taken alone, some summary statistics jibe with (although they do not directly correspond to) those reported above: 76 percent of all House "opposition" actions and 65 percent of all such actions by Senators between 1861 and 1988 were performed by members of their houses' majority parties.[80]

In general, there are obvious reasons a majority-favoring "action bonus" might obtain in oppositional and many other realms of congressional activity. Members of a majority party, either because they have enough natural allies to work with or because they enjoy the rules or positional prerogatives that come with majority status, are better placed than members of a minority party to be consequential and thus get noticed.[81] On the latter count, is it revealing that three of the "oppositions" listed in Table 3.3 were spearheaded by chairmen of the Senate Foreign Relations Committee (Sumner, Lodge,[82] and Fulbright)—a powerful office. One likely reason the Senate's "action bonus" is smaller than the House's is that Senate minority members enjoy better rules prerogatives (they can filibuster, for example) than do their House peers.[83] It helps to have levers to pull.

79. That would mean a Republican in 1953, but a Democrat in 1955.

80. I calculated these figures using all the MC "opposition" items since 1860, not just those grouped for some purposes here into "opposition clusters."

81. For an observation on this point, see Randall B. Ripley, *Power in the Senate* (New York: St. Martin's, 1969), pp. 174–75.

82. Lodge was also Republican Majority Leader at the time.

83. Note also that more senators than House members run for president. That counts

Whatever its causes, the centering of prominent oppositions in Congress's majority parties gives a distinctive flavor to American national politics. Branch versus branch tends to displace party versus party. Or perhaps it would be better to say that the U.S. system offers two different basic processes of opposition. The first, described here, is rooted in the constitutional system of separation of powers and allows or generates opposition *between* presidential elections. The second offers challenges by the party not holding the White House *during* presidential elections. The theoretical motifs are, respectively, "ambition checking ambition" as in Madison's *Federalist* #51, and party competition as in, for example, Anthony Downs's *Economic Theory of Democracy*.[84] It is true that the processes have sometimes blended; congressional oppositions have occasionally spilled over into presidential elections. Still, leaving aside the Madison-led and Clay-led oppositions that grew into new major parties themselves in the 1790s and 1830s, the presidential elections that have followed the prominent congressional oppositions documented here have always offered fresh candidate choices from outside Washington, D.C. Those choices have often been opted for. For example, Buchanan versus Douglas gave way in the 1860 election to the Republican Lincoln; Taft versus the La Follette Progressives gave way in 1912 to the Democrat Wilson; and Lyndon Johnson versus the anti–Vietnam War doves gave way in 1968 to the Republican Nixon (who was arguably an outsider again by then, having spent eight years in private life). The system allows two different kinds of shots at those in executive power.

---

as a member "action," and it is an option just as available to minority party members as to majority members.

84. Anthony Downs, *An Economic Theory of Democracy* (New York: Harper and Row, 1957).

Legislatures and Executive Branches

How can a legislature rival an executive branch in influence and legitimacy? This chapter's MC "action" profile during the past two centuries offers one kind of empirical answer. Legislating is a key ingredient, but so are investigating (along with impeaching and censuring public officials, and approving appointments), and constantly injecting "stands" into the proceedings of the "public sphere." Also, Congress is not a city council or a state legislature: To hold its own at the level of the nation state, its members have needed to assert a role in foreign policymaking. Finally, and as important as anything, its members, by exercising various techniques, have needed to be able to stage significant "oppositions" to presidential administrations.

Aside from the American Congress, where does one find an "action" mix like this? One answer, I came to see in my recent reading of Mark Kishlansky's excellent narrative account, is England in the seventeenth century, where, for several generations, the rising English Parliament shared power with the Stuart monarchy.[85] This earlier English experience is arguably worth citing here for reasons of both analogy and ancestry. On the first count, actual political parity between a legislature and an executive branch that lasts several generations is a historical rarity— twentieth-century Chile comes to mind, but there seem to be few other good instances. On the second count, I presume (though I will not try to demonstrate any particulars here), the political culture of seventeenth-century England carried down in many relevant ways to the American nation a century later. The Americans, like the English, have a Stuart past.

This is not a past that we would rush to emulate today. It featured treason trials, executions of public officials after impeachments, regi-

85. Mark Kishlansky, *A Monarchy Transformed: Britain 1603–1714* (New York: Penguin Press, 1996).

cide, exile, civil war, and chronic extreme dissonance between, on the one hand, a parliament that represented local interests and championed Protestantism and, on the other, a monarchy based on divine right that leaned toward Catholicism (until 1689) and was not averse to accepting funds from Catholic monarchies elsewhere to finance its projects—largely wars. But neither of these two institutions could vanquish the other. In the shadow of their coexistence, England became a world power, nourished liberalism, and generated in the late seventeenth century—according to Habermas's terminology and account, which match Kishlansky's account—the world's first "public sphere."[86]

What were the notable kinds of actions of the members of Parliament during the Stuart era? Legislative actions, of course.[87] Occasionally, they investigated.[88] Of great significance throughout the century, they tried to impeach executive officials, often succeeding.[89] One mid-century MP is cited as a filibustering obstructionist.[90] The members in-

86. Jürgen Habermas, *The Structural Transformation of the Public Sphere: An Inquiry into a Category of Bourgeois Society* (Cambridge: MIT Press, 1989), ch. 3, especially pp. 58–59. See also David L. Smith, *The Stuart Parliaments, 1603–1689* (London: Arnold, 1999), pp. 29–30.

87. For some notable instances, see Kishlansky, *A Monarchy Transformed*, pp. 170–71, 202–3, 302–3.

88. Kishlansky, *A Monarchy Transformed*, pp. 61, 254 (Titus Oates testified in the House of Commons in 1678 about the Popish Plot), 303–4.

89. For example, see Kishlansky, *A Monarchy Transformed*, pp. 57, 98–100 (targeting Lord Chancellor Bacon), 106 (Lord Treasurer Cranfield), 108 (the Duke of Buckingham), 143–44 (Archbishop Laud and the Earl of Strafford), 239 (the Earl of Clarendon), 254–56 (the Earl of Danby), 310 (a Whig junto in the 1690s). See also Smith, *The Stuart Parliaments*, pp. 34–38.

90. In the late 1650s: "[Sir Arthur] Haselrig had spent nearly two decades mastering the techniques of obstruction. He was unrivalled at impeding debate, stalling committees and thwarting bills. . . . Now he determined to make mischief, to bring down the parliament and if possible the Protectorate. To these ends, Haselrig seconded every expression of opposition from those who represented what was coming to be called 'the

cessantly took public stands, in the form of grievances, petitions, resolutions, declarations, programs, debates, and, simply, speeches. Over three and a half centuries ago in the 1640s, "Printed speeches brought national prominence to [John] Pym and his allies."[91] The members contributed to several ideological impulses that invested the country such as the ultra-Presbyterianism of the 1640s and the ultra-royalism of the 1660s —a pattern of action I discuss in Chapter 5. From the 1620s onward, they intruded into foreign policymaking—a necessary proclivity if they were to matter politically in the circumstances of the time—by passing laws, supplying or not supplying funds, impeaching officials, and taking stands. Finally, the members staged oppositions to the crown—not continuously, but in a variety of resolute, episodic exercises that are central to the history of the seventeenth century—among them, the Long Parliament's challenge to Charles I in the 1640s, the Whig challenge to Charles II spearheaded by Shaftesbury from the House of Lords, and the cross-party, backbench "country" opposition that dogged William III in the 1690s.[92] If it were resolved into MP "actions," the record of the Stuart era would offer the names of, among others, Sir Edward Coke, Sir John Eliot, Denzel Holles, the Earl of Warwick, John Pym, Sir Arthur Haselrig, the Earl of Shaftesbury, and Robert Harley.

As noted earlier, the English abandoned their explosive dualism of the seventeenth century as they shifted to cabinet government in the eighteenth and nineteenth centuries. The Crown vanished from politics as

---

good old cause.' He organized a filibuster against the recognition of Richard Cromwell. He backed parliamentary attacks upon the Army, and then he supported military grievances against Parliament. He opposed the elevation of Fleetwood to Lord General while he entered into negotiations with the Wallingford House leaders to bring Richard down. Month after month he stymied the Council's efforts to govern, until the Army precipitated a crisis." Kishlansky, *A Monarchy Transformed*, p. 218.

91. Kishlansky, *A Monarchy Transformed*, p. 152.

92. Kishlansky, *A Monarchy Transformed*, chs. 6, 10, 12. See also Smith, *The Stuart Parliaments*, chs. 8, 9.

an independent force. In form, prime ministers and cabinets continued to speak for the king, but in fact they came to depend on parliamentary majorities. His or her majesty's "loyal opposition" became the now conventional designation of the minority party in the House of Commons.[93]

In contrast, the Americans of in the post-Revolution 1780s gave new life to branch-versus-branch dualism by creating the strong and independent Congress and presidency of the new U.S. federal government. Looked at one way, the new American institutional package was an alternative solution—that is, a different one from cabinet government—to the problem of extreme dissonance that had embroiled the Stuart era. The trick was to anchor both executive and legislative branches in constituencies that were popular as well as more or less identical; that solution would help ward off political explosions like those of the 1640s and 1680s. The English impeachment process, which was so prominent—not to mention life-threatening—as a means of controlling the executive branch during the Stuart era, seems to have forked down into three discrete, generally more routinized, processes in the new American regime: the presidential election, which became the key route to legitimizing presidents;[94] the Senate's authority to approve presidential appointees; and the formal congressional impeachment power itself, which, though shriveled by seventeenth-century standards, still exists.

Notwithstanding these American innovations, the commonalities (at least in broad terms) between the "action" profiles of the Stuart era and those of the later American Congress offer clues about what it takes for a national parliamentary body to hold its own against an executive. In addi-

93. See Archibald S. Foord, *His Majesty's Opposition, 1714–1830* (Oxford: Clarendon Press, 1964).

94. Samuel H. Beer discussed this lineage in his testimony before the House Judiciary Committee as it considered impeaching President Clinton in December 1998. The English shifted to the parliamentary vote of confidence as the chief means for popular control of the executive; the Americans to presidential elections.

tion, for a congressional specialist, reading about the Stuart era can have a sensitizing effect: certain traits of American politics are brought out. One is the *spasmodic* quality of congressional activity. As in the seventeenth century, American MC "action" has tended to occur not randomly or evenly but in scattered, intense outbursts—for example, the lawmaking binges of the 1930s and 1960s, the various clusters of "opposition" listed in Table 3.3, or, as documented in Table 5.4, a series of "ideological impulses" during the twentieth century. Events or societal demands no doubt explain much of this spasmodic quality, yet far from all of it. Times are often quiet on Capitol Hill, but wait around and another major congressional manifestation is likely to occur.

A second trait that the Stuart era shares with American congressional politics is *inventiveness*. The boundaries of possibility are never clear. New kinds of moves can be made.[95] The maximally assertive Long Parliament of the 1640s, for example, bears a resemblance to the Reconstruction Congress of the 1860s: Who would have envisioned a John Pym or a Thaddeus Stevens? The cross-party "country" opposition led by Robert Harley in the 1690s was no less innovative. In the twentieth-century American Congress we have witnessed, among other things, Progressive era investigations as social exposés, a flowering of the Senate filibuster (from Robert La Follette, Sr., through Richard Russell and Robert Dole), the use of legislative research staffs to generate legislation (Robert F. Wagner pioneered in this area), loyalty hearings where names are named (from Martin Dies through Joseph McCarthy), the cross-party "conservative coalition" of the late 1930s through the 1950s (courtesy of Howard Smith and others), the use of presidential primaries to challenge incumbent presidents (from Estes Kefauver through Eugene McCarthy and Edward Kennedy), a revival of the impeachment power (as used against

95. In the context of this paragraph, that can mean shades of newness *within* the "action" categories listed in Table 2.6.

Nixon and Clinton—one can only imagine how it might have been used against Vice President Henry Wallace if he had somehow succeeded to the presidency in the mid-1940s), judicial appointments as showdown events (as with the opposition to the Bork nomination), House Speakers as aggressive television performers (Tip O'Neill and Newt Gingrich), and, in the 1990s, Gingrich's Contract with America.

Third, American congressional politics tends to be *accusatory*, often harshly so. Conflict is often personalized. Individuals, notably but not limited to officials of the executive branch, tend to be demonized. Instances would include Andrew Jackson, Franklin Roosevelt, and Bill Clinton—but also Newt Gingrich. I do not know how to locate this trait securely in comparative perspective, but the Stuart era with its vilification of the monarchs and their top officials certainly shared it. Perhaps it is built into the dynamics of branch-versus-branch dualism, which so often centers on executive officials who cannot easily be removed but at least can be demonized.

Somewhere, in some alternative universe, a textbook legislative branch may exist that calmly and evenly goes about its business of passing laws, and that's that. But that is not the American congressional experience, which has instead exhibited all the characteristics discussed above. Congressional politics in the 1990s, for all its combustibility, harshness, surprises, and general messiness, was a typical exercise of American history, not an aberrant one.

The House, the Senate, and the Presidency

It is said that American politicians operate within an "opportunity structure." This is the familiar hierarchy of public offices wherein, in the most familiar scenario, they start out as state or local officials, rise to the U.S. House, aspire to the Senate, and possibly climb beyond that to a cabinet post or the vice presidency or presidency.[1] Roles in the political parties are available on the side. This chapter is designed, first, through exhibits of MC "action," to illuminate the opportunity structure that has engaged American politicians by addressing a selection of topics that bear on it. How has the House compared with the Senate as an "action" stage? For various eras, what is the MC "action" record in terms of rising to the cabinet and other key appointive offices, meshing their Capitol Hill careers with roles as leaders of state or local party organizations, trying to influence who wins the vice presidency or presidency, or aiming for those two top offices themselves?

As earlier, the logic here is that it can be useful to examine what MCs are noticed for—by historians of public affairs and, through

1. See Joseph A. Schlesinger, *Ambition and Politics: Political Careers in the United States* (Chicago: Rand McNally, 1966).

plausible inference, by inhabitants of the American "public sphere" at relevant times in history. If, by means of this methodology, the Senate of an era is sized up as a collection of state party bosses, that is taken to be a finding worth reporting. If running for president is seen to be a major preoccupation of senators, that too is a finding. At two points in the chapter, I introduce statistics about what actually happened (as opposed to what historians or citizens noticed or recorded); that aside, MC "actions" as employed earlier are the data source. More than in Chapter 3, change during the two centuries of American history, not constancy, emerges as an emphasis here. In certain respects, it is striking how the fit of members of Congress into the larger political system, thus gauged, has changed since 1789.

My second task in this chapter, in a concluding section, is to identify some implications of this exhibited change. The discussion centers on institutions, not on individual MCs. In general, I argue, the "action" trends tracked here suggest that the major elective institutions of the American system have become at once more democratized, more distinct from each other, and more equal. What does this say about the country's separation of powers system today? I review some relevant, contrasting ideas about separation of powers expressed two centuries ago by Jefferson and Madison, then consider the connection between having a separation of powers arrangement like the current American one and sustaining a national "public sphere."

House and Senate

Today, the relative standings of the House and Senate are obvious in the "opportunity structure" confronting American politicians. House members aim to become senators, not vice versa.

As is well known, however, the House of Representatives began in

1789 with certain advantages. It was designed to be the popular body. In the 1790s, Madison led his opposition from there.[2] A decade and a half later, Henry Clay served briefly in the Senate but soon gave it up for the House, where he immediately won the Speakership and dominated the national policy agenda from that office for most of the time between 1811 and 1825. As for the Senate, deliberating in secret as it did during its first half decade kept the institution from building a public following, and in general, "For a generation there was continuing confusion over the intended role of the Senate." As of 1816, "it was still widely regarded as a rather inconsequential body, substantially inferior to the House."[3] In 1789 through 1809, the House led the Senate in national newspaper coverage by twenty-three to one; in 1809 through 1829, by four to one. Coverage equalized only in 1829 through 1841, thanks to that decade's familiar "virtual revolution in the position of the Senate," as Clay (a member there again), Webster, and Calhoun forged the upper chamber into an opposition base for use against Jackson, much as Madison had used the lower one against Hamilton in the 1790s.[4] The 1830s was to become "the golden age of the Senate." Presidential hopefuls gathered there. "Men

2. If Madison had become a member of the Senate rather than the House in 1789, how would the two institutions have evolved? This is an intriguing question.

3. H. Douglas Price, "Careers and Committees in the American Congress: The Problem of Structural Change," in William O. Aydelotte (ed.), *The History of Parliamentary Behavior* (Princeton, N.J.: Princeton University Press, 1977), pp. 29–36, quotations at pp. 32, 33.

4. Coverage statistics are from Elaine K. Swift, *The Making of an American Senate: Reconstitutive Change in Congress, 1787–1841* (Ann Arbor: University of Michigan Press, 1996), pp. 60–63, 121–23, 165–67. These results are based on counts of column inches of coverage by three national newspapers during sessions of, respectively, the Second, Fifth, and Eighth Congresses; the Eleventh, Seventeenth, and Twentieth Congresses; and the Twenty-third and Twenty-sixth Congresses. Quotation is from Price, "Careers and Committees," p. 33.

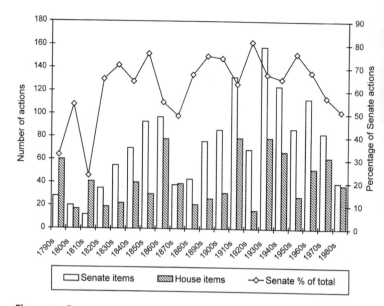

Figure 4.1. Senate versus House actions

and women flocked to the Capitol to hear [Clay, Webster, and Calhoun]; all across the country their speeches were read as if the fate of the nation hung on them."[5]

How do this study's "action" data map onto that early congressional history? Figure 4.1 sorts the full 2,304-item dataset into actions performed by senators (in the open bars) and House members (in the patterned bars) during each decade from 1789 through 1988. See especially the line-connected bullets, which denote the proportion of each decade's actions performed by senators. If a bit raggedly, the story of early House domination is borne out. Notably, senators registered a low 32 percent in the 1790s when Madison was staging his opposition and an even lower 23

5. Merrill D. Peterson, *The Great Triumvirate: Webster, Clay, and Calhoun* (New York: Oxford University Press, 1987), p. 234.

percent in the 1810s when Clay was exercising his new Speakership.[6] The 1830s did set a new standard, with a 71 percent Senate share (although the 1820s evidently paved the way for that), and senators have normally registered in the 60s and 70s since then—falling only once below 50 percent (to 46 percent in the 1870s).

Even more impressive is the senators' post-1820 "action" edge when we take chamber size into account. Since 1800, the Senate has had between 19 percent and 27 percent as many members as the House. That means that, in ten of the seventeen decades since 1820, senators have outstripped House members by at least ten to one in actions *per member,* and in the other seven decades by at least four to one. In two ways, the Senate's action edge is congruent with that chamber's higher rank in the "opportunity structure." For one thing, House members unquestionably aim for the Senate because its size, prestige, and member prerogatives make it easier to be consequential and get noticed there. For another, consider Congressman and then Senator Phil Gramm, co-author of Gramm-Latta II (the winning version of Reagan's omnibus expenditures cut) as a House sophomore in 1981, then winner of a Texas Senate seat in 1984, then co-author of the Gramm-Rudman-Hollings budget control act in 1985 and a presidential candidate later on: House members who are by nature major movers and shakers tend to aim for the Senate, where they keep on performing.

Certain wrinkles or nonwrinkles in Figure 4.1 are of interest. Not in evidence is any effect of the constitutional shift to the direct election of senators in 1913. But note that twice since the 1830s (or three or four times, depending on the threshold chosen) the House has staged something of a comeback in action percentage. In the 1860s, House mem-

6. The intervening decade of the 1800s, for which the curve juts up, has a uniquely small dataset (thirty-seven items), for what that is worth. Senators were particularly active regarding appointments and trade policy during Jefferson's late years and Madison's early ones.

bers led by Thaddeus Stevens put their stamp on Reconstruction policy. During Wilson's first administration in 1913–17, House members took the lead in advancing domestic reforms (thus generating a relatively high House action percentage for the full decade, even though senators came to dominate the foreign policy deliberations during 1917–20). The House assumed a similar legislative role in the 1930s.

Also noteworthy is the thrust toward equal shares in the 1970s and 1980s. What is responsible for this relatively recent House surge? No single theme stands out, and, again, the dataset for these decades is shaky, but here are some developments that apparently counted: Tip O'Neill brought new influence and prominence to the House leadership as Democratic Majority Leader and then Speaker (thus earning for himself fifteen action items).[7] The House stood in relief as the only branch controlled by the Democrats during the first six years of Reagan's presidency (its members out-"actioned" senators by thirty-five to twenty-eight during that time). The House struck first in attracting women and minority group members who could win notice such as Shirley Chisholm (D-N.Y.), Patricia Schroeder (D-Colo.), Geraldine Ferraro (D-N.Y.), and Andrew Young (D-Ga.). House members with these demographic traits registered fifteen action items during 1971–88; such senators, only one item.[8] And the House better than held its own in the new highly publicized budgetary politics that began its long run as deficits emerged in the mid-1970s: House members registered a twenty-six to sixteen edge on

7. O'Neill drew heavy media attention. During every year from 1977 through 1986, he was mentioned far more often than any other House member on televised network evening news. See Timothy E. Cook, *Making Laws and Making News: Media Strategies in the U.S. House of Representatives* (Washington, D.C.: Brookings, 1989), Appendix B and pp. 63–64. In a content analysis of coverage of Congress (both houses) by ten big-city newspapers during April 1978, Speaker O'Neill and Senator Edward Kennedy emerged as the most mentioned members. See Charles M. Tidmarch and John J. Pitney, Jr., "Covering Congress," *Polity* 17 (1985), 473.

8. Senator Daniel Inouye (D-Hawaii) co-chaired the Iran-Contra inquiry in 1987.

tax and budget items during 1975–88. All this activity largely counterbalanced a customary Senate edge on foreign policy items during 1971–88 (it was thirty-three to ten). To go beyond this study's dataset, consider also the prominence of the House in the 1990s with Gingrich's rise to power and his Speakership. The 1990s probably witnessed a third consecutive decade of, going by historical benchmarks, quite high "action" standing for the House.

Taking Appointments

One way Congress can fit into the country's "opportunity structure" is as a springboard to appointive offices—as when Congressman Dick Cheney (R-Wyo.) became Secretary of Defense in 1989 or Senator Hugo Black became a justice of the Supreme Court in 1937. For purposes of this study, the MC appointments to be dwelt on are those that, for one reason or another, achieved notice and became "actions"—they entered the history books.[9] A cabinet appointment might do that, for example, by lending a presidential administration sectional or ethnic diversity, thus helping to legitimize it with the public. Looked at relatively, noticed appointment moves can take up a smaller or larger slice of MC "action" during a decade or the tenure of a Congress.

Figure 4.2 graphs all this dataset's actions in which a president nominated a House or Senate member to an administrative, diplomatic, or judicial office that required resignation from Congress to be accepted.[10] The data are grouped into five time spans, each lasting four decades. For

9. To avoid possible confusion, I should make it clear that this section deals with actions in which MCs *take* appointments. Not of relevance are actions in which MCs help to *make* (or unmake) appointments, as when Senator Edward Kennedy led the derailing of the Bork nomination to the Supreme Court in 1987.

10. This precludes presidential appointments like the temporary ones to the United Nations conference in 1945 that could be accepted without resigning from Congress.

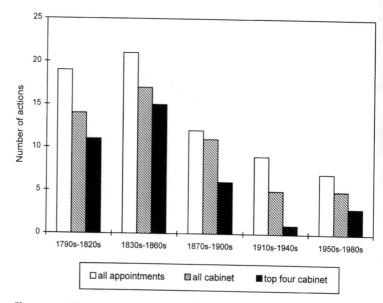

Figure 4.2. Take appointments actions

each time span, the vertical bars show data totals for three nested categories of appointments—to all offices (a total of sixty-eight items during
the two centuries), as heads of cabinet departments (fifty-two items),[11]

11. A general rule of this study is that "actions" refer to things done by people *while*
they are members of Congress; no membership, no action. This rule causes a coding em-
barrassment for "take an appointment" actions. Incoming presidents ordinarily decide
on their cabinet nominees after being elected but before being inaugurated—that is, during the final weeks of an outgoing Congress—and sometimes they pick members *of* an
outgoing Congress (of whom some have won election to the incoming Congress, some
not). But nominations are not formally made until an incoming Congress convenes (in
January of an odd year now; in March of an odd year before the "lame duck" amendment
was adopted in the 1930s), and cabinet picks who served in the outgoing Congress *and*
have been elected to the incoming Congress may take their seats at the start of the incoming Congress and then quickly resign them. For these scenarios, how was I to code
for "actions"? I decided that, to do justice to how decisions actually tend to be made, I

and as heads of just the top four cabinet departments—State, Treasury, War (Defense, beginning in 1947), and Justice (thirty-six items). Notable among the dataset's appointments *not* to head cabinet departments are those of Speaker Henry Clay as a U.S. representative to peace talks with Britain to end the War of 1812 (he resigned from Congress to take that assignment); the antisecessionist Senator Andrew Johnson (D-Tenn.) as military governor of Tennessee in 1862; Senator Edward White (D-La.) as

---

would credit all nominations formally made during the first month after an outgoing Congress lapses (that is, odd-year Januaries now, odd-year Marches before 1935) to the *outgoing* Congress. This method has the merit of allowing nonreelected MCs to enter the dataset even if they have not been formally nominated to administrative posts until after they have formally exited Capitol Hill. But even if they have been reelected, such January or March nominees are identified here for coding purposes with the outgoing Congresses. The rule pertains to all presidential appointees, not solely appointees to the cabinet. Thus, David Stockman's (R-Mich.) "take an appointment" action scored for his nomination to head the Office of Management and Budget identifies him as a member of the outgoing Congress of 1979–80, not that of 1981–82, even though Stockman had been reelected to the House in November 1980 and Reagan formally nominated him as OMB director in early 1981.

Other wrinkles exist. In two nineteenth-century cases where a president had not formally made a fresh nomination to a cabinet post during March or April of an odd year (political time was lazier in the first few decades of America's history), I allowed a formal *April or May* nomination to accrue to an outgoing Congress if it involved a nonreelected member. This yielded, notably, the appointment of Albert Gallatin to the Treasury in 1801. Gallatin had been the leading Republican in Congress during the late 1790s, and he did not seek reelection in 1800 (which means he ceased being a House member on March 3, 1801), but Jefferson formally nominated him as his first secretary of the treasury in May 1801.

Finally, notwithstanding all the above, I did not want to lose sight of a very small set of MCs who had *not* been members of an outgoing Congress, but who *were* elected to an incoming one, and who were formally nominated to an executive post at the very beginning of the next Congress. I counted such items as "actions" and identified them with an incoming Congress. Notable here is the case of Senator Salmon P. Chase (R-Ohio), who was a senator-elect, not a sitting senator (though he had served in the Senate in earlier years) when—to key on the actual presidential decision—President-elect Lincoln decided to ask him to be secretary of the treasury in early 1861.

the first Roman Catholic member of the Supreme Court in 1894; Senator Black as an associate justice of the Court in 1937 (this caused a stir because of his left-wing ideology, a disclosure then of his past Ku Klux Klan activity, and his status as FDR's first Court nominee); Congressman Andrew Young as Carter's ambassador to the United Nations in 1977; and Congressman David Stockman (R-Mich.) as Reagan's budget director in 1981.[12]

Obviously in Figure 4.2, the MC move to "take an appointment" has fallen off considerably in frequency. Correspondingly, approached in relative terms, appointments items (whether to cabinet or noncabinet positions) amounted to 8.2 percent of all MC actions during 1789–1831, 4.3 percent during 1831–71, and 3.3 percent during 1871–1911, but only 1.2 percent during 1911–50 and 1.4 percent during 1951–88. In absolute terms, the dramatic result in Figure 4.2 is the slump in appointments actions associated with the top four cabinet departments. As can be seen from differences in the heights of the bars, the dropoff in the top-four category accounts almost entirely for the slumps in the other two categories it is a part of.

This is one place where statistical reality intrudes. As it happens, the falloff in MC appointments actions shown in Figure 4.2—again, these are just the items that entered the thirty-eight public affairs history books —has a basis in real staffing statistics. At least with cabinet appointments, it is possible to find out from a relevant directory the actual

12. Others of the residual sixteen are five more ambassadors or emissaries, a commissioner on the Interstate Commerce Commission, and an undersecretary of the treasury. Also netted by the coding scheme are three instances of not-quite-appointments in which a senator angled for a combination military-diplomatic assignment but did not get it, a nominee for minister to Austria was rejected, and a senator was being groomed for a Supreme Court position but died before any opened up. The last-mentioned instance was the highly important case of Senate Majority Leader Joseph Robinson (D-Ark.), who led the drive for FDR's doomed court-packing scheme in 1937, an effort that exhausted and possibly killed him.

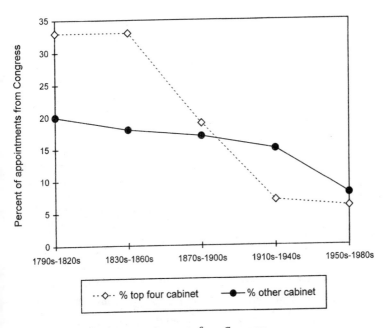

Figure 4.3. Actual cabinet appointments from Congress

percentages of heads of departments during various phases of American history who were members of Congress when they took their jobs.[13] Figure 4.3 presents such "real" data for, separately, the top four cabinet departments and the rest of the cabinet.[14] Again, the top four departments reflect the major change.[15] In the first few generations of Ameri-

13. See Joel D. Treese (ed.), *Biographical Directory of the American Congress, 1774–1996* (Alexandria, Va.: CQ Staff Directories, 1997), pp. 1–26 on cabinet members, pp. 549–2108 on MC careers.

14. Excluded from the denominator here are cabinet heads who moved musical-chairs fashion from one department to another; the appointments had to be fresh from the outside. The criteria for deciding whether someone was an MC at the time of appointment are those elaborated in footnote 11.

15. The residual category generates a downward curve in Figure 4.3 also, though be aware that the *size* of the president's cabinet has expanded considerably since 1789. The

can history, presidents drew about a third of their outside appointees to the State, Treasury, War, and Justice departments from Congress; in the twentieth century, they have drawn a mere 5 percent.

Both the "action" data and the real staffing data illuminate a familiar story. Presidential administrations used to be constructed differently. Until the 1830s, James Sterling Young has written, cabinets tended to be composed of powerful ex-House and Senate members who still kept a hand in as leaders of various Capitol Hill factions. This was because presidents during those years, lacking personal staff and independent popular bases or access to a mass audience (there was an "insufficiency of a President's authority alone to confer leadership") saw fit to surround themselves with cabinet secretaries "whose support they needed to carry their programs both on the Hill and into the lower levels of the administrative structure" and who supplied "political liaison with Congress."[16] There were other factors. Geographic balance was sometimes achieved by choosing leading members of Congress for the top positions. The lack of a lockstep congressional seniority system—which came into existence after 1900—made it agreeable for leading MCs to cycle themselves through the cabinet and back to Capitol Hill again, which some did.[17]

---

fact that Congress has been the source of a lower percentage of non-top-four appointees does not imply that the absolute number from that source has diminished. Congress itself, of course, has also greatly increased in membership size and therefore as a potential cabinet pool since 1789.

16. See James Sterling Young, *The Washington Community, 1800–1828* (New York: Columbia University Press, 1966), pp. 176–77, 222–24, 232–45, quotations at pp. 240, 232. Young paints the general picture: "As to cabinet posts, two of every three appointees from the administration of John Adams through Jackson's second administration had seen previous service on Capitol Hill, and well over half of the 49 cabinet appointees during this period (28, or 57 percent) were initially brought into the executive branch [some at first into diplomatic or other noncabinet ranks] from a last preceding government service in Congress." Young, p. 176.

17. See H. Douglas Price, "The Congressional Career—Then and Now," in Nelson W.

All this brought an early line of prestigious appointments that included Congressman John Marshall (F-Va.) as Secretary of State in 1800,[18] Congressman Albert Gallatin as Secretary of the Treasury in 1801, Congressman John C. Calhoun as Secretary of War in 1817, Speaker Henry Clay as Secretary of State in 1825, Senator Daniel Webster as Secretary of State in 1841 and again in 1850, Senator Robert J. Walker as Secretary of the Treasury in 1845, and Senator James Buchanan (D-Pa.) as Secretary of State in 1845. All these appear as "action" items in the dataset. As a collection of ex-congressional influentials who also happened to be White House prospects themselves, no cabinet offers a better example than Lincoln's in 1861, which featured Senator William Seward as Secretary of State, Senator Salmon P. Chase (R-Ohio) as Secretary of the Treasury, and Senator Simon Cameron (R-Pa.) as Secretary of War. To appease a variety of factions, Lincoln found it essential to build that way—as did his contemporary Jefferson Davis, a senator himself (D-Miss.) until the South seceded, who chose half a dozen recently resigned U.S. House or Senate members for high cabinet or ambassadorial posts with the new Confederate government in 1861.[19] In effect, the country's political "opportunity structure" suddenly doubled its top positions in 1861. Both North and South drew on Congress to assemble their governments.

During the twentieth century, however, presidents have switched toward anchoring their administrations in their personal popularity and,

---

Polsby (ed.), *Congressional Behavior* (New York: Random House, 1971); Nelson W. Polsby, Miriam Gallaher, and Barry S. Rundquist, "The Growth of the Seniority System in the U.S. House of Representatives," *American Political Science Review* 63 (1969), 787–807.

18. Soon after that he became chief justice of the Supreme Court.

19. Among them were Senator Robert Toombs as secretary of state and Senator Judah P. Benjamin (D-La.) as attorney general. These six Confederate appointments are not represented in Figure 4.2, but I did include them as "take appointment" items in this study's full dataset. They seemed to meet the criteria for "actions." (The six MCs appointed to top Confederate posts account for the discrepancy between the seventy-four appointments listed in Table 2.6 and the sixty-eight mentioned in the text of this section.)

except vice president!

from their top appointees, professional expertise. Figures like Clay, Webster, and Seward with their own formidable independent power bases have largely ceased to help *constitute* presidential administrations. For their part, members of Congress have tended toward building uninterruptible careers in the Capitol Hill seniority system. On the Senate side, the switch to direct elections in 1913 evidently made it harder for members to shift back and forth between legislative and executive branches; the state legislatures had been more agreeable to such maneuvering.[20] For these various reasons, action items for MC administrative appointments—notably, to the very top posts—have accordingly dropped off, although they have not disappeared. In the 1990s, for example, an extension of the present dataset would probably turn up, as "noticed," Senator Lloyd Bentsen's appointment as Secretary of the Treasury and Congressman Leon Panetta's as budget director in 1993, and Senator William Cohen's (R-Maine) as Secretary of Defense in 1997. Note that the recent primacy of budget politics has motored two House members, Stockman and Panetta, to top White House positions.

20. See Vikram David Amar, "Indirect Effects of Direct Election: A Structural Examination of the Seventeenth Amendment," *Vanderbilt Law Review* 49 (1996), 1347–1405. Direct popular election of senators "systematically reduces rotation between the Senate and Executive Branch offices. This is so because involvement of the People of each State [as opposed to the state legislatures, as earlier] makes more difficult deals by which Senators leave the Senate voluntarily to perform other public service on the implicit understanding that they will be reelected to the Senate when openings present themselves. . . . In particular, I posit that direct election systematically reduces the ease with which Senators can sandwich senatorial tenures around presidential Cabinet service." Amar, pp. 1350, 1357–60. Amar shows that, in the relevant statistical data, of the thirteen instances where a senator went to the cabinet and then returned to the Senate within three years after ending cabinet service, every one occurred before the ratification of the Seventeenth Amendment in 1913.

Party Bosses as MCs

PARTIES

How do legislatures intersect with political parties? For political scientists, that is one of the more important questions that can be asked about modern representative bodies, and it can be tackled in many ways. In this study's dataset, the route to answers is a more specific question: Which members of Congress have been noticed when for what party roles? Again, the assumption is that notice indexes a certain kind of importance.

Of course, there are many kinds of party roles. Even excluding those inside Congress itself such as serving as majority or minority leaders, the party-related "actions" documented in this dataset include such varied ones as: James Madison co-founded the Democratic Republican party in the 1790s, Senator John J. Crittenden (W-Ky.) took the lead in forming the Constitutional Union Party in 1859, Senator Matthew Quay (R-Pa.) managed Benjamin Harrison's presidential campaign in 1888, Senator Mark Hanna (R-Ohio) managed William McKinley's campaign in 1900,[21] and Senator George McGovern and Congressman Donald Fraser (D-Minn.) co-chaired the commission to reform Democratic nominating procedures after the party's disastrous Chicago convention of 1968.

One way to proceed here is to address a few specific party or quasi-party roles. This and the next two sections do that, without exhausting the dataset's party-related items.

A dual role that once had considerable public prominence is that of the MC serving simultaneously as head or boss of a state or local party organization. Figure 4.4 sorts into twenty-year time spans all the dataset's "actions" mentioning such a "boss" or leader role. (Many of these items are multiply coded. Senator Quay, for example, is referred to as the Republican state boss of Pennsylvania in actions where he blocked a

21. Hanna had also figured in McKinley's 1896 campaign, but that was before he became a senator.

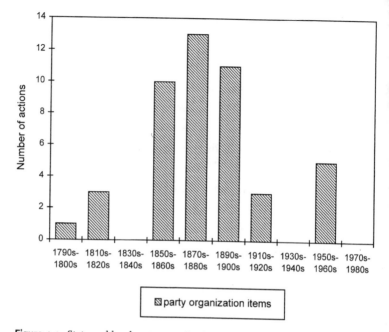

Figure 4.4. State and local party organization actions

currency reform bill and pressed for statehood for Arizona, New Mexico, and Oklahoma in 1901; the senator was a skilled legislator.) At the left in the graph, three items appear from the 1820s for Senator Martin Van Buren (D-N.Y.), the leader of that state's Albany Regency, the era's model state party organization, who helped weave together the new national Democratic party and elect Andrew Jackson president.[22] In the 1860s and 1870s a buildup of Republican state organization heads occurred in the Senate—among them Alexander Ramsey (R-Minn.), Philetus Sawyer (R-Wis.), ex–cabinet member Simon Cameron (R-Pa.), Zachary Chandler

22. The first bar on the graph denotes only one action: for Senator Timothy Pickering (F-Mass.) in 1804 as a leader of the quasi-party Essex Junto, a group of Massachusetts Federalists.

(R-Mich.), Oliver P. Morton (R-Ind.), John A. Logan (R-Ill.), and the power-hungry Roscoe Conkling (R-N.Y.). A successor generation in the 1880s and 1890s included Senators James McMillan (R-Mich.), Arthur P. Gorman (D-Md.), Thomas Platt (R-N.Y.), and Matthew Quay (R-Pa.). As late as 1912 and 1920, Pennsylvania's Republican organization remained strong enough to generate "action" items for Senator Boies Penrose, Quay's successor as leader.

Obviously, the chief feature of the time series in Figure 4.4 is its bulge in the middle; these organization actions had their heyday in the latter half of the nineteenth century.[23] The chief exception is a kind of Indian summer in the middle of the twentieth century when, for example, Senator Harry F. Byrd headed a Virginia state organization still powerful enough to mount "massive resistance" to the Supreme Court's order to desegregate local schools, and Congressmen William Green, Jr. (D-Pa.), and Charles Buckley (D-N.Y.), the local bosses of Philadelphia and the Bronx, swung their county organizations behind John F. Kennedy's drive to win the Democratic presidential nomination in 1960.

Today, looking back particularly at the late nineteenth century, there is a tendency to pooh-pooh the considerable notice given back then to organizations and bosses. Why wasn't everybody focusing on important things, like working conditions in the mines and factories? But that perspective is anachronistic. Witnesses in the "public sphere" at that time had their reasons, and those reasons can be appreciated. It is worth noticing when politicians find new ways to stockpile and use power. In the 1860s and 1870s, federal job patronage made possible a new kind of Senate baron—notably, Roscoe Conkling. By staffing the New York Custom

23. On the distinctive relation between party organizations and MCs during this era, see also David Brady, Kara Buckley, and Douglas Rivers, "The Strong Parties Hypothesis Revisited: Evidence from the Turn of the Century," manuscript presented at the Annual Meeting of the American Political Science Association, Atlanta, September 2–5, 1999.

House with hundreds of workers paid in effect to be his election opera-tives,[24] Conkling could bid to dominate his state's Republican nominat-ing processes and legislature; he could control Republican delegations to presidential nominating conventions where, in collaboration with other big-state bosses, he could swing weight and hope to influence presiden-tial candidates and presidents; and, finally, he could join with like-minded senators on Capitol Hill to lean on presidents to keep the necessary pa-tronage flowing. It was an ingenious system. As a use of federal authority to generate political influence (at least in the eyes of nervous observers of the time), it bears comparison with Alexander Hamilton's system of pub-lic debt and credit in the 1790s, the Second Bank of the United States that was brought down by Andrew Jackson, and Franklin Roosevelt's Works Progress Administration relief agency as it was allegedly deployed in elec-tion campaigns in the 1930s. In the Conkling case, Presidents Hayes and Garfield repulsed him in highly publicized showdowns over patron-age. The Pendleton Act of 1883, which inaugurated a federal civil service, made it harder for senators to build such empires of influence by using federal jobs.[25]

In the 1880s and 1890s, a new generation of organization leaders—notably, Quay and Platt, who represented the country's two largest states at that time[26]—built multiple roles as senators, state party chieftains, in-fluence wielders in state legislatures (as noted earlier, this influence was

24. "The collectorship of the New York Custom House was the most important ad-ministrative post outside the cabinet. It now controlled 1,300 appointments." Whether a Conkling favorite would get the collectorship became the issue between the senator and, respectively, Presidents Hayes and Garfield. See Sean Dennis Cashman, *America in the Gilded Age* (New York: New York University Press, 1993), pp. 252–56, quotation at p. 255.

25. The enterprising Senator George Pendleton (D-Ohio) is credited with an "action."

26. New York and Pennsylvania within the United States a century ago looked some-thing like Germany and France within the European Union today.

needed to get and keep their Senate seats), power brokers in presidential nominating conventions, and sympathetic government contacts for the era's newly muscular private corporations. Rather than federal jobs, the key organizational resources this time were corporate money and state government jobs—or in Quay's case, kickbacks from banks where the Pennsylvania state government deposited its money. It was this turn-of-the-century breed of senator that reformers of the Progressive era took aim at in promoting direct election of senators. That reform, it was thought, would break up the Senate-capped hierarchies of business-oriented influence. Earlier, we saw that the adoption of the Seventeenth Amendment in 1913 was not associated with any change in senators' "action advantage" over House members (see Figure 4.1), but Figure 4.4 shows that the reform does coincide with the plummet in organization-related actions shown for the early twentieth century. In fact, a close inspection of the order of events around 1900 suggests that moves by the era's reformers caused *both* the downfall of the senator-led party organizations *and* the adoption of the Seventeenth Amendment, rather than that the amendment, once implemented, caused the downfall.[27]

For the most part, state and local party kingpins on Capitol Hill are a story from the middle segment of American history. Since that time, leaving aside the small spike evident after 1950, there is little to tell. In Figure 4.4, the reading for the 1970s and 1980s is zero. That does not mean that MCs have stopped making new moves to stockpile and use power. In the 1970s, for example, Senator Jesse Helms (R-N.C.) developed his Congressional Club as a direct-mail technique for funding right-wing candidates around the country. In the 1980s, Congressman Tony Coelho (D-Calif.) shored up the electoral position of House Democrats by

27. On the turn-of-the-century state organizations and their demise, see David R. Mayhew, *Placing Parties in American Politics* (Princeton, N.J.: Princeton University Press, 1986), ch. 8.

shifting them toward money from business-based political action committees (PACs). But action items of this contemporary kind have not involved state or local party organizations.[28]

Choosing Presidents

In American politics, no task ranks higher than the selection of presidents, and members of Congress have often ranked high in that selection process. Ordinarily this has been a party-related role in one way or another, although its locus has varied: At three junctures, in 1801, 1825, and 1877, Congress had to step in and make, or at least help arrange, a final decision after the usual sequence of party nominating processes, a November election, and an automatic electoral college result failed to work. Normally, MCs have made their influence felt during the familiar nominating drives and November elections.

For purposes here, I have devised a catchall category of "actions" in which MCs have played a role of any kind in presidential or vice presidential selection—*except* where they just aimed for those offices themselves. The subject here is MCs as selectors, not as candidates.[29] Members have, for example, endorsed presidential candidates, called on people to run, funded candidates, managed campaigns, launched third-party movements, wheeled and dealed at nominating conventions, and, in

28. On these two items, see Michael Barone, *Our Country: The Shaping of America from Roosevelt to Reagan* (New York: Free Press, 1990), pp. 571, 624–25. In recent times, Senators Lloyd Bentsen (D-Tex.) and Alphonse D'Amato (R-N.Y.) may come as close as anybody to the old Quay or Platt role of state party boss, but that is not very close.

29. In some multiply coded actions, a member was both. In 1932, for example, Speaker John Nance Garner (D-Tex.) ran for the Democratic presidential nomination, fell short, helped FDR get the nomination, then was nominated for vice president. All that is coded as one action. It counts in this section because Garner helped FDR get the nomination; his own candidacies are irrelevant.

those cases where the final decision ended up being made in the House, helped build winning coalitions there. By stipulation, I have included here all "actions" of all kinds performed at presidential nominating conventions—captivating speeches, for example—even if they were not explicitly candidate-related. This inclusion is made on the ground that all kinds of events at a nominating convention tend to feed into electoral coalition building—either in the convention itself, where some candidate needs to assemble a majority on the last day, or in the election to come, where a party that exited a convention unified and exuberant may stand a better chance. Finally, I have included a handful of actions that have borne in any way on the *process* of selecting presidents. Senator Robert J. Walker, for example, won a key reaffirmation of the Democrats' "two-thirds" rule—the fraction of delegates needed to win a nomination—at the party's convention of 1844 (the rule had made a first appearance in 1832 and lasted until 1936). Senator Birch Bayh (D-Ind.) engineered the Twenty-fifth Amendment, governing presidential succession, in 1967. The McGovern-Fraser commission rewrote the Democratic party's nominating rules during 1969–72. Process changes—Senator Bayh's is an exception—tend to be, to some degree, related to coalitional advantage. For example, Senator Walker helped ex-Speaker James K. Polk (once D-Tenn.) win the presidential nomination; the McGovern-Fraser commission made it easy for antiorganization reformers including McGovern to take over the Democratic Party in 1972.[30]

Thus defined, MC actions bearing on presidential selection numbered 143, or 6 percent of all data items, between 1789 and 1988. Table 4.1 presents a selection of examples,[31] and Figure 4.5 sorts the data totals into twenty-year time spans. Taking the data by individual elections, the

30. See Byron E. Shafer, *Quiet Revolution: The Struggle for the Democratic Party and the Shaping of Post-Reform Politics* (New York: Russell Sage, 1983).

31. A few of these items also appear in the "stand-taking" list presented in Table 3.2.

Table 4.1 Selected MC Actions Involving Choice of Presidents or Vice Presidents

1792	James Monroe (DR-Va.)	S	Helps ward off Aaron Burr as vice-presidential candidate
1801	Albert Gallatin (DR-Va.)	H	Key strategist in Jefferson's electoral college victory
1801	Joseph Nicholson (DR-Md.)	H	Rises from sickbed to save Maryland's vote for Jefferson
1825	Henry Clay (DR-Ky.)	H	Backs J. Q. Adams as House chooses pres., gets cabinet job
1825	S. Van Rensselaer (DR-N.Y.)	H	Casts key House vote in election of John Quincy Adams
1828	Martin Van Buren (D-N.Y.)	S	Key party organizer in election of Andrew Jackson
1836	Sherrod Williams (W-Ky.)	H	Devises public interrogation of two top presidential candidates
1844	Robert J. Walker (D-Miss.)	S	Wins reaffirmation of 2/3 rule for selecting Democratic nominees
1848	John J. Crittenden (W-Ky.)	S	Deserts homesteater Clay for W. H. Harrison as Whig nominee
1852	William Seward (W-N.Y.)	S	Kingmaker at 1852 Whig nominating convention
1860	Jefferson Davis (D-Miss.)	S	Presses pro–Dred Scott resolutions as anti-Douglas move
1863	Samuel C. Pomeroy (R-Kans.)	S	Launches anti-Lincoln boom for Salmon P. Chase
1872	Carl Schurz (R-Mo.)	S	A leader of Liberal Republican third-party movement
1876	Abram Hewitt (D-N.Y.)	H	Personally bankrolls Tilden campaign
1877	James A. Garfield (R-Ohio)	H	In on high-level Wormley House Bargain to select Hayes
1892	Matthew Quay (R-Pa.)	S	Maneuvers against Benjamin Harrison at GOP convention
1896	William V. Allen (Pop-Nebr.)	S	Permanent chair of Populist convention
1896	Henry M. Teller (R-Colo.)	S	Silverite leader at GOP convention
1896	William F. Vilas (D-Wis.)	S	Helps organize gold Democrats
1896	James K. Jones (D-Ark.)	S	Reads anti-Clevelandite platform at Democratic convention
1900	Thomas Platt (R-N.Y.)	S	Plays key role in choice of Theodore Roosevelt as GOP VP nominee
1900	Mark Hanna (R-Ohio)	S	Manages McKinley's election campaign
1908	Nelson W. Aldrich (R-R.I.)	S	Writes labor and tariff planks at GOP convention

Table 4.1 (*continued*)

1920	Henry Cabot Lodge (R-Mass.)	S	Writes League of Nations plank at GOP convention
1920	Boies Penrose (R-Pa.)	S	Kingmaker at GOP convention
1924	Thomas J. Walsh (D-Mont.)	S	Permanent chair of long, deadlocked Democratic convention
1928	George Norris (R-Nebr.)	S	Bolts GOP to back Democrat Al Smith for president
1932	Samuel Rayburn (D-Tex.)	H	Delivers Texas to FDR at Democratic convention
1932	Huey Long (D-La.)	S	Maneuvers for FDR at Democratic convention
1940	James F. Byrnes (D-S.C.)	S	Promotes "draft" of FDR at Democratic convention
1948	Alben Barkley (D-Ky.)	S	Delivers rousing keynote address at Democratic convention
1948	Claude Pepper (D-Fla.)	S	Proposes draft of Eisenhower as Democratic nominee
1951	Henry C. Lodge, Jr. (R-Mass.)	S	Promotes Eisenhower as Republican nominee
1952	Robert A. Taft (R-Ohio)	S	Makes postconvention peace with Ike at Morningside Heights
1956	Adam Clayton Powell (D-N.Y.)	H	Backs Eisenhower for reelection
1960	William Green, Jr. (D-Pa.)	H	Swings his Philadelphia machine behind JFK nomination
1964	Kenneth Keating (R-N.Y.)	S	Leads anti-Goldwater walkout of moderates from GOP convention
1964	Hubert H. Humphrey (D-Minn.)	S	Handles racial conflict over seating Mississippi delegation
1967	Birch Bayh (D-Ind.)	S	Engineers constitutional amendment covering presidential succession
1968	Strom Thurmond (R-S.C.)	S	Key southern backer of Nixon nomination
1968	Abraham Ribicoff (D-Conn.)	S	Assails Chicago Mayor Daley from convention podium
1968	Eugene McCarthy (D-Minn.)	S	Won't back Humphrey after Chicago Democratic convention
1969+	George McGovern (D-S.Dak.)	S	Co-chairs McGovern-Fraser commission re Dem. nominating rules
1976	Jesse Helms (R-N.C.)	S	Heads Reagan drive in key North Carolina primary
1980	David Stockman (R-Mich.)	H	Helps prepare Reagan for 1980 television debates

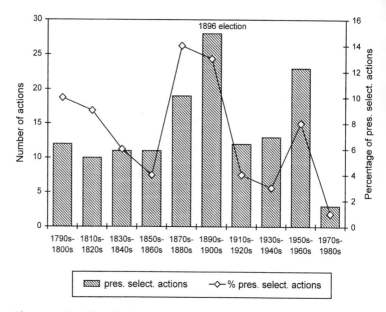

Figure 4.5. Presidential selection actions

high-count elections are those of 1896 (fourteen items), when both major parties, aided by many House and Senate members, split spectacularly into gold and silver factions at their nominating conventions;[32] 1876 (twelve items), when MCs of both parties took steps to help solve the Hayes-Tilden electoral college deadlock; 1800 (eight items), when the House chose Jefferson as president over Aaron Burr (the Republicans' intended *vice* presidential nominee) after those two men embarrassingly tied in the electoral college under the Constitution's original counting rules; 1824 (seven items), when the House chose John Quincy Adams as

32. This high count for 1896 bears out "party realignment theory," which elevates the 1890s to the high status of the 1860s and 1930s in historical importance. But of course the count here reflects only party activity. In Figure 2.1, which records total MC "actions" of all kinds by decade, the 1890s does not stand out. In the congressional "action" sphere generally, unlike the 1860s and 1930s, the 1890s was a humdrum decade.

president after a fragmented election result; and 1952 (seven items—all involving Republicans), when Senator Henry Cabot Lodge, Jr. (R-Mass.), and others figured in Eisenhower's nomination drive or ensuing campaign. In Figure 4.5, the contentious election of 1896 pumps up the total for the 1890s–1900s, though the surrounding contests helped also. The high total for the 1950s–1960s is rather evenly attributed to the elections of 1952 (seven items), 1956 (two items), 1960 (four items), 1964 (two items), 1968 (four items), and four interelection moves involving process.

To me, the main story in Figure 4.5 is the paltry reading for the 1970s–1980s. Both absolutely and relatively—that is, as a proportion of all data items—MC presidential selection actions have fallen to all-time lows. I do not think that this is an artifact of problematic recent data. It ratifies what we otherwise already know about presidential nominating politics since the late 1960s: That process reforms and media practices have greatly diminished the role of professional politicians—including members of Congress—in the selection process.[33] The way in which the occupants of the White House are selected is more completely detached from Capitol Hill than ever before. For better or worse, we live in an era of Dick Morris rather than of Martin Van Buren, Matthew Quay, or even —as its reform activism slips away into an ever less familiar past—the McGovern-Fraser commission.

Running for President

Of course, some members of Congress also aim for the White House themselves. Surprisingly, only three have ever moved there directly— Congressman James Garfield (R-Ohio) in 1880, Senator Warren G. Hard-

33. See Nelson W. Polsby, *Consequences of Party Reform* (New York: Oxford University Press, 1983).

ing (R-Ohio) in 1920, and Senator John F. Kennedy (D-Mass.) in 1960.[34] But this number greatly understates the importance of upward congressional ambition. Many members have moved directly to the vice presidency—in recent times, Senators Harry S. Truman (D-Mo.), Alben Barkley (D-Ky.), Richard M. Nixon, Lyndon B. Johnson, and Hubert Humphrey, Congressman Gerald Ford (R-Mich.), and Senators Walter Mondale (D-Minn.), Dan Quayle (R-Ind.), and Albert Gore, Jr. (D-Tenn.). Scores of members have aimed for the White House without making it, in some cases imprinting the politics of an era anyway—good examples are Henry Clay, Stephen A. Douglas, James Blaine (R-Ohio), Robert A. Taft, Hubert Humphrey, Barry Goldwater (R-Ariz.), and Edward Kennedy.[35] Several members have figured as prominent third-party candidates— Senator John P. Hale (N.H.) as a Free Soiler in 1852, Speaker Nathaniel Banks (Mass.) as a Know-Nothing in 1856, Congressman James B. Weaver (Iowa) as a Greenbacker in 1880, Senator Robert La Follette, Sr., as a Progressive in 1924, and Congressman William Lemke (N.Dak.) as Union Party candidate in 1936. Congressman John B. Anderson (R-Ill.) ran as an independent in 1980.

Congress is always there as a presidential stable. In this study's dataset, I coded 150 items—amounting to 6 percent of all MC actions during the two centuries—as "run for president or vice president."[36] Included are all noticed instances where an MC ran, or was seriously considered, for one of those two offices—either in a party's nominating process or in

34. This analysis does not encompass the many members of Congress who rose to the presidency *eventually* rather than directly. A long list begins with James Madison and ends, as of the 1990s, with President George Bush (once R-Tex.) and an expectant Al Gore (once D-Tenn.).

35. These are all Senate-based politicians except Clay and Blaine, who made a mark while in both houses. (Douglas also served early and briefly in the House.)

36. Again, some items are multiply coded. John Nance Garner's 1932 action counts here even though it also counted earlier under presidential selection.

a general election. Today, politicians openly run; in earlier times, "being seriously considered" could draw notice. Stray items accommodated by the coding category are Gerald Ford's rise to the vice presidency in 1974 (he was nominated by President Nixon and confirmed by Congress after Vice President Spiro Agnew resigned under a corruption cloud), as well as three cases where senators loomed as presidential possibilities outside the normal election cycle—Benjamin Wade as the constitutional successor if Andrew Johnson's impeachment had been upheld by the Senate in 1868, Mark Hanna as a background rival of Theodore Roosevelt until Hanna's death in 1904, and Huey Long as a rival of Franklin Roosevelt before Long was assassinated in 1935.[37]

In Figure 4.6, the 150 actions are sorted into twenty-year intervals. The result is a pattern of punctuated growth during the two centuries.[38]

37. Included in the full dataset (and in the relevant category total in Table 2.6), though *not* in any calculations for this section, are two 1861 Confederacy items: Senator Jefferson Davis assumed the presidency of the Confederate States of America, and Senator Robert Toombs was seriously considered for that office.

38. A methodological discussion is in order. In assembling the dataset, as explained in Chapter 2, I reserved the right to exclude mentions of MC activity that were trivial by the relied-on authors' own standards, and I gave as a leading instance certain nineteenth-century favorite-son presidential candidacies. This raises the possibility that the pattern in Figure 4.6 is an artifact of measurement. In fact, it is not. Using this exclusion license, I excluded from the dataset a total of eighteen candidate items (not all of them involving "favorite sons"): four for the 1850s–1860s, two for the 1870s–1880s, four for the 1890s–1900s, one for the 1910s–1920s, three for the 1930s–1940s, three for the 1950s–1960s, and one for the 1970s–1980s. Adding these items to Figure 4.6 would not greatly change its configuration. I should emphasize the low standing or fleeting mention given to these excluded items by the historians who brought them up. In one account of nominating prospects, for example, the historian noted: "and such men as [five are named, including a senator] had but minor and scattered constituencies." That is all. In another account, after eight leading possibilities for a nomination are listed, we are told that "less likely possibilities included [eight more men are named, including two senators]." That is all. In another account, "There were also the 'favorite sons'—[a senator and another politician]—but their candidacies were not entirely serious." In another account, "[three

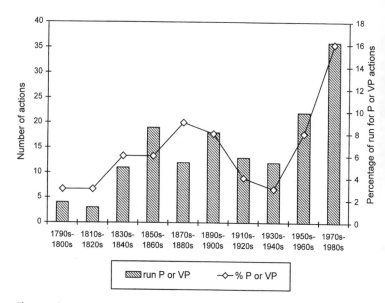

Figure 4.6. Running for president or vice president

Three eras emerge. The country's original, pre-popular system for selecting presidents was supposed to tamp down open displays of ambition;
at least among members of Congress, judging from the bar-graph values
for the era of the "Virginia dynasty" and the Adams presidencies ending in the 1820s, perhaps it did.[39] The more democratic system intro-

---

named politicians, including two senators] received a few [delegate] votes from their own
states." In another, a named senator, "who was less conservative than [another politi-
cian], also had strong friends in the South." That is all. Another named senator won nine
delegate votes during a winning candidate's first-ballot victory. At various times, five
senators refused to be considered, or were dismissed for consideration, for vice presidential nominations. And so on. True, some of these old-time also-rans might have had
as good a chance of getting nominated as did, for example, House members John Ashbrook (R-Ohio) or Shirley Chisholm in 1972. But it is also true that the old-timers did
not conduct public, nationwide campaigns the way the recent also-rans have done.

39. See the discussion in James W. Ceaser, *Presidential Selection: Theory and Development* (Princeton, N.J.: Princeton University Press, 1979), chs. 1, 2.

duced during the Jacksonian era—with its expanded electorate, popular presidency, strong party organizations, and control of nominations by party conventions—coincides in Figure 4.6 with a series of middle-sized bars extending from the 1830s through the 1940s. After that, the time series rises to a new high in the 1950s and 1960s and explodes upward in the 1970s and 1980s. The McGovern-style reforms that opened up the presidential nominating process are one obvious cause of this explosion: Around 1970, party organizations and deliberative conventions gave way entirely to free-form initiatives by ambitious individual politicians, of whom many have made an appearance. The dataset's all-time high is ten MC "run for president or vice president" actions for 1972 —by House members John Ashbrook (R-Ohio), Shirley Chisholm, Paul McCloskey (R-Calif.), and Wilbur Mills; and by Senators Thomas Eagleton (D-Mo.), who was nominated for vice president but withdrew after his psychiatric past was disclosed, Mike Gravel (D-Alaska), who nominated himself for president on the floor of the Democratic convention, Hubert Humphrey, Henry Jackson (D-Wash.), George McGovern, and Edmund Muskie. After that, the elections from 1976 through 1988 continued the brisk pace with, respectively, eight, five, five, and seven candidacy actions. Since 1988, we have witnessed the candidacies of, among others, Senators Al Gore, Bob Kerrey, Tom Harkin (D-Iowa), Bob Dole, Phil Gramm, Richard Lugar (R-Ind.), and John McCain. To put it briefly, the country has evolved since 1789 from tamping down presidential ambition among MCs to generously encouraging it.

Separation of Powers Today

Do the trends and events noted in this chapter have broader implications? I believe they do. Consider the basic set of American elective institutions—the presidency, the Senate, the House of Representatives, and, for some purposes, the state governments. What emerges here regarding their development, and the evolution of relations among them, during the past two centuries?

First, through changes involving the presidency and the Senate, the system has grown more uniformly *democratized*—that is, rooted in open, competitive processes for nominating and electing candidates. On the presidency side, Figure 4.6, which tracks the "run for president" variable (though of course it says nothing about the large number of presidential candidates who have been non-MCs), indexes two junctures of popularization: The 1830s, when party nominating conventions triumphed over the more elitist congressional caucus as a way of sorting White House aspirants; and the 1970s, when today's wide-open, candidate-rich presidential primary system made its appearance. The Senate's chief democratizing event was, of course, the adoption of the Seventeenth Amendment in 1913; yet Figure 4.4, with its time series tracking party bosses as MCs (almost all of them were senators) offers testimony also. In the context of the nineteenth century, the intrusion of party organization leaders into congressional politics was no doubt a democratizing move. Party organizations—notably, Martin Van Buren's but also later ones—were at least thought to be Jacksonian trailblazers of democracy. Yet by 1900 or so—from the standpoint of democracy as that era's reformers were recasting it to mean direct voter choice—party organizations (certainly the senator-led state ones) had shifted from a plus to a minus. Thus, both the upslope and the downslope in Figure 4.4 can be said to have been good news for democracy. At any rate, the state of affairs at the end of the twentieth century, tarnished as it might have been through campaign-finance developments, is clear enough otherwise: Similar, open selection processes for all three national institutions (as well as the state governments).

Second, the major elective institutions have grown more *distinct* from each other. In several significant ways, they impinge on each other less than they once did. As shown in Figures 4.2 and 4.3, twentieth-century presidents tapped MCs with major followings less often in constituting the top stratum of their cabinets. The Seventeenth Amendment distanced the Senate from the state governments, as did the related disappearance of state party bosses doubling as MCs. As shown in Figure 4.5, since 1970 members of Congress have virtually abandoned any prominent role in selecting presidents or vice presidents. It is true that late-twentieth-century MCs set new "action" records as White House aspirants themselves, but that does not mean they succeeded. Here is the second insertion of "real" statistical data into this chapter: As it happens, *fewer* presidents have been originating in Congress. From Washington's administration through McKinley's (this cuts American history at the beginning of the twentieth century and just before the style-setting modern presidency of Theodore Roosevelt), 83 percent of presidents had served previously in Congress, and former MCs held the White House 81 percent of the time.[40] Since McKinley, the comparable statistics have been a much lower 41 percent and 31 percent. In the twentieth century, presidents with spotless non-MC backgrounds like Carter, Reagan, and Clinton became standard fare. Increased distinctness of one institution from another is the multiply bolstered message of this paragraph.

Third, although there are conflicting trends, the major institutions have arguably grown more *equal* in influence and legitimacy. The Senate, which began as a weak question mark in 1789, surged as an "action" arena during the age of Clay, Calhoun, and Webster (see Figure 4.1), then a few generations later probably fended off a serious sag in legitimacy—

40. That includes pre-1789 service by the first three presidents, Washington, Adams, and Jefferson, in the Continental Congress. This inclusion is awkward, but by 1789 those three men had risen above the legislative level (they never held seats in the new Congress), and this is one way to score them. If the first three presidents are omitted entirely from the calculations—the relevant time span becomes Madison through McKinley— the results fall slightly to 81 percent and 77 percent.

at least on the Progressive left—through the Seventeenth Amendment. Today, the House and Senate are virtually political equals—a rare, possibly unique condition among the world's national bicameral legislatures.

As is well known, the presidency began as something of a question mark also, notwithstanding George Washington, and it operated in the shadow of Congress during much of the nineteenth century—hence Woodrow Wilson's 1885 work, *Congressional Government*[41]—but it surged in prominence and influence during the twentieth century. Yet here is the conflicting trend: Has the presidency surged too much? Did its twentieth-century rise generate a fundamental *in*equality among the major institutions? Particularly since the New Deal, Theodore J. Lowi has argued, we have witnessed a "displacement of parliamentarianism by executive government"—a switch to a "plebiscitary presidency."[42] A whiff of support for Lowi's case appears in Figure 4.6, where the upward-exploding "run for president" statistic does after all index *notice* of MC candidacies, not just actual candidacies. What kind of republic is it where, as in the United States in the 1970s and 1980s, one-sixth of the notice taken of national legislators is of their trying to become vice presidents or presidents? Figure 4.6 also shows that even before the McGovern nominating reforms around 1970, the "run for president" series had already jutted up to a record plateau in the 1950s and 1960s.[43] All the graph's post-1940s

41. Woodrow Wilson, *Congressional Government: A Study in American Politics* (New York: Meridian, 1956).

42. Theodore J. Lowi, *The Personal President: Power Invested, Promise Unfulfilled* (Ithaca, N.Y.: Cornell University Press, 1985), quotations at pp. 97, 65.

43. Even more striking is the showing of the "run for president" series in the "A"-level data taken alone—that is, the mentions in the "general" history books. When American history is divided into quintiles, "run for president" contributed two of twenty-six, or 8 percent, of all "A"-level "action" items from 1789 through 1831; nine of fifty-nine, or 15 percent, from 1831 through 1871; one of fifty-nine, or 2 percent, from 1871 through 1911; seven of seventy-two, or 10 percent, from 1911 through 1950; but twenty of thirty-nine, or a huge 51 percent, from 1951 through 1988. In absolute terms, note the plummet in

evidence is at least consistent with the idea of a takeoff in the relative standing of the presidency.

Still, whether Congress has been left in the dust is open to question. (This murky subject is touched on again in Chapter 6.) Yet, anyone who takes a close look at the 1990s might ask: Can it really be said that the presidency has been overshadowing or dominating Congress? That would have been news to the Bush or Clinton White House. In general, it seems a plausible conclusion that the United States finished the twentieth century with its legislature and presidency more or less political equals,[44] as well as, within the former, its two congressional houses roughly equals.

If the major American elective institutions have grown at once more democratized, more distinct, and more equal during the past two centuries, why is that result worth noting? The answer largely depends on how one thinks about separation of powers. If the classical idea of a one-to-one relation between estates of society and branches of government is rejected—as it was by Americans in the late eighteenth century[45]—why have a separation of powers system at all? Relevant to considering the American case, I believe, are three sharply different lines of political analysis. I take them up here as stylized views associated with, respectively, Jefferson, Madison, and Habermas.

For Jefferson and other proponents (notably, John Taylor—DR-Va.) of the distinctive brand of democratic, antiaristocratic republicanism

---

mentions of *non*-candidate-related MC actions by the general texts in their coverage of recent decades. For the five historical quintiles, the non-candidate-related "A"-level totals are, respectively, twenty-five, fifty, forty-eight, sixty-five, and nineteen.

44. For what it is worth, according to recent opinion surveys, when the public has been asked which branch—Congress or the presidency—is a better bet for handling a specified policy area, Congress has typically fared well.

45. See Gordon S. Wood, *The Creation of the American Republic, 1776–1787* (New York: Norton, 1969), pp. 387–89.

that emerged in America around 1800, the reason for having a separation of powers system was clear and simple. In modern terminology, it was to minimize shirking by government officials in a hoped-for perfect principal-agent relation between the people and the government.[46] That could be done by letting "the people"—who were seen as an uncomplicated, unified entity—elect, watch, and hold separately accountable the officials of *each* of a set of government institutions defined strictly by function.[47] That included the judicial function. Given such clean, readily comprehensible lines between people and institutions, and as little connection as possible between institutions (Jefferson "emphasized the absolute independence of each branch from the others"),[48] the odds could be minimized that government would grow into a confusing, dangerous, all-purpose concentration of power separate from society—the ultimate nightmare in all brands of republicanism.[49]

How would a resurrected Jefferson react to the trends exhibited in this chapter? The third trend, the alleged equalizing of the major institutions in influence and legitimacy, might find him indifferent. Government institutions are not supposed to have any influence of their own—that is

46. Two excellent sources on this subject are: Samuel P. Huntington, "The Founding Fathers and the Division of Powers," in Arthur Maass (ed.), *Area and Power: A Theory of Local Government* (Glencoe, Ill.: Free Press, 1959), pp. 160–68; M. J. C. Vile, *Constitutionalism and the Separation of Powers* (London: Oxford University Press, 1967), pp. 161–72.

47. "All governmental bodies are simply agents or servants of the people who have delegated to them certain specific tasks." Huntington, "The Founding Fathers," p. 164.

48. Huntington, "The Founding Fathers," p. 166.

49. If applied today, this theory of institutions would favor liberals sometimes and conservatives sometimes. For example, a true Jeffersonian republican would presumably be pleased that the Senate acquitted President Clinton after his impeachment, on the ground that a president should enjoy a direct principal-agent relation with the public, uncluttered by congressional intrusion; elections and possibly opinion polls are all the system needs. But a true Jeffersonian would be appalled by the modern liberal bent for judicial activism.

axiomatic—and if they are democratic enough they will automatically be legitimate anyway. But the other two trends—toward democratization and institutional distinctness—would no doubt delight him. Democratized yet distinct institutions is exactly what the Jeffersonian republicans were aiming for, and in both regards that is the way the system has evolved. For a century, it has been obvious that American political scientists who favor party government have been at war with Madison,[50] but they have also been at odds with Jefferson. For a Jeffersonian, an ideal American political universe would be one in which, among other things, citizens are perfectly adept at distinguishing and appraising both individual politicians and particular institutions—not just political parties, possibly not parties at all. "Is the president doing a good job?" "Would you vote to re-elect Senator Jones?" "Is the Senate handling the impeachment trial appropriately?" These are the kinds of questions that would be asked repeatedly and would count.[51]

Madison's reasoning is well-known from his writing in *The Federalist*. The rationale for having a system of separation of powers, liberally laced with checks and balances, is to constrain factions of society with harmful aims, to constrain elements of the government with their own harmful aims, and, in general, to ensure balance among society's various interests.[52] If confronted by this chapter's trends, how would a resurrected Madison (of 1787 vintage) react? He would probably be unnerved by the democratization, and he might be upset by the trend toward institutional

50. For example, James MacGregor Burns, *The Deadlock of Democracy: Four-Party Politics in America* (Englewood Cliffs, N.J.: Prentice-Hall, 1963).

51. In fact, a similar question was asked about the Clinton impeachment trial in a New York Times–CBS News poll in early 1999, and possibly its results counted. The response was 37 percent approve, 56 percent disapprove. See Richard L. Berke and Janet Elder, "Damaged by Trial, Senate's Standing Sinks in New Poll," *New York Times*, February 3, 1999, pp. A1, A16.

52. For Madison's views as contrasted with Jefferson's, see Huntington, "The Founding Fathers," pp. 179–96.

distinctness (although the Constitution's formal checks and balances do remain in place).[53] Yet after reflecting for awhile on today's overall institutional configuration, he might arrive at a net positive judgment because of the third trend toward institutional equality. Constraint and balance, after all, were his goals. A hegemonic House of Representatives was one of his fears. In today's circumstances where, judges aside, legitimacy tends to derive from being directly elected, what could be a better route to constraint and balance than a system of three powerful, democratically based, and mutually checking institutions like the U.S. presidency, Senate, and House? In general, then, albeit for decisively different reasons, Madison might join Jefferson in approving the overall drift in U.S. separation of powers arrangements, at least in the respects considered here.

Yet there exists a third, quite independent justification for having a system of separation of powers that I associate here with Habermas—in his roles both as characterizer of the "public sphere" of the eighteenth century and advocate of "discursive democracy" today. How, at the level of a nation-state, can politics and policymaking be effectively endogenized into a "public sphere"? One way is exactly to create a system of separation of powers with several mutually constraining decision points, all anchored in electoral processes. That way, arenas and incentives are supplied for a multiplicity of elected officials and others to make moves in public that are worth noticing. With luck, an atmosphere of contingency and competitive persuasion and mobilization will result. Tough, lengthy, open pulling and hauling and deliberation are virtually guaranteed because often no other route to policy success is available—particularly if, as in the American case, hurdles such as the presidential veto, the Senate filibuster, or the cumbersome Capitol Hill committee system may need

53. Nationalist that Madison was, one move toward distinctness might please him—the removal of the influence of state legislatures (as well as the state party bosses who sometimes dominated them) from the affairs of the national government.

to be cleared. This is a kind of political process that Jefferson and Madison experienced in their own lives, and in fact helped shape yet stopped short of writing theories about. Of course, American processes, whether of 1789 or today, do not meet Habermas's exacting criteria for "discursive democracy"; in his recent work *Between Facts and Norms,* however, Habermas is notably sympathetic to the idea of separation of powers.[54] "Indeed," according to one commentator, "his entire procedural structure displays the Madisonian quality of balancing and separating governmental and popular power, for the sake of a discursively based legitimacy."[55] A stylized Habermasian, if confronted by this chapter's reported trends, might be indifferent to the second (distinctness), but should applaud the first (democratization) and the third (equality)—the latter because the equality among independent institutions helps *force* an endogenization of politics and a deliberative mode.

Plainly, a "public sphere" model of politics and policymaking anchored in separation of powers clashes with a more conventional party-centered model in which parties offer programs, voters make choices, a party that wins a majority of the vote implements those choices between elections, and voters hold that party accountable in the next election. Party linkage of this sort is unquestionably a *part* of the American story,[56] but only a part. It is a good bet that the American public would never accept a

54. Jürgen Habermas, *Between Facts and Norms: Contributions to a Discourse Theory of Law and Democracy* (Cambridge: M.I.T. Press, 1996), ch. 4.3.

55. John L. Brooke, "Reason and Passion in the Public Sphere: Habermas and the Cultural Historians," *Journal of Interdisciplinary History* 29 (1998), 43–67, quotation at p. 63.

56. In the current scholarship about Congress, one particularly illuminating modeling move centers on party-related signals sent biennially by voters as being largely determinative (once strained through preexisting constitutional and congressional rules) of policy results in the ensuing two years. See Keith Krehbiel, *Pivotal Politics: A Theory of U.S. Lawmaking* (Chicago: University of Chicago Press, 1998); David W. Brady and Craig Volden, *Revolving Gridlock: Politics and Policy from Carter to Clinton* (Boulder, Colo.: Westview, 1998).

party linkage system taken straight. It would be too blunt and clumsy as a connection between voters and government, too centralized, too unsmart between elections, and too authoritarian between elections—citizens would see themselves as relegated to the status of subjects. And as an analytic matter, party linkage models tend to be incomplete. They construe politics too restrictively as preference execution rather than as a complicated blend of formation and execution; preference fixedness wins out too easily and quickly over preference contingency.

As an empirical matter, American history offers many significant instances of policymaking that seem to fit a "public sphere" and separation of powers model better than a party linkage model. Here are the ingredients: The government's separation of powers processes were difficult to navigate; the policy outcome was in doubt and took a long time; many noticed moves were made by MCs and others; election returns did not affect the result in any direct, causal way;[57] and, so far as one can tell, opinion change and crystallization occurring at both mass and elite levels *outside* the biennial election process was critical to the result. Specific instances include: The defeat of the Versailles Treaty in 1919, the defeat of Franklin Roosevelt's court-packing plan in 1937, the defeat of Clinton's health-care package in 1993–94, and the defeat of the Republicans' "shut down the government" budget drive in 1995–96.

These were defeats, it will be countered. Defeats in any process rich in veto points and cumbersomeness are a dog-bites-man story. But victories have occurred bearing such a process profile also. Consider two modern instances—the U.S. commitment to trans-Atlantic defense in 1947–49 involving, as Capitol Hill decision junctures, the Truman Doctrine, the Marshall Plan, and the creation of NATO (for a total of eight MC "action"

---

57. How about indirectly? It is of course always possible to claim that elected officials behave the way they do because of the prospect of a *future* election. Often that is true, but often it is less true, and at any rate the proposition often borders on being undisconfirmable.

items in this study's dataset); and the enactment of the Civil Rights Act of 1964 (fifteen "action" items). These two commitments were probably as thoroughly and openly considered, and as decisive (notwithstanding intense opposition in both cases), and they have proven to be as enforceable and irreversible as any public commitments entered into in American history.[58] There may be a causal connection; that is, the two outcomes have probably been so decisive, enforceable, and irreversible at least in part because the enactment processes that led up to them were so strenuous, dramatic, and crystallizing.[59]

58. Currently, there is a drive to roll back affirmative action, but that complex of policies dates back to decisions made by chiefly judges and executive officials after 1964, not to that year's Civil Rights Act itself. See Hugh Davis Graham, "Legacies of the 1960s: The American 'Rights Revolution' in an Era of Divided Governance," *Journal of Policy History* 10 (1998), 267–288.

59. Obviously, it is possible to write rules that make it easier to enact policies than does the American system. But major policies enacted quickly by narrow majorities may come apart later in implementation processes or in the streets, as has often happened, according to John T.S. Keeler, in the French Fifth Republic. See "Executive Power and Policy-Making Patterns in France: Gauging the Impact of Fifth Republic Institutions," *West European Politics* 16 (1993), 518–44.

F I V E

Action Patterns in Capitol Hill Careers

Notwithstanding the existence of a broader American opportunity structure, time spent in Congress is a career pattern all by itself. What can an analysis of MC "actions" suggest about the nature and significance of Capitol Hill careers?

That is the concern of this chapter, which begins with a consideration of particularly notable "action careers" during American history, then, with an emphasis on the twentieth century, addresses several interrelated topics: To what degree have committee leaders, party leaders, and southerners dominated the "action" realm? At what points in their careers, at different times during American history, have MCs engaged in "actions"? Have early performers differed in any interesting ways from late performers? How have the major ideological impulses of American society worked their way through Congress's structure of "action careers"? What are the implications of the various "action" findings here, if any, for a reform that would impose term limits on members of Congress? In its conclusion, the chapter circles back to notable "action careers" as a device for indexing Congress's place in public affairs history.

Notable Action Careers

In the performance of "actions," members of Congress, like those of probably any profession or complex organization, turn out to be radical un-
equals. Most members perform none; a few perform a great many. On
the very high side, exhibited in Table 5.1, is a list of forty-four members
who were responsible for at least ten actions apiece during the two centuries from 1789 through 1988.[1] At the top of the list, with forty entries, is
Henry Clay. At the bottom, with a still very appreciable ten items apiece,
are four well-known politicians of the twentieth century plus Senator
Samuel Smith (DR-Md.), a power on appointments and foreign policy
questions under Madison and other early presidents. Shown in the fourth
column is each member's "action career"—which means the dates of an
MC's first and last "actions," not the dates of his or her first becoming and
finally ceasing to be a member of Congress, which are ordinarily farther
apart. It bears repeating that action totals like those presented here need
to be read as if they were bracketed by confidence intervals. In the background are not only historians' tastes but also my own coding practices
as I decided, for example, how many items to credit to Henry Clay's energetic activity during the ascendant Whig years of 1840–42.

What comes to light in Table 5.1? For one thing, the list is made up
entirely of white males (almost all now deceased).[2] That reflects the overall picture of congressional "action."[3] In gender and race terms, studying the history of Congress is not greatly different from studying that
of the American presidency. Even in the recent decades of this dataset,

1. Note that one member listed here, Senator Edward Kennedy, continued his congressional career beyond 1988.

2. In addition, note that virtually all the surnames are northwestern European.

3. Males have also dominated the scholarship on U.S. public affairs, as the alert reader
of Table 2.1 might have noticed. All thirty-three "era" histories relied on for this study are
by men, although three of the five recent "general" histories have a woman as coauthor.

Table 5.1 Members of Congress Who Performed Ten or More Actions

N Actions	Member	Chamber	Action Career	Historians' Rank (Sens.)
40	Henry Clay (DR,W-Ky.)	H,S	1811–1850	1 (tie)
37	Henry Cabot Lodge (R-Mass.)	H,S	1890–1921	14
30	Robert A. Taft (R-Ohio)	S	1939–1953	6
27	William E. Borah (R-Idaho)	S	1917–1939	
27	Robert La Follette, Sr. (R-Wis.)	S	1906–1924	1 (tie)
27	Charles Sumner (D/FS,R-Mass.)	S	1851–1872	10
24	George Norris (R,I-Nebr.)	H,S	1909–1940	5
23	John Sherman (R-Ohio)	H,S	1856–1897	16 (tie)
22	Stephen A. Douglas (D-Ill.)	S	1845–1861	7 (tie)
21	Nelson W. Aldrich (R-R.I.)	S	1899–1910	16 (tie)
21	Daniel Webster (DR,W-N.H.,Mass.)	H,S	1813–1850	3 (tie)
20	Robert F. Wagner (D-N.Y.)	S	1927–1949	11
19	James Madison (DR-Va.)	H	1789–1796	
17	Samuel Rayburn (D-Tex.)	H	1914–1961	
17	Arthur Vandenberg (R-Mich.)	S	1933–1948	16 (tie)
16	John C. Calhoun (DR,W,D-S.C.)	H,S	1811–1850	3 (tie)
16	Lyndon B. Johnson (D-Tex.)	S	1953–1960	9
16	Thomas P. O'Neill (D-Mass.)	H	1967–1985	
15	Thaddeus Stevens (R-Pa.)	H	1861–1868	
14	John Randolph (DR-Va.)	H,S	1800–1826	
14	Burton K. Wheeler (D-Mont.)	S	1923–1941	
13	James G. Blaine (R-Ohio)	H,S	1872–1881	
13	Barry Goldwater (R-Ariz.)	S	1960–1984	
13	Matthew Quay (R-Pa.)	S	1887–1902	
13	William Seward (W,R-N.Y.)	S	1849–1861	
12	J. William Fulbright (D-Ark.)	H,S	1943–1968	12
12	Hiram Johnson (R-Calif.)	S	1919–1945	
12	Lyman Trumbull (R-Ill.)	S	1861–1872	
11	John Quincy Adams (F,DR,NR,W-Mass.)	H,S	1803–1842	
11	Thomas Hart Benton (D-Mo.)	S	1829–1848	13
11	Harry F. Byrd (D,I-Va.)	S	1937–1964	
11	Arthur P. Gorman (D-Md.)	S	1881–1904	
11	Henry Jackson (D-Wash.)	S	1957–1976	
11	Edward Kennedy (D-Mass.)	S	1968–1987+	
11	Robert La Follette, Jr. (R,I-Wis.)	S	1928–1939	
11	Mike Mansfield (D-Mont.)	S	1962–1973	
11	Edmund Muskie (D-Maine)	S	1963–1980	
11	Thomas B. Reed (R-Maine)	H	1889–1897	
11	Benjamin F. Wade (R-Ohio)	S	1851–1868	

Table 5.1 (*continued*)

N Actions	Member	Chamber	Action Career	Historians' Rank (Sens.)
10	Hubert H. Humphrey (D-Minn.)	S	1949–1977	7 (tie)
10	Huey Long (D-La.)	S	1932–1935	
10	Wilbur Mills (D-Ark.)	H	1960–1972	
10	Richard Russell (D-Ga.)	S	1948–1970	15
10	Samuel Smith (DR-Md.)	H,S	1800–1827	

members *not* in the category of white males contributed only 2.6 percent of all MC actions in the 1950s, 6.1 percent in the 1960s, 7.6 percent in the 1970s, and 6.4 percent in the 1980s.[4] Among African-American members, Congressman Adam Clayton Powell, Jr.'s "action career" is the most noteworthy—seven items from 1947 through 1967.[5] Congresswoman Edith Green (D-Oreg.) ranks first among women members (four actions) for her role as skeptical overseer of the Democrats' antipoverty program during the 1960s.[6] It is true that recent elections in the 1990s have broadened the demography of Congress somewhat, but the institution is still overwhelmingly a white males' club.[7]

4. From the 1970s, five of the eleven items relied on here are coded principally as "descriptive representation." That is not true of any item from the 1950s, 1960s, or 1980s.

5. On Powell's career, see Charles V. Hamilton, *Adam Clayton Powell, Jr.: The Political Biography of an American Dilemma* (New York: Macmillan, 1991).

6. The four Green items all derive from Allen J. Matusow, *The Unraveling of America: A History of Liberalism in the 1960s* (New York: Harper and Row, 1984), pp. 113–14, 115, 265, 269. It is worth remembering that the data sources for the 1970s and 1980s are somewhat lean.

7. That is certainly evident in recent statistics on the committee hierarchy. Of the eighty MCs serving as (Republican) chairs or (Democratic) ranking minority members of the forty House and Senate committees during the twentieth century's last two Congresses, *not one* was a woman in 1997–98 and *only one* was a woman in 1999–2000 —Nydia M. Velázquez (D.-N.Y.), ranking minority member of the House Small Busi-

Note also the variety of roles in Table 5.1. Of the forty-four members listed, five were Speakers of the House: Henry Clay (until 1825), James Blaine, Thomas B. Reed (R-Maine), Samuel Rayburn (D-Tex.), and Thomas P. O'Neill.[8] Since 1910, two others have been formal leaders of their congressional parties: Senate Majority Leaders Lyndon B. Johnson and Mike Mansfield (D-Mont.).[9] In previous times when "majority leader" and "minority leader" were not yet formalized posts, a few others were de facto leaders of their parties—certainly Nelson W. Aldrich and Arthur P. Gorman in the Senate around 1900 and arguably James Madison and Thaddeus Stevens before that. That makes eleven leaders altogether.[10] If the focus is limited to members whose "action careers" have occurred chiefly or entirely since 1910—there are twenty-four in all—four have been official leaders (the aforementioned Johnson, Rayburn, Mansfield, and O'Neill), and another seven have contributed a large share of their actions while chairing (or serving as their parties' rank-

ness Committee. Four women had held such positions during the earlier Congress of 1995–96, but Senator Nancy Kassebaum (R-Kans.) and Congresswomen Cardiss Collins (D-Ill.) and Jan Meyers (R-Kans.) retired in 1996, and Congresswoman Nancy Johnson (R.-Conn.) gave up chairing the House Committee on Standards of Official Conduct at that time.

8. Speaker Joseph G. Cannon was responsible for nine actions during 1901–10.

9. Though a more recessive figure than his predecessor Johnson, Mansfield made a series of notable moves on domestic and foreign policy and as manager of the Senate.

10. In the full dataset, 13 percent of the 1,226 actions coded for the eight decades starting in 1911 were performed by MCs who, at the relevant time, held the office of Speaker, House Majority Leader, House Minority Leader, Senate Majority Leader, or Senate Minority Leader. That includes runs for the presidency or vice presidency by, for example, Speaker John Nance Garner in 1932 and Senate Majority Leader Johnson in 1960. By decades, the percentages are: 14 percent in the 1910s, 11 percent in the 1920s, 8 percent in the 1930s, 6 percent in the 1940s, 26 percent in the 1950s, 16 percent in the 1960s, 15 percent in the 1970s, and 14 percent in the 1980s. The bulge in the 1950s is due to Lyndon B. Johnson; sixteen of the thirty actions performed by official leaders during that decade were his as Senate Majority Leader.

ing members of) House or Senate standing committees whose jurisdictions accommodated those actions. Those seven are Henry Cabot Lodge,
William E. Borah, Arthur Vandenberg, and J. William Fulbright as leaders
of the Senate Foreign Relations Committee, and Harry F. Byrd, Richard
Russell, and Wilbur Mills as heads of, respectively, the Senate Finance
Committee, the Senate Armed Services Committee, and the House Ways
and Means Committee.

But that leaves half the listed "action careers" since 1910, and probably a similar share before that,[11] that have *not* been heavily associated
with holding leadership positions or heading relevant standing committees. Top official positions have been far from a necessary (to say nothing of a sufficient) condition of member "action." For example, Senator
Robert F. Wagner set the legislative pace in the Senate during the New
Deal without benefit of a relevant committee chairmanship,[12] and Senator
Robert A. Taft became the upper chamber's leading conservative legislator and taker of stands during the 1940s without holding his party's
top leadership post or, for most of his important moves, a relevant top
committee rank.[13] Those two senators found other ways to take the initiative and make themselves felt as backbenchers early in their careers.[14]

11. It is hard to draw the comparison, given the less formal leadership structures and
less prominent standing committees of the nineteenth century.

12. Wagner moved up to the chairmanship of the Senate Banking and Currency Com-
mittee in 1937, but that came after his major work in advancing the National Industrial
Recovery Act of 1933, unemployment insurance as an ingredient of the Social Security
Act of 1935, and the National Labor Relations Act (that is, the Wagner Act) of 1935.

13. Taft became formal leader of the Senate Republican party only in 1953, the last year
of his life, although he had been de facto leader (at least on domestic policy) for several
years before that and formally head of the party's Senate policy or steering committee
(which Taft breathed life into) starting in 1944. In designing the Senate version of the
Taft-Hartley Act in 1947, Taft worked from a relevant committee chairmanship.

14. For both Taft and Wagner, the bracketing dates of their "action careers" are identical to those of their full Capitol Hill careers. That is true also for John C. Calhoun, Daniel

As for the rest of the twentieth-century high scorers, George Norris, Burton K. Wheeler, Senator Hiram Johnson (R-Calif.), and both the La Follettes were Progressive activists and critics of presidents' foreign policies. Senators Hubert Humphrey, Barry Goldwater, Edmund Muskie, Henry Jackson, and Edward Kennedy have been all-purpose public figures—legislators, takers of stands, and White House aspirants.[15] Huey Long is difficult to classify. Many of the high scorers in Table 5.1 have not held top official positions, and, also, many have not been principally legislators: Consider Charles Sumner, Matthew Quay, Huey Long, J. William Fulbright, and Barry Goldwater.

To document what politicians did is one thing, to appraise them is another. As it happens, American senators of the past two centuries, like presidents, have been ranked according to "greatness" in a survey of historians, and it might be of peripheral interest here to see how the resulting judgments map onto this study's "action" scores. Specifically, twenty-six historians responded to a survey conducted by David L. Porter in 1982 asking them to rank the "ten greatest Senators in the nation's history," using as broad criteria: "1) their accomplishments in office and 2) their long range impact on American history."[16] The returns allowed a rank-

Webster, William Seward, Benjamin F. Wade, and Huey Long, and very close to true for James Madison and Hubert Humphrey. For the busy early years of Wagner's and Taft's careers in the Senate, see J. Joseph Huthmacher, *Senator Robert F. Wagner and the Rise of Urban Liberalism* (New York: Atheneum, 1971), chs. 5–7; James T. Patterson, *Mr. Republican: A Biography of Robert A. Taft* (Boston: Houghton Mifflin, 1972), chs. 12–17.

15. In none of these five cases has an "action career" been chiefly associated with a standing committee chairmanship, although committee roles of one kind or another have been relevant. Muskie launched his important environmental initiatives as head of a relevant Senate subcommittee. Jackson, whose actions were primarily in the defense or foreign policy area, held a high (though not until the end of his career, the top) rank on the Senate Armed Services Committee. In his later years, Kennedy has been ranking Democrat on the Senate Labor and Human Resources Committee.

16. David L. Porter, "America's Ten Greatest Senators," in William D. Pederson and

ing of the top nineteen senators, not only the top ten, and those ranks appear in the right-hand column of Table 5.1.[17] Henry Clay and Robert La Follette, Sr., tied for first place. John Sherman, Nelson W. Aldrich, Arthur Vandenberg, and William B. Allison (R-Iowa)—the lone absentee of the nineteen from the table, because his "action" count was only six—scored lowest in a four-way tie for sixteenth place.

By what formula does "action" convert into "greatness"? For one thing, old energetic icons remain icons: Clay, Webster, and Calhoun are in the top four. For another, major liberal or Progressive entrepreneurs of the twentieth century tend to score high: Witness the "greatness" ranks of La Follette, Sr., Norris, Wagner, and Humphrey. There is a nod to Senator Taft, perhaps partly because the Senate itself, in 1959, officially designated him, La Follette, Sr., Clay, Webster, and Calhoun as the five outstanding senators in American history. But in general, orthodox Republicans fare poorly. Given their very high "action" scores in this study, note particularly the low "greatness" ranks of John Sherman, Nelson W. Aldrich, and Henry Cabot Lodge. Probably on exhibit here is the familiar Progressive or liberal bias of twentieth-century American historiography. To have promoted slavery may not earn "greatness" demerits (witness Calhoun), but to have promoted capitalism or nationalism probably does. One likely legacy of that bias is, still today, the relative scantiness of scholarship on U.S. national politics and policymaking between Reconstruction and the Progressive era.[18] Recently, both the Federalists and

---

Ann M. McLaurin (eds.), *The Rating Game in American Politics: An Interdisciplinary Approach* (New York: Irvington, 1987), quotations at pp. 110, 111.

17. House members were not considered in the survey.

18. "We still have much to learn about the nature of governance and policy-making in the Gilded Age; about the impact of ideas and political philosophy on party leaders; about the relationship among parties, leaders, public policy, and voting behavior.... There has never been a published scholarly biography of John Sherman, despite, or perhaps because of, the availability of 600-plus volumes of his papers in the Library of Congress.

Whigs have been given interesting new life by historians,[19] but that has yet to be done for the Republicans who presided over the mushrooming American economy after the Civil War.[20] The statutory foundations of that economy owed much to, among others, Sherman and Aldrich.

Committee Roles

High performers are of interest in themselves—the forty-four MCs listed in Table 5.1 did contribute an ample 31 percent of this study's "action" items—but for most questions involving Capitol Hill careers the study's full 2,304 items are the appropriate data base. Several questions to be asked here address change during the two centuries.

One question is: How differently have committee roles figured in MC "actions" during different eras? In the twentieth century, "Wilbur Mills, Chairman of the House Ways and Means Committee" has rolled off the tongue as if it were one long word. In nine of the ten actions by Mills coded for this study—all his moves on trade, tax, and social security legislation from 1960 through 1972, though not his surprising bid for the presidency in 1972—historians discuss the congressman's role on the

Other leading figures also lack biographies or have been treated in studies that are now woefully out of date." Charles W. Calhoun, "Late Nineteenth-Century Politics Revisited," *History Teacher* 27 (1994), 325–37, quotation at p. 335. Calhoun himself is contributing the kind of work called for, as evidenced in his "Political Economy in the Gilded Age: The Republican Party's Industrial Policy," *Journal of Policy History* 8 (1996), 291–309.

19. See Stanley Elkins and Eric McKitrick, *The Age of Federalism: The Early American Republic, 1788–1800* (New York: Oxford University Press, 1993); Daniel Walker Howe, *The Political Culture of the American Whigs* (Chicago: University of Chicago Press, 1979); John Ashworth, *Slavery, Capitalism, and Politics in the Antebellum Republic* (New York: Cambridge University Press, 1995).

20. Real per capita income, for example, nearly tripled between 1870 and 1910. See Stuart Bruchey, *The Wealth of the Nation: An Economic History of the United States* (New York: Harper and Row, 1988), p. 67. It should come as no surprise that the Republicans kept winning elections.

Ways and Means Committee or at least mention his committee title. To do otherwise would be remiss. Mills is possibly Exhibit A of a twentieth-century congressional opportunity structure that has allowed some MCs —given suitable talent, which Mills had—to rise to great influence as heads of standing committees.[21] These are the standard, familiar congressional units that are permanently authorized (they do not need to be renewed every two years), can report legislation to the House or Senate floor, have chairmanships that are ordinarily gained and ensured by seniority, and enjoy subject-area jurisdictions that are more or less constant and guaranteed.[22] Lower-ranking members, not just chairs, exercise influence from committee niches. Standing committees have been the organizational backbone of the twentieth-century Congress.

All this is familiar. But the nineteenth-century committee system is said to have been another story. The late H. Douglas Price wrote in 1977: "The modern House and Senate are committee-centered. . . . But it was not always so. It seems to me that the current view of the House and Senate can be extrapolated back, with rather minor modification, to around 1920. But as one moves further backward in time most of the familiar congressional landmarks drop from sight, one by one, until 1890 when the House and Senate appear as very different structures from their modern counterparts. Long-run careers and stable committees, the twin pillars of the modern Congress, are largely missing in the pre-1896 House or the pre-1876 Senate."[23]

21. On Mills, see John F. Manley, *The Politics of Finance: The House Committee on Ways and Means* (Boston: Little, Brown, 1970), ch. 4.

22. Though less constant than was once thought. Through a kind of common-law decision process as new bills are introduced and referred in Congress, committees do lose or gain areas of jurisdiction. See David C. King, *Turf Wars: How Congressional Committees Claim Jurisdiction* (Chicago: University of Chicago Press, 1997).

23. H. Douglas Price, "Careers and Committees in the American Congress: The Problem of Structural Change," in William O. Aydelotte (ed.), *The History of Parliamentary*

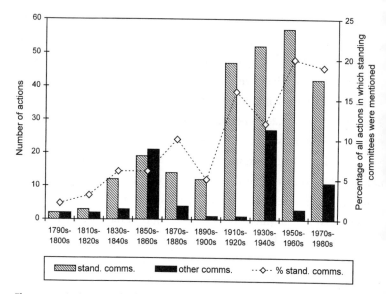

Figure 5.1. Actions in which committees mentioned

Congress's standing committees, in short, amounted to more in the general scheme of things in the twentieth century than they did in the nineteenth. This study's dataset allows a roundabout evaluation of that claim. When historians have written about members' "actions" during various eras, how often have they *mentioned* a standing committee context or membership in discussing those actions? The assumption is that mention indexes a kind of importance—as with Mills's much-noticed role on Ways and Means. In Figure 5.1, the patterned vertical bars show numbers of "actions" (of all kinds) that, when discussed in the history texts, drew mention of a relevant MC's role or position on a House or Senate standing committee by at least one "general" or "era" historian. In

Behavior (Princeton, N.J.: Princeton University Press, 1977), p. 29. See also Nelson W. Polsby, "The Institutionalization of the U.S. House of Representatives," *American Political Science Review* 62 (1968), 153–56, 160–61.

addition, the black bars show the same for all other kinds of congressional committees—a residual category that includes special, select, joint, and conference committees, and in one case the House's Committee of the Whole.[24] Tracked by the line-connected bullets are percentages of all ac-

24. Note that to record historians' mentions like this is very different from finding out whether actions *really were* connected in some fashion to committee positions. Here is some relevant "real" information for the four decades since both houses' standing committee systems assumed more or less their current configuration, thanks to the Legislative Reorganization Act of 1946. From 1951 through 1988, the dataset's total number of actions is 503. Of these, 225, or 45 percent, were moves made by members who belonged to committees (of any kind) that had subject-area jurisdictions accommodating the moves. Any kind of action (including taking a stand) might count. Thus, Congressman Mills helped engineer the Trade Expansion Act of 1962 as chairman of the (subject-relevant) Ways and Means Committee. Senator Fulbright advised President Kennedy on the Bay of Pigs invasion in 1961 while chairing the Foreign Relations Committee. Senator Ervin investigated Watergate as head of a committee created to do exactly that. Senator Gaylord Nelson (D-Wis.) called for celebration of "Earth Day" in 1970 when he was a member of the Senate Interior and Insular Affairs Committee (that seems relevant enough, though it is a judgment call). The committee-related total of 45 percent breaks down as follows: 17 percent by chairs or ranking members of House or Senate standing committees; 3 percent by chairs or ranking members of other kinds of committees; 24 percent by other members of House or Senate standing committees; 1 percent by other members of other kinds of committees. Excluded from all these calculations are actions performed by Speakers or House or Senate Majority or Minority Leaders, even if those persons simultaneously held "action"-relevant committee positions. From 1951 through 1988, 18 percent of all actions were performed by holders of these five leadership positions. When this 18 percent is added to the committee-related 45 percent, the result is a figure of 63 percent of all actions during the four decades that had at least a surface connection to official leadership or committee positions. But note that such a connection, at least as it is established here, is an uncertain guide to the importance of the official positions. To show, for example, that nineteenth-century actions were similarly accommodated by committee positions would not prove much. What if, for example, important mark-up decisions were really made on the House or Senate floor? In that event, in a limiting-case scenario that assumes de facto self-selection onto panels, committee memberships might just index the sort of subjects members were interested in, not their committee-facilitated moves or influence on those subjects.

tions that drew mentions of just standing committees—a coding measure that bows to the primacy of that particular kind of unit in both actual practice and much political science theory.

The twentieth century does stand out in Figure 5.1. For one thing, standing committees in the nineteenth century had to compete with short-term committees crafted on the spot to handle extraordinary problems—notably, as seen in the tall black bar for the 1850s–1860s, the House's "Committee of 33" and the Senate's "Committee of 13," which were created to manage the secession crisis in 1860–61, and the Joint Committee on Reconstruction of 1865–67. (Altogether, twelve actions were associated with these special panels.) For another, committees of all kinds are mentioned less often, both absolutely and relatively, in discussions of nineteenth-century actions. According to the evidence here, the twentieth-century standing committee system kicked into place around 1910 and was still going strong in 1988. H. Douglas Price's time line is borne out. During the twentieth century, the chief residual "action" role for other types of committees was investigation, not, as in the 1860s, crisis management:[25] The black bars for the 1930s through the 1980s include items from specially authorized investigations headed by, among others, Congressman Dies (un-American activities)[26] and Senators Nye (munitions makers), Black (lobbyists), La Follette, Jr. (anti-union practices), Byrd (war agencies), Truman (defense production in World War II), Kefauver (organized crime), Russell (the Korean War), McClellan (union malpractices), and Ervin (Watergate).

25. Although standing committees can investigate also, as did the Senate Government Operations Committee under Joseph McCarthy in 1953–54.

26. The House Un-American Activities Committee did not become a standing committee until 1945. Before that, Dies's unit had to be reauthorized repeatedly.

The South

This discussion of standing committee careers of the twentieth century brings to mind southerners—Wilbur Mills, Richard Russell, Howard Smith of the House Rules Committee, Russell Long (D-La.) of the Senate Finance Committee, and the many other southern Democratic barons who flourished under the congressional seniority system. Might that southern emphasis appear somehow in a time series plotting MC "actions" according to region?

Figure 5.2 shows, for each decade from the 1790s through the 1980s, the percentage of all MC actions performed by southerners—that is, by House or Senate members representing any of the eleven states that seceded in 1861 or Kentucky or Oklahoma.[27] As a kind of equity yardstick, a second time series (denoted by the broken line) shows the percentage of the American population that was southern during each decade. The vertical space between the two time series can be thought of as an "action bonus" enjoyed by the South or non-South.

Witness the South's bonus before the 1850s—an achievement of, among others, James Madison (Va.), Congressman and Senator John Randolph (DR-Va.), John C. Calhoun (S.C.), and Henry Clay (Ky.). According to Figure 5.2, that southern edge was lost during the turbulent politics of the 1850s, and a new northern hegemony took hold with the Civil War that lasted until the Democrats, dominated by southerners in their congressional ranks, took office under Woodrow Wilson. But it was somewhat later, from the 1930s through the 1960s—an era of rigid seniority rules and seldom unbroken Democratic Party control of Congress—that the South came to enjoy its second major "action bonus" in American history.

27. This is probably as good a dividing line as any between South and non-South, though it poses problems. For one thing, states change. Maryland, to name one, had more of a southern texture in the 1790s than it does now.

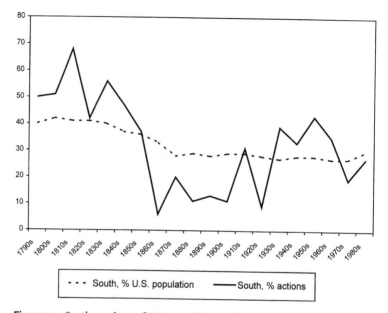

Figure 5.2. Southern share of U.S. population and actions

What explains this pattern across the two centuries? For one thing, to take the early part of the time series, it has often been remarked that the southern, slaveholding states possessed an edge in leadership talent,[28] and Figure 5.2 certainly accommodates that idea.[29] But more fundamentally, recall that "actions" tend to accrue to members of a congressional

28. For example, see Henry Adams, *History of the United States during the First Administration of Thomas Jefferson,* vol. 1 (New York: Antiquarian Press, 1962), pp. 114–16, 131–34, 264–66.

29. This is without scoring as "southern" three slaveholding states of the border area: Delaware, Maryland (home of Samuel Smith: ten "actions" through 1827), and Missouri (home of Democratic Senator Thomas Hart Benton: eleven "actions" through 1848). Of course, not all politicians from slaveholding states held the same views. Clay, a border stater, was a far cry from the South Carolinian Calhoun. Benton was hostile to the slave interest of the Deep South.

majority party. Therefore, if party MC holdings correlate with region, as they have always done in American history, an "action bonus" may accrue to a region because of party holdings alone. Thus, for example, Congress tilted North in the 1920s because it tilted Republican.

That relationship helps to account for Figure 5.2 from start to finish, but the mid-twentieth century bulge still merits comment. The southern "action bonus" then was rather large, it obtained *within* the majority party as well as within Congress as a whole—southern Democrats' "action" shares within their own party during the four decades were, respectively, 53 percent, 59 percent, 63 percent, and 42 percent, well beyond their membership proportions in the party[30]—and finally, of course, how was the bonus used? For certain conservative Democratic committee leaders such as Martin Dies, Howard Smith, Harry F. Byrd, James O. Eastland, and John McClellan, to perform "actions" meant to engage in free-lance activities, to shape or cater to their own societal constituencies outside Congress, or, insofar as they were agents answerable to any Capitol Hill body, to serve chiefly a conservative cross-party floor coalition.[31] In general, the South's seniority edge within the Democratic Party very likely added size to the mid-twentieth-century bonus shown in Figure 5.2, and the mix of animations described above added memorable content to it.

In Figure 5.2, the curves draw even in the 1970s and 1980s. This reflects, for one thing, a disappearance of the South's seniority advantage within the Democratic Party, which may have, in itself, helped induce

30. Even in the 1960s, the fading southerners enjoyed an intraparty "action bonus" (according to one technique of measurement) of 6 percent. Across the two houses and the five Congresses of that decade—that is, ten values in all—southern Democratic MCs held a mean 36 percent of all Democratic seats.

31. On the last point, particularly regarding Dies and Smith, see Eric Schickler, "Collective Interests, Institutional Innovation, and the Development of the U.S. Congress," ch. 4, Ph.D. dissertation submitted to the Department of Political Science, Yale University, 1997.

the region's conservative voters to shift Republican as they have recently done. Still, given the new Republican leadership structure on Capitol Hill in the 1990s, the South may have compiled an "action bonus" again.

Locating Actions in Careers

Another question that can be asked about MC actions is: At what points in careers are they performed? In search of answers, I coded each "action" in the dataset for three pieces of information: The biological *age* of the performing member at the time of the action; the member's *one-house seniority* at that time (that is, the number of Congresses the MC had served in then consecutively in the same house); and the member's *total congressional service* at that time (that is, the total number of Congresses the MC had served in then, regardless of which house or whether the service was consecutive). One-house seniority is important because it underpins the formal seniority rights of House members or senators. Total congressional service indexes overall Capitol Hill experience. For many members—notably those in the twentieth century like Richard Russell, who came to the Senate early and spent a full continuous career there—the two service measures are always identical. For many others—notably MCs in the nineteenth century like Henry Clay, who cycled in and out of the House, the Senate, the executive branch, and private life—the measures are almost always different. Clay promoted the Compromise of 1850—his last "action"—while serving in his first Congress by one measure but his fifteenth by the other.

I have plotted median values of these three measures for twenty-year time segments of each of two datasets. Figure 5.3 is based on all 2,304 MC actions. Figure 5.4 is based only on the 1,079 actions coded as "legislate" or "legislative eponym." This distinction is in order because some kinds of actions—for example, running for president—have varied less than others across the two centuries in the points when they have oc-

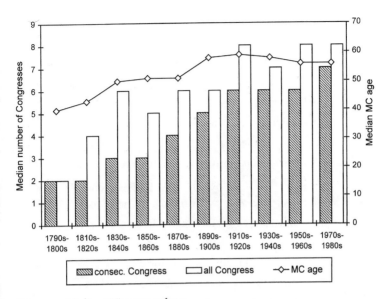

Figure 5.3. Median MC terms and age

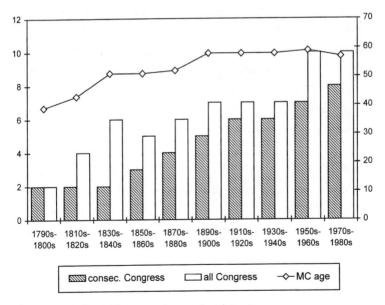

Figure 5.4. Median MC terms and age on legislative items

curred in Capitol Hill careers. Also, the legislative role probably deserves its own analysis.

Note, first of all, the median member ages associated with actions, as shown by the line-connected bullets across the tops of both graphs. (It bears emphasizing that these data are "action"-specific, not member-specific. For example, Joseph McCarthy's in 1953–54 count as five separate data points toward the total for the 1950s–1960s.) The pattern is one of phases. Actions were performed by relatively young MCs during the first few decades of American history, then the median age jumped to the low fifties and stayed there for awhile, then it ratcheted to the high fifties around 1900 and has stayed flat there since. In the "action" realm, at least going by these medians, members of Congress are roughly the same age as CEOs of large corporations and are not a bit older today than they were a century ago. An equilibrium seems to have been reached around 1900.

In contrast, at least during the twentieth century, the two measures of Capitol Hill tenure in Figures 5.3 and 5.4 exhibit increase without any apparent end. In both the one-house-seniority series (labeled "consec. Congress") and the total-congressional-service series (labeled "all Congress"), the action medians begin a monotonic (or nearly so) climb in the early nineteenth century and do not stop climbing.[32] In our own lifetimes, congressional "action" performers have not been getting older but they certainly have been getting more senior. As shown in Figure 5.4, this is particularly true in the legislative sphere, where the medians have surged to all-time highs in recent times—to a record eighth Congress of consecutive service in one house (that is, a member's fifteenth or sixteenth year) and a record tenth Congress all told (that is, a member's nineteenth or twentieth year). These are strikingly high figures, and they may help to

32. Note that in the 1790s, given the coding rules of this dataset, it was impossible to have accumulated a great deal of seniority. Pre-1789 service in the Continental Congress is not counted.

explain the pressure for congressional term limits. In the 1970s–1980s—an era that featured Speaker O'Neill, Russell Long, Robert Dole, Edward Kennedy, Daniel Rostenkowski, and the veteran Barry Goldwater, not to mention the octogenarian champion of senior citizens, Congressman Claude Pepper (D-Fla.)—the members who won prominence through "actions" were routinely ones who had been operating on Capitol Hill seemingly forever. Fresh blood, to be guaranteed by term limits, could understandably become a powerful anti-Congress mobilizing theme by around 1990.

Early versus Late Actions

How should we think about the idea of congressional term limits? There exist many lines of consideration, but I pursue a particular one in this section and the next: In American history, what have been the actual patterns of MC "action" at low levels of congressional service or seniority, as opposed to at higher levels? This analysis has a point. To limit House and Senate members to, say, twelve years in office—the reform that seems most likely to win approval, if any does[33]—might, for better or worse, alter or eliminate certain career-related features of congressional performance. Exactly so, and for the better, the advocates of term limits would confidently claim—but we cannot be sure of that.

I am aware that the analysis I am about to undertake here will provide indirect illumination at best. For one thing, no one can say what types of

33. The campaign for congressional term limits is not finished yet, if experience with the Seventeenth (direct election of senators) and Nineteenth (women's suffrage) Amendments is any guide. These earlier reforms also threatened the electoral bases of Capitol Hill incumbents. Accordingly, the eventual victories required circuitous methods involving process innovations at the state level, as well as time. See Kris W. Kobach, "Rethinking Article V: Term Limits and the Seventeenth and Nineteenth Amendments," *Yale Law Journal* 103 (1994), 1971–2007.

members would appear, or how they would behave individually or collectively, in a U.S. Congress undergirded by a system of electoral incentives that does not now exist. Perhaps nothing really important would change; perhaps a great deal would. I am also aware that nothing I argue or exhibit here has any relevance for positive theories that stipulate MCs to be undifferentiated commodities — seekers of reelection, for example, or "agents" of outside "principals" (notably, their home constituencies). For purposes here, the idea needs to be entertained that members who differ in any of several attributes — age, generation, Capitol Hill experience, public renown, or personality — might behave or be received by their peers or the public differently. This is in the interest of cutting closer to reality (which a term-limits reform might, after all, intrude upon) than do such positive theories.

I begin by examining a selection of "action careers" of recent decades. Listed in Table 5.2 are all MCs credited in the dataset with six or more actions who performed the majority of them after 1930. From top to bottom, in the two right-hand columns under "All Cong. service," the qualifying forty-five members are stratified according to the proportions of their actions that took place during the first six Congresses they served in — regardless of which house or whether the service was consecutive — and after that. Thus, at the top of the list, all seven of Senator Hugo Black's actions occurred *during* his first six Congresses; at the bottom, all ten of Senator Richard Russell's occurred *after* his first six Congresses. Unless complications having to do with part-terms interfere, six Congresses means twelve years. In the two central columns of Table 5.2, consecutive service in one house is the comparable organizing principle[34] with

34. For example, Barry Goldwater held a Senate seat during 1953–64 and again during 1969–86. Eleven of his thirteen "actions" occurred during the first six Congresses of one stint or the other. Another example: Lyndon Johnson held a House seat during 1937–48 and a Senate seat during 1949–60. All of his sixteen "actions" occurred during

results that in most cases repeat or resemble those in the "All Cong. service" columns. The chief interesting disparities involve Senator Democratic leaders Mike Mansfield, Lyndon B. Johnson, and also James F. Byrnes (D-S.C.) (the latter was a powerful informal Democratic leader in the 1930s), all ex-House members whose notable performing came early in their Senate careers though rather later in their total congressional careers. I have let total congressional service dictate the vertical order in Table 5.2—although, of course, term-limits proposals vary regarding the specifics of what they would ban when.

What emerges in Table 5.2? Above all, diversity rather than commonality: We do *not* see just one generic brand of "action career." The bottom half of the table lists primarily party and committee leaders who began their careers on Capitol Hill unflashily, gathered experience and seniority, and gradually rose to the positions where they did their "action" performing. Caution and insiderism characterize this late-performing breed, though not necessarily ideological conservatism—Democratic presidents have relied on members such as Sam Rayburn, James F. Byrnes, Mike Mansfield, and Senator Joseph Robinson (D-Ark.). Wilbur Mills, we are discovering, was an important designer (in his own way) of the contemporary American welfare state.[35]

Scattered in the top half of Table 5.2 are a few members—though only a few—who performed heavily both early and late in their careers. Senators Wagner and Taft kept going after their twelfth years. Senators Humphrey and Goldwater started out as brash, iconoclastic propagators of new ideas, got caught up in presidential politics, and also evolved into congressional senior statesman types.

---

the first (and, as it happens, the only) six Congresses of one stint or the other (and, as it happens, all sixteen came during his Senate years).

35. See Julian E. Zelizer, *Taxing America: Wilbur D. Mills, Congress, and the State, 1945–1975* (New York: Cambridge University Press, 1998).

Table 5.2 Actions by High Performers since 1930 during Their First Six Congresses, and After That

Action career	Member	Consecutive in One House		All Cong. Service	
1932–37	Hugo Black (D-Ala.)	7	0	7	0
1931–35	Edward Costigan (D-Colo.)	6	0	6	0
1965–68	Robert F. Kennedy (D-N.Y.)	7	0	7	0
1932–35	Huey Long (D-La.)	10	0	10	0
1950–54	Joseph McCarthy (R-Wis.)	9	0	9	0
1948–52	Richard M. Nixon (R-Calif.)	7	0	7	0
1967–76	Birch Bayh (D-Ind.)	5	1	5	1
1939–53	Robert A. Taft (R-Ohio)	25	5	25	5
1928–39	Robert La Follette, Jr. (R,I-Wis.)	9	2	9	2
1927–49	Robert F. Wagner (D-N.Y.)	15	5	15	5
1965–79	George McGovern (D-S.Dak.)	6	1	5	2
1963–80	Edmund Muskie (D-Maine)	8	3	8	3
1960–84	Barry Goldwater (R-Ariz.)	11	2	7	6
1934–44	Martin Dies, Jr. (D-Tex.)	4	3	4	3
1973–82	Howard Baker, Jr. (R-Tenn.)	4	4	4	4
1949–77	Hubert H. Humphrey (D-Minn.)	5	5	5	5
1945–83	Claude Pepper (D-Fla.)	3	3	3	3
1937–64	Harry F. Byrd (D-Va.)	5	6	5	6
1947–67	Adam Clayton Powell, Jr. (D-N.Y.)	3	4	3	4
1965–76	Frank Church (D-Idaho)	3	5	3	5
1968–87+	Edward Kennedy (D-Mass.)	4	7	4	7
1923–41	Burton K. Wheeler (D-Mont.)	5	9	5	9
1958–73	Samuel Ervin (D-N.C.)	2	4	2	4
1934–41	Gerald P. Nye (R-N.Dak.)	2	4	2	4
1914–38	Byron P. (Pat) Harrison (D-Miss.)	2	5	2	5
1943–68	J. William Fulbright (D-Ark.)	3	9	3	9
1950–62	Estes Kefauver (D-Tenn.)	6	2	2	6
1937–64	Howard Smith (D-Va.)	2	7	2	7
1934–50	Millard Tydings (D-Md.)	5	1	1	5
1972–88+	Robert Dole (R-Kans.)	3	4	1	6
1941–68	Everett Dirksen (R-Ill.)	2	6	1	7
1933–48	Arthur Vandenberg (R-Mich.)	2	15	2	15
1914–61	Samuel Rayburn (D-Tex.)	1	16	1	16
1937–48	Alben Barkley (D-Ky.)	2	4	0	6
1937–41	James F. Byrnes (D-S.C.)	6	0	0	6
1913–35	Carter Glass (D-Va.)	0	6	0	6
1957–76	Henry Jackson (D-Wash.)	2	9	0	11
1953–60	Lyndon B. Johnson (D-Tex.)	16	0	0	16
1961–78	Russell Long (D-La.)	0	6	0	6
1962–73	Mike Mansfield (D-Mont.)	8	3	0	11

Table 5.2 (*continued*)

Action career	Member	Consecutive in One House		All Cong. Service	
1960–72	Wilbur Mills (D-Ark.)	0	10	0	10
1967–85	Thomas P. (Tip) O'Neill (D-Mass.)	0	16	0	16
1933–40	Key Pittman (D-Nev.)	0	6	0	6
1928–37	Joseph Robinson (D-Ark.)	0	6	0	6
1948–70	Richard Russell (D-Ga.)	0	10	0	10

And witness the top stratum in the table, the heavy early performers —Hugo Black, Senator Edward Costigan (D-Colo.), Robert F. Kennedy, Huey Long, Joseph McCarthy, and Richard M. Nixon. Admittedly, a data-censoring problem arises here because none of these six figures stayed in Congress long enough to become a late performer as well: There were two assassinations (Long and Kennedy); one death, possibly from alcoholism (McCarthy); one retirement (Costigan); and two upward moves (Black to the Supreme Court and Nixon to the vice presidency). Accordingly, an alternative, counterfactual universe no doubt exists in which these men have stayed on Capitol Hill and slowly morphed into Wilbur Mills types. But that does not seem a good bet. Senator Costigan aside, in all of American history it would be hard to find better specimens of young men in a hurry than Black, Kennedy, Long, McCarthy, and Nixon—they were aggressive, impetuous, not easily curbable, and powerfully ambitious in an existential sort of way.[36] To invoke two classical prototypes,

36. Hugo Black in the 1930s was an aggressive ideologue, notably as a committee investigator of business lobbyists and conservative interest groups during 1935–36, where his operating style prefigured that of Joseph McCarthy in the 1950s. In 1935: "Black needed publicity and his methods turned rough. Committee agents roused a New Jersey advertising man from bed at 1 A.M. and immediately took him to Washington to testify." In general: "It was politics as theater. His natural showman's instinct came to the fore. Black thrived in the white glare of publicity. Black's hatred of business interests caused him to trample over witness's rights protected by the Fourth Amendment." The American Civil Liberties Union and also Walter Lippmann criticized him for these

if the bottom of Table 5.2 offers some sage-like Nestor figures, the top offers some swashbuckling Alcibiades ones.

What can we conclude from these data? Obviously, to enact a reform curtailing or interrupting congressional careers would cut into the patterns of Table 5.2—but how, and for better or worse? I urge the reader to take a close look at the particulars of the table and speculate. Possibly nothing important would change: For example, the functional equivalents of Wilbur Mills and Tip O'Neill might somehow materialize young and operate early anyway. But then again they might not. Suppose it takes experience to bring out qualities like those of Mills or O'Neill, and do we value those qualities? In the long run, it seems to me, one risk of term limits is that the Nestor component of Congress would decrease and the Alcibiades component would increase. It is a prospect that the authors of *The Federalist*, young though they were, would probably recognize.

Here is another question relevant to term limits: What have been the *highly* prominent MC actions in American history performed *very* late in members' careers? For purposes here, the relevant MCs need not have been overall high performers; the emphasis is on actions rather than on members. For a distillation of such moves, see Table 5.3, which lists all thirty-seven actions that survived the stiff "A"-level test for inclusion in the dataset—that is, they were mentioned in at least two "general" his-

---

practices, and a federal court restrained him. See Roger K. Newman, *Hugo Black: A Biography* (New York: Pantheon, 1994), ch. 12, quotations at pp. 180, 193; Virginia Van der Veer Hamilton, *Hugo Black: The Alabama Years* (Baton Rouge: Louisiana State University Press, 1972), ch. 11. At the time of Black's appointment to the Supreme Court in 1937: "He was, in fact, probably the most radical man in the Senate. . . . He was intensely partisan and an unforgiving fighter. . . . Men who had crossed swords with him rarely forgot or forgave the experience, and his friends on the floor were few. His many enemies accused him of meanness and small spiritedness, and even the friends regretted his excesses—such as some incidents of his lobbying investigation—into which his partisanship sometimes led him." Joseph Alsop and Turner Catledge, *The 168 Days* (Garden City, N.Y.: Doubleday, Doran and Co., 1938), p. 301.

Table 5.3 "A"-Level Actions by Members Serving in Their Tenth or Later Congresses

Member	Year	Consec. Cong.	All Cong.	Action
Henry Clay	1833–36		10–11	Leader in forging Whig opposition
Henry Clay	1841		14	Promotes ambitious American System program
Henry Clay	1841		14	Advances measure to create U.S. bank
John Quincy Adams	1835–44		–10	Ends campaign to admit antislavery petitions
John C. Calhoun	1847		11	Offers his slavery noninterference doctrine
John C. Calhoun	1850		13	Southern partisan as Compromise of 1850 passes
Henry Clay	1850		15	Chief promoter of Compromise of 1850
Daniel Webster	1850		14	Key role in arranging Compromise of 1850
John C. Crittenden	1860–61		11	Crittenden Compromise to settle 1860–61 crisis
Charles Sumner	1870	10	10	Blocks Grant's annexation of Dominican Republic
Charles Sumner	1871–72	11	11	Defects from Grant to back Greeley for president
John Sherman	1875		10	Author of Specie Resumption Act
Roscoe Conkling	1877–80		–10	Makes patronage demands against President Hayes
Roscoe Conkling	1877–81		–11	Leader of GOP stalwarts
Roscoe Conkling	1880		10	Promotes Grant for president
Roscoe Conkling	1881		11	Resigns seat over Garfield patronage denials
George F. Hoar	1898–99	11	15	Opposes annexation of the Philippines
Nelson W. Aldrich	1901–2	11	12	Pro-business GOP leader of the Senate
Joseph G. Cannon	1903–10		15–18	Runs House as GOP conservative "czar"
Nelson W. Aldrich	1905–6	13	14	Drags feet against T. Roosevelt RR regulation drive
Joseph G. Cannon	1910		18	Loses out to insurgent House rules challenge

Table 5.3 (*continued*)

Member	Year	Consec. Cong.	All Cong.	Action
Henry Cabot Lodge	1919	13	16	Leads anti-League round-robin of 37 senators
Robert La Follette, Sr.	1919		11	An "irreconcilable" against League of Nations
Henry Cabot Lodge	1919	14	17	Engineers defeat of Wilson's League
Robert La Follette, Sr.	1924	10	13	Third-party Progressive candidate for president
George Norris	1924		11	Blocks private development of Muscle Shoals
George Norris	1933	11	16	Steers TVA through the Senate
Millard Tydings (D-Md.)	1950	12	14	Heads committee to parry Joe McCarthy's charges
Lyndon B. Johnson	1955–60		10–12	Powerful Senate leader with distinctive style
Wayne Morse	1964	10	10	One of two dissenters vs. Tonkin Gulf resolution
J. William Fulbright	1966–67	11–12	12–13	Stages televised hearings against Vietnam War
Eugene McCarthy	1968		10	Antiwar challenger to LBJ renomination
Samuel Ervin	1973	11	12	Runs televised Watergate hearings
Hugh Scott	1974		16	Calls Nixon tapes disgusting
Gerald Ford	1974	13	13	Chosen as vice president by Nixon and Congress
John Anderson	1980	10	10	Independent candidate for president
Robert Dole	1988	10	14	Runs for GOP presidential nomination

tories—*and* were performed in a member's tenth (or later) Congress.[37] This is regardless of whether the service was consecutive or in the same

37. Excluded are "A"-level items regarding nominations for the vice presidency, or where a member's name became attached eponymously to a bill or act. Note that for a senator who has served consecutively, the tenth Congress means the beginning of a fourth term.

House (see the "All Cong." column in the table), although consecutive one-house service is reported also if it extended to ten Congresses (see the "Consec. Cong." column).[38]

Again, I urge the reader to examine Table 5.3 and assess the particulars, which are generally well known. On balance—that may mean, for example, weighing John Quincy Adams's ultimately victorious drive to admit antislavery petitions to the House[39] against Roscoe Conkling's quest for patronage jobs—would the country have been better or worse off without these moves? And how likely is it that less-veteran MCs would have made them? In a term-limited Congress, would they not have happened at all, or happened in a lesser or different way? Such a counter-scenario is at least plausible to the degree that any actual move depended on a member's age (the median member age of the actual performances here is sixty-four), long experience on Capitol Hill,[40] or authority derived from

38. In the "All Cong." column of Table 5.3, three entries are preceded by a dash. Those reflect instances when an MC "action" stretched across more than one Congress *and* the first Congress of the action was not yet the member's own tenth Congress of service. In these cases, the number after the dash is the MC's "All Cong." reading for the *last* Congress of the action.

39. That decade-long drive by former President Adams (and others), targeting a southern-inspired "gag rule" that barred the House from officially receiving such petitions, is a classic instance of an MC "action" aimed at mobilizing the public: "Adams made the most of the controversy, baiting his Southern colleagues, pulling oratorical and procedural stunts on the floor of Congress—knowing all the while that, though he might be ruled out of order or even shouted down, his performances would be reported to the country, burnishing his name and rallying support to his cause." Sean Wilentz, "The Mandarin and the Rebel: John Quincy Adams, *La Amistad*, and Democracy in America," *The New Republic*, December 22, 1997, pp. 25–34, quotation at p. 33.

40. The bright side of congressional experience (if combined with talent) was suggested by James Madison in *The Federalist* #53: "A few of the members, as happens in all such assemblies, will possess superior talents; will, by frequent re-elections, become members of long standing; will be thoroughly masters of the public business, and perhaps not unwilling to avail themselves of those advantages. The greater the proportion of new members and the less the information of the bulk of the members, the more apt will

having gradually accumulated a national reputation. As of 1966, for example, Senator Fulbright had been building a reputation as a foreign policy expert among a nationally aware constituency for nearly a quarter of a century.[41]

The items in Table 5.3 are a mixed bag by any standard, but certain patterns appear. In nearly half the cases, the veteran MCs were offering major opposition to presidential administrations. The opposition motif appears here again. And in eight of those cases—22 percent of the table's total—that opposition was over foreign policy. A recurrent aim was to stop the government from expanding or exercising American power or commitments abroad. Thus Senator Sumner blocked Grant from annexing the Dominican Republic in 1870, Senator George F. Hoar (R-Mass.) prominently opposed U.S. annexation of the Philippines in 1898–99,[42] and three senior senators took the lead against the Vietnam War in the mid-1960s—Wayne Morse (D-Oreg.) through his much-noticed roll-call vote against the Tonkin Gulf resolution, Fulbright by way of his tele-

---

they be to fall into the snares that may be laid for them." Madison (New York: Mentor, 1961), p. 335.

41. In an argument offered by Edward G. Carmines and James H. Kuklinski, certain MCs develop national "policy reputations." Singled out as instances are the veteran members Edward Kennedy, Jesse Helms, and Claude Pepper. Such reputations are "common knowledge, public information that is widely disseminated to ordinary people." A result can be top-down information flow about issues or events that cues people across the country about what or how they should think. "What will increase people's willingness to use reputationally based information? Legislators who have accumulated a 'track record' over a long duration, and who tend to be consistent in their statements and behaviors, should be more attractive inside sources than unknown lawmakers; in the latter case, reputations may be nonexistent." See "Incentives, Opportunities, and the Logic of Public Opinion in American Political Representation," ch. 10 in John A. Ferejohn and James H. Kuklinski (eds.), *Information and Democratic Processes* (Urbana: University of Illinois Press, 1990), pp. 252–56.

42. See Robert L. Beisner, *Twelve Against Empire: The Anti-Imperialists, 1898–1900* (New York: McGraw-Hill, 1968), ch. 7.

vised hearings, and Eugene McCarthy through his New Hampshire challenge to President Johnson's renomination in 1968. In addition, Senators Lodge and La Follette, Sr., helped defeat the collective security commitment (Article X) associated with joining the League of Nations in 1919.

This record is surprisingly long-lived and consistent. Yet a caveat needs to be entered. The discussion would be incomplete without referring to Arthur Vandenberg, the ex-isolationist Republican senator from Michigan who, during his tenth and eleventh Congresses in 1945 through 1948, played a key public and committee role in helping launch the United Nations, the Truman Doctrine, the Marshall Plan, and NATO. Probably through a quirk of historians' writing, none of these moves satisfied this study's "A"-level test (hence no entries for them appear in Table 5.3)— although Vandenberg did generate more "B"-level items than any other MC during the two centuries, and all of them are foreign policy items. Vandenberg in the wake of World War II offers an obvious contrast to Lodge in the wake of World War I: Lodge opposed a White House– led thrust toward international collective security, and Vandenberg supported such a thrust. Still, even if one or two Vandenberg "actions" are admitted to Table 5.3 in a stipulated status, a generalization remains available. In all of the table's foreign policy moves by senior MCs, none is a call for unilateral U.S. expansion or aggressiveness abroad; the emphasis is toward reluctance and caution in using or committing American power.

Ideological Impulses

In Chapter 3, I grouped and analyzed certain subsets of data items as "oppositions" to presidential administrations. I undertake here a similar analysis of item subsets I will call "ideological impulses"—although in this case only during the twentieth century, which has enough data points to offer a suitable kind of analytic traction.

What is an "ideological impulse"? To take a current example, the Republican conservatism heralded by Newt Gingrich that invested Congress during the 1990s is one. I cannot reach the 1990s with this dataset. But I can try to reach earlier manifestations that are arguably comparable. Allowing for impulses that have been largely defensive (for example, those symbolized by Nelson W. Aldrich or Tip O'Neill) as well as ones that have been insurgent or change-oriented (as in the cases of, say, the La Follette Progressives, the New Dealers, or recently the Gingrich Republicans), here is the blueprint for coding: For the twentieth century, isolate every subset of twenty-five or more temporally clustered MC actions in which members pursued the same policy goals or ideological cause (or at least a family of related goals or causes). This is somewhat loose around the edges: Disagreements could arise, for example, about when an impulse began or ended or exactly which items belong in it. But I believe that anyone who has followed the history of the twentieth century will recognize the impulses I have identified.[43]

43. The reader will notice that certain of this chapter's impulse clusters overlap and resemble Chapter 3's opposition clusters. But the blueprints differ in two ways. First, in order for an MC action to be included in an opposition cluster, that action had to be directed against a presidential administration, but that criterion is not required for impulses. Accordingly, the Progressive activism under Theodore Roosevelt and Taft generated only five opposition items but thirty-four impulse items. That is because many Progressive moves—such as those vehemently opposing the Payne-Aldrich tariff in 1909 —are not coded as anti–White House. Second, in coding for oppositions I tried to stay close to what the relevant historians themselves characterized as clusters of MC moves. Here I have wandered farther afield, using my own judgment to group items into impulses. Thus the Progressive "opposition" of the 1920s is a narrowly focused cluster of twelve items during 1922–24. I have let the Progressive "impulse" of the 1920s encompass a series of moves by Senators Norris, La Follette, Sr., Borah, Wheeler, and Walsh, the eponymous promoters of the McNary-Haugen agricultural support program, and several others during the full decade of 1921–31. For a recent discussion of this family of moves during the 1920s, see David A. Horowitz, *Beyond Left and Right: Insurgency and the Establishment* (Urbana: University of Illinois Press, 1997), ch. 3 and pp. 81–82. Another good general source (not just on Borah) is LeRoy Ashby, *The Spearless Leader:*

These ideological impulses are listed in Table 5.4. There are fifteen in all, starting with the Old Guard Republican conservatism led by Senator Aldrich and Speaker Cannon during 1901–10 and ending with the Democratic Party's policy thrust under Reagan in the 1980s. In three cases, the impulses exhibit the congressional sides of domestic reform pursued by Democratic presidents—Wilson in the 1910s, Franklin Roosevelt in the 1930s, and Kennedy and Johnson in the 1960s.[44] Five of the congressional impulses center on foreign policy: The opposition to U.S. entry into World War I and then the League of Nations in 1917–20;[45] the pre–World War II isolationism of 1933–41;[46] the post–World War II internationalism of 1945–54; the anti-internationalist mix of isolationism, Asia First sentiment, and anti-Communist disloyalty-hunting that raged during 1947–54;[47] and the anti–Vietnam War thrust of 1964–75. In several

---

Senator Borah and the Progressive Movement in the 1920's (Urbana: University of Illinois Press, 1972).

44. Not enough allied MC actions accumulated to exhibit a congressional side of Reagan's policy drive in the early 1980s.

45. For the Progressive side of this impulse, see Horowitz, *Beyond Left and Right,* pp. 19–35.

46. See Horowitz, *Beyond Left and Right,* ch. 8.

47. See Horowitz, *Beyond Left and Right,* pp. 223–70. This awkward mix is difficult to label succinctly. It combines: the isolationist opposition, led by Senator Taft, to the trans-Atlantic or more broadly "internationalist" commitments then being undertaken by the Truman and Eisenhower administrations; the era's anti-Communist disloyalty-hunting that came to be symbolized by Senator McCarthy (which had as one of its prime targets the U.S. national security establishment then busy at work forging those trans-Atlantic or internationalist commitments); and the aggressive "Asia Firstism" of the time symbolized by Senator William Knowland (a thrust that was anything but truly "isolationist") that would have shifted U.S. attention and commitments from Western Europe to East Asia. Uniting these three strains was a passionate, sometimes venomous, opposition to the policies and personnel of the post–New Deal political elite then running the executive branch—notably its diplomatic and national security sector. Feisty young World War II veterans who won House or Senate seats in 1946 provided much of the energy of this "ideological impulse."

Table 5.4 Major MC Ideological Impulses in the Twentieth Century

Years	N	Ideological Impulse	Notable Participants
1901–10	37	Old Guard domestic conservatism under Theodore Roosevelt and Taft (on currency and tariff legislation, regulation of RRs, etc.)	Nelson W. Aldrich (R-R.I.), Joseph Cannon (R-Ill.), John C. Spooner (R-Wis.)
1905–12	34	Progressive insurgency under late TR, Taft (on tariff duties, RR regulation, Cannon's Speakership, etc.)	Albert Beveridge (R-Ind.), George Norris (R-Nebr.), Robert La Follette (R-Wis.), Jonathan Dolliver (R-Iowa)
1912–17	41	New Freedom domestic reform under Wilson (plus warmup for it in 1912–13)	Claude Kitchin (D-N.C.), Robert La Follette (R-Wis.), Oscar Underwood (D-Ala.), many single-shot actors
1917–20	32	Antiwar and anti-League opposition to Wilson's foreign policy	William Borah (R-Idaho), Robert La Follette (R-Wis.), Henry Cabot Lodge (R-Mass.)
1921–31	41	Promotion of Progressive causes under Harding, Coolidge, and early Hoover	Robert La Follette (R-Wis.), George Norris (R-Nebr.), Thomas Walsh (D-Mont.), Burton Wheeler (D-Mont.)
1931–37	73	New Deal domestic reform under FDR (and warmup under late Hoover)	Edward Costigan (D-Colo.), Sam Rayburn (D-Tex.), Robert La Follette, Jr. (I-Wis.), Robert Wagner (D-N.Y.)
1933–38	39	Left-populist challenge to New Deal: more inflation, nationalization, relief, wealth taxes, or antimonopoly than FDR wanted	Hugo Black (D-Ala.), Huey Long (D-La.), Elmer Thomas (D-Okla.), Burton Wheeler (D-Mont.), William Lemke (R-N.Dak.)
1934–39	36	Right opposition to New Deal (incl. to court-packing and gov't. reorganization)	Josiah Bailey (D-N.C.), John J. O'Connor (D-N.Y.), Burton K. Wheeler (D-Mont.) after 1936
1933–41	28	Isolationist opposition to U.S. involvement in internat'l. orgs. and European affairs	William Borah (R-Idaho), Hiram Johnson (R-Calif.), Gerald Nye (R-N.Dak.), Burton Wheeler (D-Mont.)
1945–54	30	Foreign policy internationalism under late FDR, Truman, Eisenhower (pro UN, Marshall Plan, NATO, vs. McCarthyism)	Thomas Connally (D-Tex.), Arthur Vandenberg (R-Mich.)

Table 5.4 (*continued*)

Years	N	Ideological Impulse	Notable Participants
1947–54	40	Isolationism, Asia Firstism, and disloyalty hunting under Truman and early Ike	Patrick McCarran (D-Nev.), Joseph McCarthy (R-Wis.), William Knowland (R-Calif.), Robert Taft (R-Ohio)
1961–68	29	Domestic reform under JFK and LBJ (civil rights, Medicare, etc.)	Hubert H. Humphrey (D-Minn.), Wilbur Mills (D-Ark.), Mike Mansfield (D-Mont.), Edmund Muskie (D-Maine)
1961–68	26	Conservative opposition to domestic reforms of the 1960s	Harry F. Byrd (D-Va.), Barry Goldwater (R-Ariz.), Richard Russell (D-Ga.), Howard Smith (D-Va.)
1964–75	36	Opposition to the Vietnam War and the national security establishment that conducted it	Frank Church (D-Idaho), J. W. Fulbright (D-Ark.), Robert Kennedy (D-N.Y.), George McGovern (D-S.D.), Eugene McCarthy (D-Minn.)
1981–88	34	Pursuit of Democratic foreign and domestic policies under Reagan	Edward Boland (D-Mass.), Patrick Moynihan (D-N.Y.), Thomas O'Neill (D-Mass.), Claude Pepper (D-Fla.), Daniel Rostenkowski (D-Ill.)

instances, one congressional impulse was the enemy of another—as with the case of GOP Old Guard conservatism and the Progressive challenge to it under Theodore Roosevelt and William Howard Taft. Such patterns of antagonism will figure in the analysis below. It bears emphasizing again that, as a statistical matter, "actions," not members, are weighted equally in these impulses; since Senator Wagner performed eleven of the seventy-three actions of the New Deal impulse—that was one reality of the 1930s—he accordingly contributes 15 percent of the content when it comes to calculating that impulse's various properties.

Let me make a pitch for this idea of "impulses." Granted certain methodological assumptions, Table 5.4 is a list of the major applications of ideological energy on Capitol Hill during the twentieth century (at least through 1988).[48] Two points are in order. First, the list is unorthodox in that it goes beyond the familiar domestic reform drives of the 1910s, 1930s, and 1960s—the three exercises of liberal or Progressive activism that typically serve as an exhaustive list of major U.S. government performances during that century.[49] That is because the methodology here is not confined to legislating or to a welfare-state teleology. Just as applicable to the "impulse" category are, for example, post–World War II internationalism and the spirited congressional opposition to it (see Table 5.5 for the forty "action" particulars of the latter),[50] both of which had considerable nonlegislative content and did not address the welfare state one way or another yet made lasting marks on the United States and, for that matter, the rest of the world, anyway.

Second, where did these MC impulses come from? The easy, conventional answer is that they were emanations of contemporary public opinion. That is plainly a part of the truth, but, as argued in Chapter 1, there is a case too for the autonomous consequentiality of elites—or at least an interactive relation between elite actors and mass views.[51] It is a commonplace that presidents sometimes set agendas and stir public support for them: Consider Theodore Roosevelt, Franklin D. Roosevelt, and Ronald Reagan. The Supreme Court can sometimes establish national norms—

48. In political science, it is customary to look for cyclical regularities when confronted by a time series of manifestations like these. In my view, that would be pointless overtheorizing in this case, as it would be for the "oppositions" analyzed in Chapter 3.

49. As in Arthur M. Schlesinger, Jr., "The Cycles of American Politics," ch. 2 in Schlesinger, *The Cycles of American History* (Boston: Houghton Mifflin, 1986).

50. As in previous tables, "Consec. Cong." reports the performer's number of Congresses served in consecutively in one house at the time of the action. "All Cong." reports total Congresses served in at that time. "A/B/C" refers to the historians' source criteria that an action satisfied, "A" being the most stringent.

51. The kind of elite influence being alleged here is possibly an aspect of "state capacity," although it does not seem to figure in today's largely bureaucracy-centered literature about "the state."

consider *Brown v. Board of Education* in 1954—or, according to a recent study, it can catalyze rights-oriented activity among social movements.[52] In the immense political science literature about Congress, possibly the most neglected topic is Congress and its members as *shapers* of mass opinion and political activism.[53] For some particularly likely instances of that role during the twentieth century, consider the Progressive era insurgency led by Robert La Follette, Sr.; McCarthyism; the relation between initiatives by senators and the evolution of public sentiment during the campaign against the Vietnam War; and the Gingrich conservatism of the 1990s.

Now for some analysis. How have the fifteen impulses listed above mapped onto congressional careers? Figure 5.5 provides three summary career-related values for each ideological impulse. As in previous exhibits, these values are median performer *age* (the line-connected bullets), median performer *one-house seniority* (the patterned vertical bars), and median performer *total congressional service* (the open vertical bars)—each calculated for the set of MC actions embraced by each impulse. The impulses are ordered chronologically in the graph, with ones of more or less the same era grouped together.

52. For the latter argument, see Michael McCann, *Rights at Work: Pay Equity Reform and the Politics of Legal Mobilization* (Chicago: University of Chicago Press, 1994), ch. 3 ("Law as a Catalyst").

53. But see Lawrence R. Jacobs and Robert Y. Shapiro, "Politicians Don't Pander: Political Leadership, Public Opinion, and American Politics," 1998 manuscript; and Edward G. Carmines and James H. Kuklinski, "Incentives, Opportunities, and the Logic of Public Opinion in American Political Representation," in John A. Ferejohn and James H. Kuklinski (eds.), *Information and Democratic Processes* (Urbana: University of Illinois Press, 1990), a chapter centering on Congress that offers a parting "conjecture" at p. 266: "Contrary to populist conceptions of political representation, American politics is elite-driven. The division of labor between those whose primary business is governing the nation and those for whom politics is secondary dictates that the former will, under most circumstances, set the agenda, define the parameters of major debates, and bring deliberations to their conclusion."

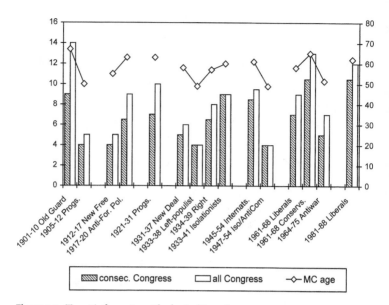

Figure 5.5. Twentieth-century ideological impulses

As earlier in Table 5.2, diversity wins out over genericness in Figure 5.5: "Ideological impulses" have registered at radically different points in Congress's tenure-and-age structure. On the extreme low side, the action medians for the left-populist challenge to the New Deal (featuring Huey Long and others)[54] and also for post–World War II anti-internationalism (featuring Taft, McCarthy, Knowland, and others, as shown in Table 5.5) are: Four Congresses of consecutive one-house service; four Congresses of total service; and forty-nine years of age. These MCs were relative youngsters. On the extreme high side, for example, the medians for the conservative opposition to New Frontier and Great Society domestic reform in the 1960s are: Ten and a half Congresses; thirteen Congresses; and sixty-five years of age. These MCs were generally old-timers. Statis-

54. See Horowitz, *Beyond Left and Right,* pp. 94–114, 119–124, 127–134.

Table 5.5 The Isolationist, Asia First, Antidisloyalty Impulse of 1947–54

Year	Member	Age	Consec. Cong.	All Cong.	H/S	A/B/C test	Action
1947	Walter Judd (R-Minn.)	49	3	3	H	C	Claims State Department sold out China
1947	John Rankin (D-Miss.)	65	14	14	H	C	Role in HUAC investigation of Hollywood
1947	Robert A. Taft (R-Ohio)	58	5	5	S	C	Has reservations about Truman Doctrine
1948–49	William Knowland (R-Calif.)	40	2	2	S	B	Notable Asia Firster
1948	Karl Mundt (R-S.Dak.)	48	5	5	H	C	Mundt-Nixon bill re internal security
1948	Richard Nixon (R-Calif.)	35	1	1	H	C	Mundt-Nixon bill re internal security
1948	Richard Nixon (R-Calif.)	35	1	1	H	A	Pursues Alger Hiss in HUAC investigation
1948	J. Parnell Thomas (R-N.J.)	53	6	6	H	A	Chairs HUAC probe of espionage
1948	Robert A. Taft (R-Ohio)	59	5	5	S	B	Chief congressional critic of Marshall Plan
1949	Karl Mundt (R-S.Dak.)	49	1	6	S	C	Spokesman for "China lobby"
1949	Robert A. Taft (R-Ohio)	60	6	6	S	C	Argues against NATO treaty
1950	Styles Bridges (R-N.H.)	52	7	7	S	C	Backs McCarthy's anti-Communist drive
1950	Homer Capehart (R-Ind.)	53	3	3	S	B	Makes key speech about internal subversion
1950	William Jenner (R-Ind.)	42	2	3	S	C	An emerging McCarthyite leader
1950	William Jenner (R-Ind.)	42	2	3	S	B	Says Gen. Marshall is front man for traitors
1950	Patrick McCarran (D-Nev.)	74	9	9	S	A	McCarran Internal Security Act
1950	Joseph McCarthy (R-Wis.)	42	2	2	S	A	His Wheeling speech launches McCarthyism
1950	Joseph McCarthy (R-Wis.)	42	2	2	S	A	Makes accusations before Tydings panel
1950	Joseph McCarthy (R-Wis.)	42	2	2	S	A	Intrudes into Conn. and Md. Senate elections
1950	Richard Nixon (R-Calif.)	37	2	2	H	B	Runs "pink lady" campaign vs. H. G. Douglas

Table 5.5 (*continued*)

Year	Member	Age	Consec. Cong.	All Cong.	H/S	A/B/C test	Action
1950	Robert A. Taft (R-Ohio)	61	6	6	S	A	Backs McCarthy's anti-Communist drive
1950	Robert A. Taft (R-Ohio)	61	6	6	S	C	Favors lower military spending
1950	Robert A. Taft (R-Ohio)	61	6	6	S	B	Demands Cong. role in Korean War policy
1950–51	Robert A. Taft (R-Ohio)	61	6	6	S	B	Takes part in major debate re foreign policy
1950	Kenneth Wherry (R-Nebr.)	58	4	4	S	C	Backs McCarthy's anti-Communist drive
1951	Joseph Martin (R-Mass.)	67	14	14	H	B	Leaks MacArthur anti-Truman letter re Korea
1951	Joseph Martin (R-Mass.)	67	14	14	H	B	Attacks Truman admin. after MacArthur firing
1951–52	Joseph McCarthy (R-Wis.)	43	3	3	S	A	Attacks Marshall, Acheson, others
1951–52	Richard Nixon (R-Calif.)	38	2	3	S	C	Attacks Acheson, others
1952	Patrick McCarran (D-Nev.)	76	10	10	S	A	McCarran-Walter Immigration Act
1952	Karl Mundt (R-S.Dak.)	52	2	7	S	B	His "Korea/Communist/ corruption" slogan
1952	Francis Walter (D-Pa.)	58	10	10	H	A	McCarran-Walter Immigration Act
1953–54	John Bricker (R-Ohio)	60	4	4	S	B	Bricker amdt. to restrict pres. treatymaking
1953–54	William Knowland (R-Calif.)	46	5	5	S	C	Hardline anticoexistence foreign policy
1953	Joseph McCarthy (R-Wis.)	45	4	4	S	B	Opposes C. Bohlen as ambassador to USSR
1953	Joseph McCarthy (R-Wis.)	45	4	4	S	B	Gets Greek shipowners to stop China trade
1953	Joseph McCarthy (R-Wis.)	45	4	4	S	A	Hunts Communists in State Department
1954	John F. Kennedy (D-Mass.)	37	1	4	S	A	Only Dem. senator silent on McCarthy censure
1954	Joseph McCarthy (R-Wis.)	46	4	4	S	A	Army-McCarthy hearings
1954	Joseph McCarthy (R-Wis.)	46	4	4	S	A	Is censured by Senate

tically speaking, some impulses have centered in actions by young and junior MCs, others in actions by old and senior MCs.

To simplify the discussion here, let us characterize entire impulses as junior, senior, or in between. Have junior impulses differed from those of seniors in any interesting ways? One answer is that, in conventional ideological terms, taking the twentieth century as a whole, junior impulses have leaned toward being progressive, liberal, or left wing, and senior ones toward being conservative or right wing; yet, in fact that relation is cloudy and probably cannot be said to have existed at all since World War II. To be specific, the left had at a decisively junior level its La Follette–led Progressives of 1905–12, its New Freedom advocates of 1912–17, and its left-populist challengers to the New Deal in 1933–35; at a still quite junior level its New Dealers and anti–Vietnam War coalition;[55] but also at a middle-seniority level its Progressives of the 1920s and Great Society reformers of the 1960s; and at a very senior level its O'Neill-centered liberals of the 1980s. The right has had its very senior Old Guard of 1901–10 and anti–Great Society contingent of the 1960s, but also its middle-seniority opposition to the New Deal[56] and its strikingly junior Nixon-Knowland-McCarthy-Taft impulse after World War II —to say nothing of its Gingrich Republicans of the 1990s.[57]

A better bet for differentiation is simply whether the impulse was de-

55. As a matter of medians, this is true of the anti–Vietnam War impulse, notwithstanding the high seniority then of Senator Fulbright.

56. For a general discussion of this impulse, see James T. Patterson, *Congressional Conservatism and the New Deal: The Growth of the Conservative Coalition in Congress, 1933– 1939* (Lexington: University of Kentucky Press, 1967); David M. Kennedy, *Freedom from Fear: The American People in Depression and War, 1929–1945* (New York: Oxford University Press, 1999), ch. 11. For the impulse's Progressives such as Senator Wheeler who had turned anti–New Deal, see Horowitz, *Beyond Left and Right*, pp. 140–51, 159–60.

57. This discussion omits three foreign policy impulses that are hard to place on a left-right dimension.

fensive or offensive. Consider the three most senior impulses in Figure 5.5—those symbolized by Senator Aldrich and Speaker Cannon in 1901–10, Senator Richard Russell and Congressman Howard Smith in the 1960s, and Speaker O'Neill in the 1980s. In all three cases an establishment of some kind or other was putting up a defense against an aggressive challenge—by, respectively, the Progressives who targeted their era's burgeoning trust-centered capitalism and its allegedly subservient congressional establishment; the Great Society reformers who targeted, among other things, the South's segregationist racial order backed up by committee seniority and the filibuster privilege on Capitol Hill; and the Reaganites who targeted their era's allegedly bloated and uncontrollable welfare and regulatory state shielded by an unevictable Democratic Congress. And consider the six most junior impulses—those of the La Follette Progressives of 1905–12, the New Freedom reformers, the New Dealers, the left-populist challengers to the New Deal, the Nixon-Knowland-McCarthy-Taft coalition after World War II, and the anti–Vietnam War coalition. These six impulses were all offensives—before World War II, against chiefly the private corporate economic sector; after that, against the U.S. national security establishment and its policies in 1947–54, when the attack came from the right, and again in 1964–75 when it came from the left.

In connection with defensive versus offensive impulses, consider also political style. Which of the fifteen impulses stand out as particularly harsh, aggressive, accusatory, and given to conspiracy theories? In both Europe and the United States during the twentieth century, on both the left and the right, those were tendencies worth watching. To me— this is not a matter of hard evidence—the impulses that first spring to mind are those associated with the La Follette–led Progressive insurgents of 1905–12 and the anti-Communist, Asia First element of 1947–54 (notably, though not solely, Senator McCarthy), followed by, in no particular order, the left-populist challengers to the New Deal (Huey Long and the others),[58] the often bitter isolationists of 1933–41, and the often abrasive anti–Vietnam War contingent of 1964–75. Four of these five impulses (all but the pre–World War II isolationists) are among the six most junior impulses shown in Figure 5.5. If this and the preceding paragraph are correct, adoption of congressional term limits, on balance in the long run, might be an effective way to aid the political offense—as opposed to defense—whatever that might mean in the way of programmatic content at various times in the future (who knows?) and also to reward and thereby reinforce the stylistic qualities specified above.

One final point emerges from Figure 5.5. It has to do with *configurations* of impulses rather than just properties of individual ones. At four junctures during the twentieth century, powerful impulses sited differently in Congress's tenure-and-age structure existed at the same time and operated *against* each other. These are: The senior GOP Old Guard against the junior Progressive insurgents early in the century; the junior left-populist challengers to the New Deal against the somewhat more senior New Deal regulars against, in turn a bit later, the yet more senior conservative anti–New Dealers during the 1930s; the senior internationalists against the junior anti-Communist Asia First element following World War II; and the middle-seniority Great Society reformers against their senior conservative opponents in the 1960s. With sensitive up-to-date data, another such reading might appear for the senior establishment

58. Like Robert La Follette, Sr., and Joseph McCarthy, Huey Long once caused a stir by publicizing a list of names. This was in the Senate in 1932. In a populist-style attack on Democratic Majority Leader Joseph Robinson, "he read to the Senate the names of the major clients of Robinson's law firm in Arkansas, a list that included many of the largest power companies, banks, and railroads of the Southeast." See Alan Brinkley, *Voices of Protest: Huey Long, Father Coughlin, and the Great Depression* (New York: Vintage, 1983), p. 43. One result of Long's move was an "action" for this study's dataset.

Democrats against their more junior Gingrich Republican challengers in the 1980s and 1990s.

For better or worse, this juxtaposition of opposing impulses during the twentieth century has added a wrinkle to—or at least accentuated a wrinkle in—congressional politics: Conflict *between generations,* which can have distinctive consequences. Every one of the fifteen impulses listed in Figure 5.5 made a significant mark on politics or policy. Where cross-generational impulses checked each other, that often helped bring policy results that took considerable time to produce or that amounted to compromises or scaled-down victories—in the early part of the Progressive era, the New Deal era (notably in 1937–38 when the Democrats enjoyed their largest congressional majorities ever, but stuttered in policy terms), the launching of the Cold War, the Great Society era, and quite likely the 1980s and 1990s.

At the seat of this generational cross-checking is the long congressional career, a twentieth-century trademark. The significance of long careers, it is customary to believe, has lain in a kind of Wilbur Mills effect: Longevity plus seniority rights equals clout for experienced oldtimers. True as that may be, there is another significant effect. Not all twentieth-century MCs pursued or enjoyed long careers, and, as this study's "action" items show, young or novice MCs can be consequential. In the 1930s, for example, Congressman Wright Patman (D-Tex.) quickly emerged as a Capitol Hill champion of populist causes including veterans' bonuses, and Congressman Maury Maverick (D-Tex.) as the embodiment of southern New Deal liberalism. In the late 1940s, Richard Nixon, William Knowland, and Joseph McCarthy made their distinctive marks (see Table 5.5).[59] The late 1970s and early 1980s brought the junior con-

---

59. Not all Nixon's "actions" appear in Table 5.5. I sorted one, for example, into the "internationalist" category dominated by Senator Vandenberg. This was a move in 1948 by Nixon and another House freshman, Charles Kersten (R-Wis.), which drew notice

servative entrepreneurs Henry J. Hyde, author of the Hyde anti-abortion amendment during his first term in the House; Congressman Jack Kemp (R-N.Y.), coauthor of the Kemp-Roth tax cut proposal; David Stockman, a major influence on budgetary thinking; and Phil Gramm, coauthor of Gramm-Latta II in 1981—as well as junior Democratic neo-liberal influentials such as Tony Coelho, Senator Bill Bradley (D-N.J.), and Senator Gary Hart (D-Colo.). In the 1990s, one legislative success story was Dianne Feinstein as a junior California senator.

The general point is: Long careers have guaranteed on Capitol Hill at any one time the *coexistence* of sizable members of high-, middle-, *and* low-tenure MCs who, regardless of their vintage, can realistically aim for "actions" of one kind or another. If MC generations are on balance at odds with each other over major issues, that can translate into spirited cross-generational conflict and an extra dose of "checks and balances" for the American system, as evidently happened during the twentieth century. Here is another feature of congressional politics that a term-limits reform would likely cut into.

Presidents, Congress, and Eras

Finally on the subject of careers, consider the sharply contrasting approaches that both scholars and citizens take to the American presidency as opposed to Congress. The presidency is ordinarily personalized, no doubt overpersonalized. We hear of the age of Jackson, the age of Roosevelt (either one), and the Reagan era. Also, it is conventionally assumed that presidents, within the broad constraints imposed by their need to be reelected and other elements in their environments, make choices and that those choices can be consequential. Some presidents impose them-

---

partly because it came from two Republican freshmen, warning the Soviet Union to back off its undertakings in Europe.

selves on society in a major way.[60] No one would seriously argue that presidents are simply "agents" of a society hovering in the background as "principal." President Clinton pressed for health-care reform, opted for economic policies favored by Robert Rubin and Alan Greenspan, spoke out on education issues, consorted with Dick Morris, legitimized "soft money" in election campaigns, sponsored the NATO military offensive in Yugoslavia, testified dubiously before a grand jury, and pardoned a group of Puerto Rican terrorists. All these were choices. At two showdown junctures during 1995–96, he vetoed the Gingrich-Dole budget package but signed the welfare-reform act, and we can all supply reelection explanations for those two moves, but as far as we know he nearly decided the other way in each case, and if he had, we would have no trouble explaining in hindsight those opposite moves as reelection-oriented also. And we know all this.

But Congress is a different story. It is typically depersonalized and its members viewed as society-driven robots. There are two good reasons for this: Legislative tasks require less discretion than executive ones, and the personal quirks and propensities of a 535-member institution do tend to cancel out.

Yet the depersonalizing tendency goes too far. Consider the decade of the 1930s, which ordinarily stars an active "Roosevelt" and a passive "Congress." In fact, it is a fair question whether the 1930s, at least as an epic legislative era, should not be labeled "the age of Wagner" as much as it is "the age of Roosevelt." Possibly the most talented and successful legislator in American history, an ingenious deployer of research information channeled to him by a first-rate staff, Senator Robert F. Wagner shaped federal statutes of the 1930s in the areas of public works, relief, government preparation of unemployment statistics, unemployment in-

60. For example, see Stephen Skowronek, *The Politics Presidents Make: Leadership from John Adams to George Bush* (Cambridge: Harvard University Press, 1993).

surance, retirement insurance for railroad workers, public housing, and of course labor-management relations (through the National Recovery Act and the Wagner Act).[61] According to one recent study, "Sometimes Wagner introduced bills on behalf of the president but, when dealing with social welfare legislation, the New York senator almost always took the lead and endeavored to bring Roosevelt onboard," and "Without a doubt, the creation of America's nascent limited welfare state owed to the political talents of both leaders, but Wagner's indomitable drive was paramount."[62] Of course other talented legislators operated in the 1930s too, and Roosevelt was Roosevelt, yet one reading of the significance of the 1932 election might be: It produced a president who would sign Wagner's bills.

Aside from "the age of Roosevelt" and its like, is there a way to code eras that captures a kind of political reality by incorporating exertions like those of Senator Wagner? Consider Table 5.6, which addresses two spans of time: The quarter century from 1851 through 1875 (twelve Congresses in all), which encompassed the growing sectional tension of the 1850s, the Civil War, and Reconstruction; and 1939 through 1954, roughly the period of the ascendant "conservative coalition" on Capitol Hill as well as of World War II and the launching of the Cold War. The data presentation for each era includes all MCs who performed at least six lifetime "actions" of which at least half came during the era in question. The members are listed in order of the time locations of the (temporally) median items of their lifetime "action careers."

I will not claim elegance for Table 5.6, but consider the content. In the top display, a rainbow of antislavery to proslavery influentials contested for advantage in the 1850s—Charles Sumner and William Seward

61. Huthmacher, *Senator Robert F. Wagner*, chs. 5–13.

62. Roger Biles, "Robert F. Wagner, Franklin D. Roosevelt, and Social Welfare Legislation in the New Deal," *Presidential Studies Quarterly* 28 (1998), 139–52, quotations at pp. 140, 150.

Table 5.6 Major Action Careers Centered in Two Eras

Pre–Civil War, Civil War, and Reconstruction (1851–75)

MC	Total actions	Congress, as indexed by its even year (18XX)									
		44	48	52	56	60	64	68	72	76	80
Robert Toombs (Ga.)	9			x·········	········	·X·····	x				
Stephen A. Douglas (Ill.)	22		x······	·········	········	·X··x					
William Seward (N.Y.)	13			x·········	····	X··x					
John J. Crittenden (Ky.)	8	←········	·········	·········	····	X··x					
Jefferson Davis (Miss.)	9		x······	·········	·····	X					
Benjamin F. Wade (Ohio)	11				x········	········	·X········	·x			
Charles Sumner (Mass.)	27				x········	········	········	X·········	····	x	
Thaddeus Stevens (Pa.)	15						x······	X··x			
Lyman Trumbull (Ill.)	12						x······	X·········	x		
Benjamin F. Butler (Mass.)	9								x·····	X··x	
John Sherman (Ohio)	23					x········	········	········	········	·X········	→

Conservative coalition, World War II, beginning of Cold War (1939–54)

MC	Total actions	Congress, as indexed by its even year (19XX)									
		28	32	36	40	44	48	52	56	60	64
Martin Dies (Tex.)	7		x········	········	·····	X··x					
Alben Barkley (Ky.)	6			x·····	····	X········	·x				
Sam Rayburn (Tex.)	17	←·······	········	········	········	·····	X········	········	········	······	x
Howard Smith (Va.)	9			x········	····	X········	········	········	········	······	x
Arthur Vandenberg (Mich.)	17		x······	········	········	·····	X··x				
Robert A. Taft (Ohio)	30				x········	·····	X········	·x			
Harry F. Byrd (Va.)	11			x········	········	····	X········	········	········	······	x
Richard Nixon (Calif.)	7						x··X··x				
Joseph McCarthy (Wis.)	9						x····X				

through Stephen A. Douglas and John J. Crittenden through Robert Toombs and Jefferson Davis; later, in the years of Reconstruction, Sumner again, Benjamin Wade, Thaddeus Stevens, the more cautious Lyman Trumbull and John Sherman, and the flamboyant Benjamin Butler took the programmatic offensive. In the bottom display, once past the Democratic Party's spear-carriers Sam Rayburn and Alben Barkley (D-Ky.) and the convert internationalist Arthur Vandenberg, opposition to presidential administrations provides the keynote—as in that era it indeed did. To be sure, these displays leave out most of the dataset's items—those by performers of fewer than six "actions"—but on the congressional side they are plausible guides to what the two eras had on offer.

The Stability of American Institutions

In analyzing the data patterns in previous chapters, I have tried to generalize and draw out certain implications along the way. Hence the emphasis on a profile of MC "action" types in Chapter 3, the trends toward democratization, distinctness, and equality among the major U.S. elective institutions in Chapter 4, and the time locations of "actions" in MC careers in Chapter 5. In this concluding chapter, I present some additional general discussion, this time about stability and change in the American system and Congress's place in it, and then finish as I began in Chapter 1 with a look at congressional politics in the 1990s.

From a comparative perspective, nothing is more striking about the American constitutional system than its stability since 1789. Congress, along with the country's other national institutions, has largely kept its form and standing during the past two turbulent centuries when very few major political institutions elsewhere have done so.

The reasons for this are many and complicated, some of them historical, centering on Anglo-American tradition. Yet one promising reason has recently emerged from a study by Matthew S. Shugart and John M. Carey based on cross-country comparative analysis. That is, once the framers of the U.S. Constitution chose to construct a presidential system anchored in separation of powers—in principle, that was not their only option—they hit on a particularly effective balance between governmental branches. They created a powerful presidency free to flex its *executive* muscles, and a Congress, compared with most legislatures that have ever existed since then in the world's collection of presidential systems, unusually well-fortified with *legislative* powers including the right to take the initiative. Surprisingly, such a strong legislature is a rare blueprint. American presidents, unlike many of their counterparts elsewhere, do not enjoy legislative prerogatives such as emergency decree powers,[1] a partial veto (now that the Supreme Court has struck down the short-lived line-item veto), an exclusive right to introduce certain kinds of legislation (with the exception of treaties), a right to introduce non-amendable, take-it-or-leave-it proposals (in practice not even necessarily treaties, as Wilson learned when Senate "reservations" came to plague the Versailles treaty in 1919; and certainly not domestic legislation, as the White House promoters of health-care reform came to be reminded in 1993–94), and an exclusive right to introduce budgets, or a license to submit proposals to national referendum decisions—to say nothing of a right to dismiss an uncooperative Congress and call a new election.[2] Why is this an apt constitutional formula? At the task of legislating, Shugart and Carey argue, heterogeneous multimember assemblies tend to be better than single-person presidencies at arranging compromises and accommodating diversity, and as a result they tend to be better at winning legiti-

1. Although they can and do issue "executive orders," a power generally underappreciated in academic writing. On this subject, see Terry M. Moe and William G. Howell, "The Presidential Power of Unilateral Action," *Journal of Law, Economics, and Organization* 15(1999), 132–79.

2. Matthew S. Shugart and John M. Carey, *Presidents and Assemblies: Constitutional Design and Electoral Dynamics* (New York: Cambridge University Press, 1992), chs. 7, 8, especially pp. 154–58.

macy for their systems among their publics. In the long run, constitutional systems that are legitimate are likely to be stable.[3]

This case certainly seems plausible, and Shugart and Carey back it up with comparative data and analysis. Compatible with it and perhaps building on it by addressing *how* its results might come to be true are five arguments I present here, drawing on patterns of MC "action" discussed in previous chapters, about Congress's possible contribution to the legitimacy and stability of the American constitutional system during the past two centuries. As in Shugart and Carey, all five arguments hinge on Congress's enjoying a considerable grant of formal authority—legislative authority, though not only that—and four of the five (the last four) dwell on balance or relations between the executive and legislative branches. These last four arguments raise once again the subject of congressional "oppositions," which seem to be as fundamental as anything to the nature of the regime.

The first argument is that Congress, from 1789 onward, by offering a taste of real power and the prospect of more, has absorbed a large share of the country's most talented and ambitious politicians into the Capitol Hill–centered "opportunity structure" discussed in Chapter 4; *and,* in doing so, it has harnessed them to roles that are largely national (as opposed to local or provincial, or for that matter cross-national), public (in the sense of involving open performances before audiences), and peaceful (at least within settled American territory, and with the exception of

3. "On matters of legislation, we suggest that relatively strong assemblies should be associated with more stable and effective government relative to strong presidencies because assemblies serve as arenas for the perpetual fine-tuning of conflicts. An assembly represents the diversity of a polity far better than an executive dependent on the president's whims is likely to do. Because of the diverse forces represented in an assembly, such a body has the potential for encompassing divergent viewpoints and striking compromises on them." Shugart and Carey, *Presidents and Assemblies,* p. 165.

the 1860s). The British House of Commons, with its magnet-like draw of politicians from around that country into ministerial positions that have a public face, has brought about similar results, but not all national legislatures have been so adept at processing ambitious people. In late nineteenth-century Germany, for example, centrists and even conservatives of high leadership potential are said to have steered clear of that country's rather toothless parliament,[4] and politicians of the left, denied any taste or promise of power, dwelt on organizing mass movements and constructing antisystem ideologies. In contemporary Brazil, parliamentary politicians are said to drain off into the bureaucracy, where the real power is; they leave the national congress because it is weak (in contrast to a presidency strong enough to often destabilize the system) and it stays weak because they leave it.[5] In Canada, many of the most talented and aggressive politicians seem to spend their careers as provincial premiers. What would Canada be like if they could aim for positions in a U.S.-style Senate in Ottawa? What would the United States be like if Henry Clay had stayed home to run Kentucky, Matthew Quay to run Pennsylvania, and Lyndon Johnson to run Texas? This is a consideration relevant to the future of the transnational parliament of the European Community.

The second argument, to move to congressional oppositions (as indexed in the eighteen historical clusters listed in Table 3.3), is that these oppositions have often been *consequential*. See Table 6.1 for a summary judgment about which side—the executive branch or Congress—has pre-

---

4. See Max Weber, "Parliament and Government in Germany under a New Political Order," in Weber, *Political Writings*, eds. Peter Lassman and Ronald Speirs (New York: Cambridge University Press, 1994), pp. 171–72.

5. Fabiano Santos, "Recruitment and Retention of Legislators in Brazil," *Legislative Studies Quarterly* 24 (1999), 209–37, at 225–26. Some of Brazil's state governorships also attract and keep very powerful leaders.

Table 6.1 Results of Manifestations of Congressional Opposition

Executive branch prevailed

1790–93   Madison Republicans vs. Hamilton's Treasury program (Hamilton won on the assumption of state debts and his plan for a U.S. bank; lost on later items)

1793–96   Madison Republicans vs. Washington administration's pro-England foreign policy

1803–8   Quid Republicans vs. Jefferson administration

1832–36   Whig challenge to Jackson administration

1869–72   Liberal Republicans vs. Grant administration (Sumner won on Santo Domingo, but the Liberals could not lever tariff reform or civil service reform or keep Grant from getting reelected)

1934–35   Huey Long's challenge to FDR

1939–41   Isolationist opposition to Roosevelt administration (FDR finally got his way, although not without forcing events such as Hitler's occupation of France)

No clear winner

1877–81   Stalwart GOP challenge over job patronage (Conkling emerged a clear loser, but Presidents Hayes and Garfield were hardly clear winners, and civil service reform came only in 1883 after they were out of the picture)

1906–12   Progressive insurgency (La Follette and the others helped to cripple the Taft administration, but without much in immediate policy payoff to show for it)

1922–24   Progressive insurgency (Teapot Dome and other moves dented the orthodox Republicans, but again without much policy payoff for the left)

1938–44   Investigative assault vs. Roosevelt administration's agencies

1947–54   Isolationist, anti-Communist, Asia First challenge to Truman and early Eisenhower administrations (The trans-Atlanticists won in their policy sphere, and McCarthy ended up discredited, but the right came to influence China policy, and the loyalty investigations cast a long shadow)

1964–72   Challenge to Vietnam War and national security establishment (Johnson backed off his policies in 1968; Nixon and congressional doves contested through 1972; final congressional victory over war finally came later in 1975)

MC opposition prevailed

1857–60   Douglas's showdown with Buchanan over chiefly Kansas policy (The Lecompton constitution favored by the Buchanan administration lost)

1864–68   Reconstruction policy (The congressional Republicans won their policies, although they could not evict President Andrew Johnson)

1917–20   Antiwar, anti-League challenge to Wilson administration (The League was a big loss)

Table 6.1 (*continued*)

1937–38	Conservative challenge to the Roosevelt administration (FDR lost on court-packing and executive reorganization, failed to purge conservative Democrats in the 1938 primaries, won mostly modest victories otherwise—although the Supreme Court did surrender in key policy areas on its own initiative)
1972–74	Watergate

vailed in each of the eighteen confrontations.[6] Across the two centuries, the pattern is roughly a wash, and with no evident trend toward presidential victories during the twentieth century. That is, measured against a constitutionally strong executive poised to claim popular mandates, MC oppositions, by drawing on Congress's legislative as well as investigative, impeachment, and appointment powers—not to mention opportunities afforded by Capitol Hill to take stands and occasionally stage White House bids themselves, such as Eugene McCarthy's in 1968—have come out roughly even. This bears out Shugart and Carey's image of a strongly empowered legislature. As for a contribution to systemic legitimacy and stability, consider the utility toward those ends of stiff, evenly matched, outcomes-at-stake competition outside the narrow time constraints of the election cycle.

Third, congressional oppositions have been *flexible,* by which I mean that the parties have often bent. The American regime is obviously not a rigid party type where a president supplied with House and Senate majorities of his own party has free rein. As discussed in Chapter 3— and as Presidents Jefferson, Buchanan, Grant, Taft, Franklin Roosevelt,

6. These are judgment calls, some of them close. Certain items could plausibly be switched to a neighboring category. I am indebted to Rogan Kersh for assistance on the judgment calls.

Lyndon Johnson, and others would testify—major MC oppositions have arisen as often within a president's own party (particularly when that party has controlled Congress) as elsewhere. One aspect of this flexibility is a service that might be called "defector signaling." Voters have been offered the inference that more than normal party-versus-party scrapping was at issue when, for example, Democratic Senator Douglas broke with Democratic President Buchanan over Kansas policy, Senator Wheeler broke with Franklin Roosevelt over court-packing, Senator Fulbright challenged Lyndon Johnson over Vietnam, or Senator Goldwater informed Nixon it was time to quit.[7] To be sure, the parties do not always bend. In the 1990s, a lack of Democratic MC defectors helped keep the Clinton administration's scandals at more or less the level of party-versus-party scrapping.[8]

Fourth, congressional oppositions taken in the aggregate over time have been *unbiased*—at least between or among the politically mobilized sectors of the society. At various times, Whigs as well as Democrats, Republicans as well as Democrats, progressives as well as conservatives, and hawks as well as doves have staged them. Note the ideological heterogeneity of the clusters listed in Table 3.3 or 6.1. (In this case, the argument also holds for the "ideological impulses" listed in Table 5.4.) Looked at from the other side, the presidential administrations trying to stave off these oppositions have logically had to be comparably unbiased—in the

7. Of the eighteen clusters of opposition MC actions listed in Tables 3.3 and 6.1, fourteen include at least one action performed by an MC who was unambiguously a member of the president's party. The only exceptions or gray cases are the Madison-led clusters of 1790–93 and 1793–96 and the Clay-led Whig cluster of 1832–36, when new opposition parties were being formed on the spot, and the not easily classifiable Reconstruction opposition to Andrew Johnson.

8. Actually, one important defection did occur regarding Whitewater, in 1994. Senator Donald W. Riegle, Jr. (D-Mich.), ran damaging hearings as chairman of the Senate Banking Committee that resulted in the resignation of Deputy Treasury Roger C. Alt-

same aggregate sense taken over time. For either the presidency or Congress, this lack of constant identification with any one mobilized societal interest has probably paid off in institutional survival. It is true that one or the other institution has occasionally *seemed* to have an enduring societal anchor—as with the connection between the New Deal presidency and liberalism. Yet, such associations have been perishable, as can be seen in the writings of partisan intellectuals, who, following the norms of their trade, cast their arguments about institutions in universalistic terms, but tend not to mean it—for example, the successive generations of conservatives who favored a strong Congress during the New Deal era but a strong presidency during the Reagan era, or the generations of liberals who favored a broad congressional impeachment power for use against Nixon in 1974 but a narrow one for use against Clinton in 1998. Over time, both the presidency and Congress have proven to be common carriers. That fact can hardly be inescapable, and it has probably contributed to the legitimacy and stability of both these institutions and the system in general.

Fifth and finally, congressional oppositions have been *dramatic*. In political science, that is an underexamined quality. High-stakes congressional confrontations with the White House are, among other things, sequences of well-reported, interconnected moves by political actors that the public can watch, appreciate, and appraise. They tend to have a beginning, a dynamic, and an end. For system purposes, it probably matters that they have an end. "It's been a fair fight, it's gone on long enough, and it's *over;* I don't want to hear about it any more," has probably been a common concluding reaction by both actors and audiences to many of these encounters of the past. By the time of the 1920 election, little taste was left for quarreling about the League of Nations. A year after the Army-McCarthy hearings of 1954, the anti-Communist loyalty investigations that had convulsed the country for years were a receding memory. In August 1974, Nixon returned to California, and that was that for Watergate; San Clemente was not to be an Elba. Deflations of this sort seem to have occurred twice during the 1990s. In the spring of 1996, Clinton and his Republican congressional opposition, after three years of furious struggling over the 1993 budget, health-care reform, and the Gingrich-Dole budget that resulted in the shutdown of the government, more or less gave up. Passions were reined in, headlines shrank, and compromise lawmaking ensued (on welfare reform, a minimum wage hike, portability health insurance, and other subjects) before a national audience that was apparently no less ready to move on. In early 1999, once the Senate voted not to convict President Clinton, the subject of his sexual and grand-jury escapades abruptly dropped from public affairs. There was no audience for it any more.

How can the American regime be so rock-solid if it functions so untidily and its policy offerings are, at least by those who draw comparisons with European nations, so often criticized?[9] The realm of MC "actions" offers clues to that puzzle that I have presented here, to which might be added, for example, the system's openness to "ideological impulses," yet also its ability to contain them, which I discussed in Chapter 5. Obviously, vastly more might be said on this subject through a discussion of the presidency, the courts, the federal system, and the nature of American society. But Congress and its members have a supportive role, and if it continues, like it or not, we are no doubt headed for yet another century of MC "actions,"—legislative moves, speeches, filibusters, impeachment motions, investigations, stands, opposition activity, intrusions into foreign policy, and all the rest. Public affairs as it involves Congress will carry on seamlessly, or at least as seamlessly as it has done in the past, into the future.

Yet for this to happen, members of Congress will need to maintain

---

9. On this subject, see James Q. Wilson, "Does the Separation of Powers Still Work?" *The Public Interest,* Winter 1987, No. 86, pp. 36–52.

their customary place in the American public sphere—that is (to refer to the discussion in Chapter 1), they will need to keep on making moves that are widely noticed by virtue of being sized up as consequential, potentially consequential, or otherwise significant. But that is not a sure thing, as the reader may have reflected by now. Given the experience around the world during the twentieth century, it is plain that representative assemblies can decline or recede. For one thing, they can decline in legitimacy—in contrast to a government's other branches (as American city councils evidently did vis-à-vis mayors during the twentieth century) or as part of an entire government's downslide in legitimacy—and as a result lose influence over events. For this or other reasons, they can decline in visibility; they can come to be noticed less. In the case of Congress and its members, declining visibility, however induced, would mean by definition a shrinking universe of MC "actions."

Is Congress headed for, or already in, such a slide? Certain strands of evidence argue yes. Public confidence in Congress (and other U.S. government institutions) has been low in recent times. Among the American public, tolerance seems to be limited these days for Congress's complex deliberative processes or its unending quarrelsomeness[10]—which the 1990s saw a good deal of.[11] MCs are thought to lose their bearings

10. John R. Hibbing and Elizabeth Theiss-Morse, *Congress as Public Enemy: Public Attitudes toward American Political Institutions* (New York: Cambridge University Press, 1995), p. xii and ch. 1. "Puzzling is the unrefined populist pining of so many citizens. They seem to expect Congress, magically, to mold sometimes bitterly divided public opinion into coherent and effective public policy without debate, disagreement, or compromise." Hibbing and Theiss-Morse, p. xii. See also Robert H. Durr, John B. Gilmour, and Christina Wolbrecht, "Explaining Congressional Approval," *American Journal of Political Science* 41 (1997), 175–207.

11. For a study concluding that civility had declined, and "bomb-throwing" had increased, on Capitol Hill in the early 1990s as contrasted with that setting in the early 1960s, see Lewis G. Irwin, "Evaluating Change in Legislative Success: Actors, Procedures, Strategies, and Product in the U.S. House of Representatives," Ph.D. dissertation

once they move inside the Washington, D.C., Beltway: "Stated simply, people think members of Congress have bought into the 'Washington system,' which seduces members away from fulfilling their responsibility to the public." They are "corrupted by special interests and lobbyists."[12] The movement to impose term limits, whatever else it may be, is a statement about Congress's legitimacy. Also, media coverage of Congress has grown more negative in recent decades—perhaps adding to the institution's legitimacy problems:[13] "In this post-Woodward-and-Bernstein era, rewards seem to flow toward reporters who expose or accentuate 'scandal and sloth.'"[14]

In addition, media coverage of Congress has grown more scanty in recent times, at least on network television; there is less of it.[15] This points

---

submitted to the Department of Political Science, Yale University, 1998, pp. 188–89, 270–73, 288–93.

12. Hibbing and Theiss-Morse, *Congress as Public Enemy,* p. 62 and more generally chs. 4, 5.

13. S. Robert Lichter and Daniel R. Amundson, "Less News Is Worse News: Television News Coverage of Congress, 1972–92," ch. 5 in Thomas E. Mann and Norman J. Ornstein (eds.), *Congress, the Press, and the Public* (Washington, D.C.: American Enterprise Institute and Brookings Institution, 1994), pp. 137–39; Mark J. Rozell, "Press Coverage of Congress, 1946–92," ch. 4 in Mann and Ornstein (eds.), *Congress, the Press, and the Public,* pp. 109–10; John R. Hibbing and Elizabeth Theiss-Morse, "The Media's Role in Public Negativity Toward Congress: Distinguishing Emotional Reactions and Cognitive Evaluations," *American Journal of Political Science* 42 (1998), 481–84.

14. Hibbing and Theiss-Morse, "The Media's Role," p. 482.

15. See Greg Schneiders, "The 90-Second Handicap: Why TV Coverage of Legislation Falls Short," *Washington Journalism Review,* June 1985, pp. 44–46; Lichter and Amundson, "Less News Is Worse News," pp. 133–35. Schneiders's time series ends in 1984, Lichter and Amundson's in 1992. See also Stephen Hess, "The Decline and Fall of Congressional News," ch. 6 in Mann and Ornstein (eds.), *Congress, the Press, and the Public.* From a 1998 report on television news in the United States and Britain: "News is also shifting its focus away from politicians. There are fewer Congressional hearings or parliamentary wrangles and more features from fly-over country or Middle England. The public sector features less and the private sector more. The number of political reporters

to a possible problem of congressional visibility, and it raises a more general question about the condition of the American "public sphere." Whatever that realm might have amounted to in the past, is it deteriorating? Given today's increasingly fragmented media audiences, spreading multicultural (as opposed to national) identities, and widespread apathy or disdain toward politics, perhaps it is.[16] The competition is stiff: In an age of channel-surfing, sound bites, smooth media personalities, and the Internet, what kind of role can there be for House and Senate members and their slow, antiquated, often distasteful processes?[17] The ability of voters to recall the names of their own House members has been gently declining since the 1950s.[18] Today's young people, according to survey data, "are more withdrawn from public affairs than earlier birth cohorts were when they were young."[19] Also, as was observed earlier, a national script does not seem to exist anymore: Gone are the imperatives of the Cold War and the confident project of erecting a welfare and

is shrinking and the number of consumer-affairs correspondents growing." "Stop Press," *The Economist*, July 4, 1998, pp. 17–19, quotation at p. 19.

16. "With advancing modernization . . . , politics in many countries seems to have degenerated into a pale replica of democratic governance, losing much of its capacity to forge citizenship, national community, civic involvement, and common forms of identity. Signs of this historical process have been increasingly visible in the United States since the late 1970s with growing anti-statism and popular anger directed against the federal government, the rise of identity-based movements, enhanced popularity of therapeutic and various new-age indulgences, emergence of a postmodern intellectual culture, and a pervasive sense of cynicism and civil privatism that has swept through broad regions of society." Carl Boggs, "The Great Retreat: Decline of the Public Sphere in Late Twentieth-Century America," *Theory and Society* 26 (1997), 741.

17. See, for example, Kyle Pope, "Impeachment? Viewers Prefer Football Game," *Wall Street Journal*, December 22, 1998, p. B1.

18. Gary C. Jacobson, "The Declining Salience of U.S. House Candidates, 1958–1994," paper presented at the annual conference of the American Political Science Association, Boston, September 3–6, 1998, fig. 2.

19. Stephen Earl Bennett, "Young Americans' Indifference to Media Coverage of Public Affairs," *PS: Political Science and Politics* 31 (1998), 535–41, quotation at p. 535.

regulatory state to fasten attention on Washington, D.C. It is against this background that, as noted in Chapter 2, historians seem to have flagged as documenters of late twentieth-century public affairs. Also (to refer to Chapter 4), today's histories have taken on something of an imperial, as opposed to republican, flavor in casting their post–World War II members of Congress so often as contenders for the White House.

Nonetheless, it is possible to supply answers to, or at least qualifications to, this recitation of decline, of which I offer five here. It is probably too early to write off Congress or its members. First, and obviously, formal powers can be worth a great deal. Many MC "actions" are probably guaranteed for the twenty-first century by Congress's as yet unimpaired powers to legislate, ratify treaties, appropriate money, impeach, investigate, serve as a platform for free speech, and issue subpoenas. These powers are likely to be used, and their use is likely to be noticed.[20] Second, congressional politicians have engaged in slow, conflict-ridden, often nasty behavior since the 1790s. Unappealing as that may be, it is a kind of normal politics. Third, we should be wary of assuming that a golden age existed somewhere in the past when we assess readings of public confidence in Congress. As far as we know, there has never been an era when Congress rode particularly high in public opinion. The institution's unattractive processes have probably always weighed it down, except for occasional blips of high ratings like the one in the mid-1960s— the time of Johnson's Great Society program—that has misleadingly figured in much time series analysis since then as a starting point and implicit yardstick.[21] Also, following the much-commented-on trough of

20. One reflection on this subject: "The unyielding truth is that, even as the ethos of anti-politics becomes more compelling and even fashionable in the United States, it is the vagaries of political power that will continue to decide the fate of human societies." Boggs, "The Great Retreat," p. 774.

21. Three studies address this question by examining spotty but illuminating survey

the early and middle 1990s, congressional ratings shot up surprisingly high during the largely idle (and not in any obvious way appealing) Congress of 1997–98. It is not clear what these time series amount to.[22] Fourth, we should take care not to romanticize about the American "public sphere"—past, present, or future. It is not an example of participatory democracy. The United States has always been a busy, commercially oriented country in which some people dwell on public affairs, many take an occasional interest, and many others show a rare interest or no interest at all.[23] That is not likely to change.[24] The significance of these last three

readings for the two decades or so before 1965: Glenn R. Parker, "Can Congress Ever Be a Popular Institution?" ch. 1 in Joseph Cooper and G. Calvin Mackenzie (eds.), *The House at Work* (Austin: University of Texas Press, 1981), pp. 31–32. "In fact, popular Congresses can be viewed as aberrations created by unusual circumstances." Cooper and Mackenzie, p. 31. As instances, Parker cites the Eighty-third Congress of 1953–54, when Eisenhower began his presidency and the Korean War came to an end, and the Great Society Congress of 1965–66. Karlyn Bowman and Everett Carll Ladd, "Public Opinion toward Congress: A Historical Look," ch. 3 in Mann and Ornstein (eds.), *Congress, the Press, and the Public*, pp. 45–51. "It would be a mistake to assume, of course, that Americans thought highly of Congress in earlier times and only soured on the institution recently. From the time of our early humorists to today's late night talk show hosts, Congress has been an inviting target." Mann and Ornstein, pp. 50–51. Hibbing and Theiss-Morse, *Congress as Public Enemy*, ch. 2. "So the low levels of positive feelings for Congress in the past twenty years [up to the mid-1990s] may be slightly more extreme and persistent than usual, but the historical norm—to the extent it can be determined from these irregular data—is for quite modest levels of support." Hibbing and Theiss-Morse, p. 35.

22. See the discussion in Rogan Kersh, "Anti-Democratic Demos: The Dubious Basis of Congressional Approval," *Critical Review* 12 (1998), 569–84. See also Gary C. Jacobson, "Impeachment Politics in the 1998 Congressional Elections," paper presented at the annual conference of the Midwest Political Science Association, Chicago, April 14–17, 1999. "In early 1998, approval of Congress reached 57 percent, the highest level recorded in the 25 years the question has been asked." Jacobson, p. 3.

23. See the discussion in Robert A. Dahl, *Who Governs? Democracy and Power in an American City* (New Haven: Yale University Press, 1961), ch. 25. *or Shklar*

24. Habermas and his followers, in addressing the twentieth century, have used the

points is: The real historical performance of Congress and its members has had institutional survival value; performance of the same kind may continue to have survival value, although we cannot be sure of that; at any rate, we should be eyes-open about imposing performance criteria that are unhistorical.

All this is not to say that no change ever occurs in American political processes or the level of interest that people take in them. In fact, change and interest tend to be episodic.[25] In the 1990s, discontent with politicians had become so pronounced that another major burst of democratizing procedural reforms, as in the Progressive era, loomed as a possibility for the early twenty-first century.[26] But the realm of MC "actions" would probably survive any such burst of reform, which after all meant in the case of the Progressive era, in effect, to trade in Senator Aldrich and Speaker Cannon for Senator La Follette and Congressman Norris.

Fifth, it is nothing new for Congress or its members to have to angle for communications links with the public. Because the relevant technologies have never been stable, permanent solutions have never been found, and openings have continually existed for entrepreneurial MCs to forge new links—often thereby scoring "actions" in this study. A lineage of such innovations runs from the 1790s to the present—from James

idea of a "public sphere" as a largely utopian standard for criticizing contemporary politics and society. See, for example, Craig Calhoun (ed.), *Habermas and the Public Sphere* (Cambridge: MIT Press, 1992).

25. See Samuel P. Huntington, *American Politics: The Promise of Disharmony* (Cambridge: Harvard University Press, 1981).

26. In one opinion survey in early 1999, 84 percent of respondents said that the public should have more influence than it has now over Congress as it makes decisions; 8 percent said the same as now; 4 percent said less than now. Steven Kull, *Expecting More Say: A Study of American Public Attitudes on the Role of the Public in Government Decisions* (Washington, D.C.: Center on Policy Attitudes, February 1999), p. 3. Note that this was during the Clinton impeachment proceedings.

Madison and his public essays and co-sponsored newspaper, through Daniel Webster and his widely circulated speech extolling the Union in the Senate's Webster-Hayne debate of 1830,[27] Senator Sumner and his techniques for circulating antislavery speeches,[28] Senator Borah and his pioneering regular press conferences with national reporters,[29] the La Follettes and their national magazine devoted to reform, Huey Long and his radio oratory, Senator Fulbright and his televised Vietnam War hearings, Speaker O'Neill and his barrage of anti-Reagan press conferences,[30] to Speaker Gingrich and his books, tapes, lectures by satellite, GOPAC organization, links with talk-show radio hosts, use of C-SPAN, marketing

27. "He knew it could be the most important speech in his entire career, so he asked Joseph Gates of the *National Intelligencer,* known for his shorthand expertise, to report the speech personally. . . . The *National Intelligencer* published the revised version in three installments, February 23, 25, and 27, 1830, and issued it in pamphlet form. Webster had personally invited Joseph Gates to report his speech but was dissatisfied with the transcript because it lacked an emotional wallop. So the *Intelligencer* waited while he revised it. . . . The speech was so heavily edited and rewritten that some thought 'it bore little resemblance' to what Webster has actually said in the Senate. The editors and publishers printed and distributed more than forty thousand copies of this second reply to [Senator Robert Y.] Hayne [D-S.C.] and acknowledged that twenty other printed editions appeared elsewhere. Webster and his wife themselves distributed it to friends, political figures, and influential leaders of industry and commerce. The response came immediately. People were overwhelmed by what they read. They could talk of nothing else." Robert V. Remini, *Daniel Webster: The Man and His Time* (New York: Norton, 1997), pp. 324, 329–30.

28. On Sumner: "It was his *own* reporting and circulation of speeches that engaged him deeply. Through the franking privilege and anti-slavery societies he built a network of readers outside party journalism." Thomas C. Leonard, *The Power of the Press: The Birth of American Political Reporting* (New York: Oxford University Press, 1986), p. 86.

29. See LeRoy Ashby, *The Spearless Leader: Senator Borah and the Progressive Movement in the 1920's* (Urbana: University of Illinois Press, 1972), pp. 17–21, 207–8. Borah inaugurated this custom in 1919. The senator had "a positive genius for newspaper publicity," in the reported estimate of Herbert Hoover. Ashby, p. 17.

30. On O'Neill as a communications pioneer in the early 1980s, see Douglas R. Harris, "The Rise of the Public Speakership," *Political Science Quarterly* 113 (1998), 196–97, 201.

of the Contract with America, and the rest. As much as anything, this is the major congressional story of the 1990s—Newt Gingrich as a communications entrepreneur. The low Gallup ratings that the ex-Speaker achieved should not obscure his effectiveness—notably in the years leading up to the 1994 election—in reaching out to and mobilizing conservative activists, donors, and candidates for House seats. This was a significant penetration of the American public. With today's rapid changes in electronic technology, this new century is likely to see continual, possibly dramatic, innovations in the Madison-through-Gingrich line, although it is impossible to guess what or by whom. Much is at stake. Recently, in one decentralized drift, MCs have been shifting the locus of their public commenting, and even their deliberating, from the House and Senate floors to the television talk shows that proliferated during the 1990s.[31]

This argues for communications links as a high-priority item in congressional studies.[32] Another range of suitable topics oriented toward the present and future, if this study of MC "actions" is to be regarded seriously, is *kinds* of MCs—the premise being that different kinds of House and Senate members might tend to perform different kinds of "actions."

31. "Who needs Congress when there's 'Crossfire'? During the House Judiciary Committee's televised debate about an impeachment inquiry yesterday, [Democratic] Representative Robert Wexler of Florida, a vehement opponent of impeaching the President, said he was scheduled to appear on 'Crossfire' later that night with [Republican] Representative Bob Barr of Georgia, one of the President's fiercest critics. 'In an effort not to ruin the show tonight, I'm going to wait to respond to Mr. Barr's comments earlier until we get on the show,' Mr. Wexler said. It was a joke and it wasn't. Television has clearly superseded Congress as the primary site of political debate." Caryn James, "It Was All Too Familiar, Like a 'Nightline' Rerun," *New York Times*, October 6, 1998, p. A21. In one report of the Senate's impeachment trial, a paragraph began: "Among 21 Republican and Democratic senators who fanned out across CBS, NBC, ABC, CNN and other networks today. . . ." Frank Bruni, "Senators Try to Restore Status as Upper House on the Higher Road," *New York Times*, January 25, 1999, p. A17.

32. As in Timothy E. Cook, *Making Laws and Making News: Media Strategies in the U.S. House of Representatives* (Washington, D.C.: Brookings Institution, 1989).

Again, this premise goes beyond the assumption that it is sufficient to see MCs as simply bundles of constituent policy preferences sent to Capitol Hill every two years. One current hypothesis, for example, is that policy-oriented professionals—people who aim to spend lifetime careers energetically writing new amendments and statutes—have entered Congress in large numbers during recent decades, replacing yesterday's part-time MCs who were allegedly more relaxed.[33] Is this beaverishness one reason Washington, D.C., has grown more unpopular? The Senate's intake of ex-governors has been falling, particularly in the 1990s; does this have implications for kinds of "actions" and for the working of that body?[34] A question arises from Chapter 5: What is the importance of age, generation, and experience among MCs, and what are the implications for term-limits reform?[35] Also, what are the "action" implications of the fact that MCs seem to be increasingly drawn from two atypical slices of the population—multimillionaires and *willing* round-the-clock fund-raisers?

Another significant question is: What are the implications of gender change on Capitol Hill? In view of current trends in American state legis-

33. See Alan Ehrenhalt, *The United States of Ambition: Politicians, Power, and the Pursuit of Office* (New York: Times Books, 1991), chs. 1, 2; Burdett Loomis, *The New American Politician: Ambition, Entrepreneurship, and the Changing Face of Political Life* (New York: Basic Books, 1988). This is a lively topic in Britain also: See Peter Riddell, *Honest Opportunism: The Rise of the Career Politician* (London: Hamish Hamilton, 1993). "So the distinguishing feature is not the scale of government but rather its level of activity. That reflects the desire of career politicians to do something, to find an outlet for their ambitions. Change is the order of the day. Active government initiating a heavy legislative programme has been as much a product of the Thatcher era as of the earlier collectivist phase since 1945." Riddell, p. 269.

34. In general, the chamber's intake of ex-governors seems to have declined gently since the 1950s. Ethan J. Bacon, "Proven Paths: The Penultimate Offices of United States Senators During the Twentieth Century," Yale course paper, fall 1998.

35. Much attention has been accorded, of course, to the importance of experience on Capitol Hill. One classic treatment is Richard F. Fenno, Jr., *Home Style: House Members in Their Districts* (Boston: Little, Brown, 1978), ch. 6.

latures and European parliamentary bodies, it is very likely that the proportion of MCs who are women will keep rising, and it might even reach the fifty-fifty mark some time during the twenty-first century. It is easy to see that female MCs might have policy orientations that are on average different from those of their male counterparts, but do women MCs, or would they, have a propensity for different *kinds* of "actions"? One hypothesis is: "In terms of personal style, some expect that women will introduce a 'kinder, gentler' politics, one characterised by cooperation rather than conflict, collaboration rather than hierarchy, honesty rather than sleaze."[36] Any results like this—as well as any distinctive policy tastes exhibited by women MCs in the particular area of military policy[37] —could leave residues in any future study of congressional "action" distributions. Considerable ingenuity has gone into addressing these gender questions,[38] but an empirical barrier persists: Few legislative bodies any-

36. Pippa Norris, "Women Politicians: Transforming Westminster?" *Parliamentary Affairs* 49 (1996), 89–102, quotation at p. 91.

37. Sidney Verba points to "systematic differences between men and women [generally] in their support for aggressive actions and policies. The data are consistent across time, across places, and across specific issues and questions. . . . [T]hey would seem to be the kind of deeply ingrained orientation that women would carry into political office." "Women in American Politics," ch. 23 in Louise A. Tilly and Patricia Gurin (eds.), *Women, Politics, and Change* (New York: Russell Sage, 1990), pp. 565–69, quotation at p. 566.

38. In addition to the Norris and Verba essays, I have the found the following works on women and politics particularly illuminating: Sue Thomas, *How Women Legislate* (New York: Oxford University Press, 1994), pp. 38–39, 50–51; Linda Witt, Karen M. Paget, and Glenna Matthews, *Running as a Woman: Gender and Power in American Politics* (New York: Free Press, 1994), ch. 11; Janet A. Flammang, *Women's Political Voice: How Women Are Transforming the Practice and Study of Politics* (Philadelphia: Temple University Press, 1997), ch. 6; Cindy Simon Rosenthal, "Once They Get There: The Role of Gender in Legislative Careers," *Extensions: A Journal of the Carl Albert Congressional Research and Studies Center,* spring 1995, pp. 15–17; Lyn Kathlene, "Power and Influence in State Legislative Policymaking: The Interaction of Gender and Position in Committee Hearing Debates," *American Political Science Review* 88 (1994), 560–76; Beth Reingold, "Conflict

where have accumulated the "critical mass" of women members needed to allow confident analysis of patterns.

Missing from this study's dataset is the 1990s, the political era we remember best, and I close by addressing directly the question of how this most recent decade, if suitable "action" data could be gathered, might fit into the overall analysis.

First, the Republican conservatives led to power by Newt Gingrich offer an obvious instance of an "ideological impulse"; this one would comfortably join the twentieth-century list of such manifestations presented in Table 5.4. In generational terms, it was a young, brash, forceful, iconoclastic offensive against one of the most inviting targets imaginable—the aging, rather smug, high-seniority, perquisite-rich Democratic congressional establishment of the 1980s that, like the Old Guard Republicans of the early twentieth century or the southern-led congressional establishment of the 1950s, virtually pleaded for a fresh challenge. (Note in Figure 5.5 the similar "action" profiles of these three establishments.) Generational challenge was obviously not the only theme of the 1990s, and it is not an inevitable reaction to a congressional establishment—but sometimes this occurs.

Also, the newly assertive Republicans staged two major "oppositions" during the 1990s—at least that is the way the MC "actions" of the decade might sort into clusters suitable for entry into Table 3.3 or 6.1. In 1993 through 1996 came the sequence of showdowns over Clinton's 1993 bud-

---

and Cooperation: Legislative Strategies and Concepts of Power among Female and Male State Legislators," *Journal of Politics* 58 (1996), 464–85; Drude Dahlerup, "From a Small to a Large Minority: Women in Scandinavian Politics," *Scandinavian Political Studies* 11 (1988), #4, 275–98; John Harwood and Geraldine Brooks, "Other Nations Elect Women to Lead Them, So Why Doesn't the U.S.?" *Wall Street Journal*, December 14, 1993, pp. A1, A9; Sam Howe Verhovek, "Record for Women in Washington Legislature," *New York Times*, February 4, 1999, p. A18. Wendy Brown, *Manhood and Politics: A Feminist Reading in Political Theory* (Totowa, N.J.: Rowman and Littlefield, 1988).

get, health-care reform, and the Gingrich-Dole budget. On balance, that was a standoff. In 1998–99 came the Republican impeachment drive. That ended in a White House victory.[39] From these manifestations one exceptional feature does stand out—as it does from the O'Neill-led challenge to the Reagan administration in the early 1980s, which failed to win entry to Table 3.3 but might have done so with ampler data sources. That is, all three of these recent opposition drives have been quite partisan; participation by members of the president's party has been minor.[40] This is in line with the general American trend toward tighter partisanship in recent times. Is purely, or at least nearly so, partisan congressional opposition a feature that is here to stay? Possibly, but it would be risky to bet on it. American history supplies plenty of instances where high-stakes issues—involving section, race, economics, corruption, alleged disloyalty, foreign policy, or White House power thrusts as in the cases of Watergate or FDR's court-packing plan—have divided one or both of the parties and brought on nontextbook oppositions, and we will probably see many more.

What can be said about the Republicans' Contract with America? I have skirted the subject of congressionally initiated legislative "programs" during American history; there does not seem to exist any clean way to code for their incidence. But here is a try: A relevant instance is, let us say, an ambitious menu of legislative aims prominently originated and advanced by one or a few de jure or de facto leaders of the House or Senate. The Contract with America fits this definition. Otherwise, using the thirty-eight

39. For what it is worth, note that the impeachment drive was not *precipitated* by people with elected politicians' instincts. Kenneth Starr, the Independent Counsel, did that.

40. Note, however, that in 1993–94, as documented earlier, the Clinton administration did encounter prominent trouble from Senators Boren, Breaux, Moynihan, and Riegle, and Congressmen Cooper and Penny—all Democrats. Senator Joseph Lieberman (D-Conn.) caused damage at a critical time during the impeachment politics of late 1998.

"general" and "era" histories listed in Table 2.1, here are the Contract's apparent predecessors. Before 1900: The agenda of Madison and others to craft government agencies, a revenue measure, and the Bill of Rights in 1789; the war hawks' agenda of military preparedness, territorial expansion, and war in 1811–12; the successive versions of Clay's American System in 1815–16 (pressed along with Calhoun and others), 1824, 1831–32, and 1841; Clay's wide-ranging collection of proposals tailored for the Compromise of 1850; the Radical Republicans' Reconstruction program of 1864–68; the later, last-gasp Reconstruction agenda (including the Civil Rights Act of 1875) pressed by Benjamin F. Butler and others in 1874–75; and possibly, although the White House had a hand in this also, the Republican agenda of tariff hikes, Civil War pension hikes, voting rights for southern blacks, naval expansion, and other items pressed by Speaker Reed, Ways and Means Chairman William McKinley (R-Ohio), and others during the Congress of 1889–91.[41] A pattern emerges here. Before 1900, many legislative programs originated on Capitol Hill, and

41. On 1789: John C. Miller, *The Federalist Era, 1789–1801* (New York: Harper and Row, 1960), pp. 14–19; on 1811–12: John Mayfield, *The New Nation: 1800–1845* (New York: Hill and Wang, 1982, revised ed. of 1961 work of the same title by Charles M. Wiltse), pp. 31–34, Marshall Smelser, *The Democratic Republic, 1801–1815* (New York: Harper and Row, 1968), pp. 208–18; on 1815–16: Mayfield, *The New Nation*, pp. 77–80, James A. Henretta, W. Elliot Brownlee, David Brody, and Susan Ware, *America's History*, 2d ed. (New York: Worth, 1993), vol. 1, p. 261; on 1824: George Dangerfield, *The Awakening of American Nationalism, 1815–1828* (New York: Harper and Row, 1965), pp. 201–8, Winthrop D. Jordan and Leon F. Litwack, *The United States*, 4th ed. (Englewood Cliffs, N.J.: Prentice Hall, 1994), p. 111; on 1831–32: Glynton G. Van Deusen, *The Jacksonian Era, 1828–1848* (New York: Harper and Bros., 1959), pp. 57–60; on 1841: Van Deusen, *The Jacksonian Era*, pp. 154–64; on 1850: David M. Potter, *The Impending Crisis, 1848–1861* (New York: Harper and Row, 1976), pp. 96–116; on 1864–68: J. G. Randall and David Donald, *The Civil War and Reconstruction*, 2d ed. (Lexington, Mass.: D.C. Heath, 1969), pp. 552–54, 566–600; on 1874–75: Eric Foner, *Reconstruction: America's Unfinished Revolution, 1863–1877* (New York: Harper and Row, 1988), pp. 553–56; on 1889–91: R. Hal Williams, *Years of Decision: American Politics in the 1890s* (Prospect Heights, Ill.: Waveland, 1978), ch. 2.

all of them came from the Federalist, Whig, or Republican side (or else were advanced by Henry Clay in his earlier days when he was still a Jeffersonian Democratic-Republican yet nonetheless, in later terms, Whiggish in outlook).[42] This reflects that side's propensity for government activism during the nineteenth century[43] as well as its doctrine of congressional supremacy in the legislative sphere that became so prominent during Andrew Jackson's presidency.[44]

Beginning with Theodore Roosevelt, of course, presidents have ordinarily dominated the legislative agenda on Capitol Hill, and that largely eliminated high-profile programs of the Clay variety during the twentieth century—at least according to the silences of the relevant history books. Possibly the best "modern" version of a nineteenth-century-type program is Senator Taft's effort to roll back the New Deal in 1947–48.[45] Democratic moves in the House in 1911–13, and the Senate in the late 1950s, might merit a mention. Speaker Wright's Democratic program of 1987–88 may make an impression in future history books. Yet there are not many instances, and none of them comes through robustly in the accounts.

Thus the Contract with America of the 1990s, looked at from one vantage point, was a throwback. It suggests Henry Clay (to whom Gingrich

42. Madison can probably be counted as a Federalist as of 1789, before Hamilton presented his Treasury program.

43. On this point see, for example, Robert Wiebe, *The Opening of American Society: From the Adoption of the Constitution to the Eve of Disunion* (New York: Vintage, 1985), ch. 11 ("Comprehensive Programs"); Robert S. Salisbury, "The Republican Party and Positive Government: 1860–1890," *Mid-America* 68 (1986), 15–34.

44. This was after the time of Alexander Hamilton, who had exemplified the first of these propensities though not, of course, the second.

45. See Dewey W. Grantham, *Recent America: The United States Since 1945* (Arlington Heights, Ill.: Harlan Davidson, 1989), pp. 36–39; Eric F. Goldman, *The Crucial Decade—And After: America, 1945–1960* (New York: Knopf, 1973), pp. 53–56.

often refers), the Whig idea of congressional legislative supremacy, even the image of failure associated with many of those nineteenth-century enterprises: As Clay found out, it is difficult to steer a legislative program past a hostile president. Yet in one respect, as a merchandising effort, the Contract was new. In the nineteenth century, it was the political parties (certainly not Congress's leaders of a Whiggish mindset) that ordinarily took charge of presenting elaborate, concrete programs to the public. In the early twentieth century, the presidency more or less preempted that role. In the 1990s, Gingrich and the other designers of the Contract with America surprisingly tried to elevate the House of Representatives to parity with the White House as a program merchandiser—not an easy thing to do.

To take up another feature of the 1990s, the major legislative show-downs of 1993–96—over the 1993 budget, health-care reform, the Gingrich-Dole budget, and also NAFTA—are among the best exhibits ever for the idea that drama and contingency are fundamental aspects of poli-tics. To understand sets of events like these, it is highly advisable to watch political actors perform and draw reactions in a context of attentive and fluid public opinion—in short, to witness moves in a process of prefer-ence formation.[46] Consider the two colossal failures—health-care reform and the Gingrich-Dole budget. In hindsight, it is fashionable to argue that both these drives were doomed to fail, that voters entered the process with relevant, fixed, first-order preferences that, once brought to bear through exposure to new information about the two legislative proposals,

46. A teacher of a course on congressional politics can do worse than to assign a nar-rative account of such a showdown—for example, Haynes Johnson and David S. Broder, *The System: The American Way of Politics at the Breaking Point* (Boston: Little, Brown, 1996), on the 1993–94 health-care drive. A classic is Joseph Alsop and Turner Catledge, *The 168 Days* (Garden City, N.Y.: Doubleday, Doran and Co., 1938), on FDR's court-packing campaign of 1937.

would sink them both—by inducing queasiness among many congressional Democrats in the first case (which in fact emerged), and a Clinton veto in the second (this happened too).

But the case for inevitability is not convincing—not least because, so far as we know, the most expert prognostications (as late as early 1994 in the first case, and late 1995 in the second) left the outcomes of the two drives very much in doubt. In principle, the case for inevitability might be clouded in two distinct ways by introducing the idea of consequential moves by political actors (including, but not limited to, MCs). First, assuming that relevant fixed voter preferences did exist in the 1990s in the areas of health-care and budgeting policy, political actors might have varied in the effectiveness with which they drew attention to connections between those preferences and the legislative proposals on offer. During 1993–94, for example, did the Democrats ever come close to matching the insurance industry's "Harry and Louise" ads? But second, how about the idea of novelty? The premise that relevant ex ante preferences can exist and predictably govern has to be undermined to the degree that items of choice are new or strange. The 1,300-page health-care plan and the many-faceted Gingrich-Dole budget were exactly that—certainly in a holistic sense, but also in terms of key ingredients. How could anyone know what the reaction would be to "health alliances" or "medical savings accounts"? Among other things, the two legislative instruments —like the movie *Titanic*, the New Coke, or the Taurus vehicle—were new products. In Schumpeter's terminology, they were "new combinations."[47] This implies the existence of producers or merchandisers who make moves (although note that in the political realm there also exist opposing actors who make anti-moves). If economic theory is to be applied to congressional politics, one strand might well be that pertaining

47. Joseph A. Schumpeter, *The Theory of Economic Development* (Cambridge: Harvard University Press, 1959), p. 66.

to producers and consumers. We have, at least in part, a system of elected producers.

The spasmodic quality of congressional politics was amply on display during the 1990s. After the eye-catching encounters of Clinton's first term, Congress more or less receded into the shadows and stayed there during his second term, emerging only for the impeachment proceedings. But MC moves did occur after 1996 that might qualify as "actions," and, without being systematic about it, I will close with a selection of them.

In 1997, as Democrats and Republicans of the House surprisingly began the new session by bringing ethics charges against each other, Newt Gingrich kept the Speakership by a precarious margin (he lost a few Republican votes) and was reprimanded for an ethics violation. Jim McDermott (D-Wash.) evidently leaked to the press a clandestine tape-recorded conversation between Gingrich and his allies, and John Boehner (R-Ohio) responded by bringing a lawsuit against McDermott (this is an "action" that would be hard to classify). In July, sophomore conservative Lindsey Graham (R-S.C.) and others staged what amounted to a coup against Gingrich, which failed[48] — but subsequent reports about the conspiring implicated and undermined Majority Leader Dick Armey and other GOP leaders. Also in 1997, freshman Senator Fred Thompson (R-Tenn.) conducted televised hearings, which failed to make much of an impression, concerning the Clinton administration's campaign-finance scandal.[49] Jesse Helms, chairman of the Senate Foreign Relations Committee,

48. See the retrospective account in Jim Vandettei and Francesca Contiguglia, "A Year Later, Rebels' Work Isn't Done," *Roll Call*, July 13, 1998, pp. 1, 30.

49. "Privately, committee staff and aides acknowledge that they blew it. . . . The real problem lay with Thompson. Although he had served as minority counsel during the Watergate hearings, he made one mistake after another in how he defined and conducted the inquiry into foreign influence over the election. . . . For an ex-Hollywood actor, Thompson also displayed surprisingly little understanding of the way nationally pub-

blocked Clinton's nomination of Governor William F. Weld (R-Mass.) to be ambassador to Mexico—a move that neither the norms nor the rules of the Senate made it clear that Helms could get away with, but he did.

On the legislative front in 1997–98, Speaker Gingrich and Senator Majority Leader Trent Lott (R-Miss.) came to a long-sought agreement with the Clinton White House to balance the federal budget; House Democratic Minority Leader Gephardt opposed the deal.[50] With Lott supplying key backing, the Senate ratified a chemical weapons treaty.[51] In league with media-savvy staff members, House Ways and Means Chairman Bill Archer (R-Tex.) and Senate Finance Committee Chairman William Roth, Jr. (R-Del.), led an unstoppable (as it turned out) drive to reform the Internal Revenue Service; one aide "fed reporters the kind of vivid examples of IRS abuses that allowed them to quickly generate big headlines."[52] Senator John McCain, soon to be a candidate for the White

licized hearings work. The campaign finance hearings were a television drama whose success would depend upon the public's impression." John B. Judis, "Bull in a China Scandal," *The New Republic,* September 22, 1997, pp. 18–23, quotations at pp. 20, 21.

50. Richard W. Stevenson, "After Years of Wrangling, Accord Is Reached on Plan to Balance Budget by 2002," *New York Times,* May 3, 1997, pp. 1, 12; Jerry Gray, "House Democratic Leader Opposes Clinton's Budget Deal," *New York Times,* May 21, 1997, p. B7.

51. "In the end, the push to gain support in the Republican Senate for the Chemical Weapons Convention turned to a significant degree on the close cooperation between the national security adviser Samuel R. Berger, and Senator Trent Lott, the conservative Republican majority leader whose 11th-hour conversion brought so many other undecided Republicans to the Administration's side." Alison Mitchell, "How the Votes Were Secured in the Push on Weapons Pact," *New York Times,* April 25, 1997, p. A1.

52. Howard Kurtz, "By Playing the Media, GOP Forced Clinton's Hand on IRS Overhaul," *Washington Post,* November 2, 1997, p. A20. This was "a victory for a handful of GOP lawmakers and strategists who spent months carefully orchestrating the shift in the media climate that forced the president's hand. From preemptive news conferences to well-timed leaks, from carefully placed op-ed pieces to exclusive arrangements with the likes of '60 Minutes,' the Republican crusaders helped sow the seeds of a new conventional wisdom."

House, promoted ambitious legislation. The "McCain tobacco bill" won considerable public and congressional acclaim in 1998, though it finally faltered and died. On Capitol Hill and in appearances across the country, McCain and Senator Russell D. Feingold (D-Wis.) marketed the McCain-Feingold bill to reform the campaign-finance system; they did well with the country's elite media but failed to generate enough enthusiasm among the public in general to get past the Senate's cloture barrier (sixty votes).[53] On the House side, moderate Republican Christopher Shays (R-Conn.) and Democrat Martin T. Meehan (D-Mass.) resourcefully assembled a cross-party coalition to pass, at least in the House, their own version of campaign-finance reform.[54]

Clinton's impeachment dominated the Capitol Hill scene from September 1998 through February 1999, during which time Senator Joseph Lieberman (D-Conn.) emerged as an early harsh critic of the president,[55] but Democratic ranks soon firmed up. Adverse November election results brought down Speaker Gingrich, but House Judiciary Committee Chairman Henry J. Hyde and House Republican Whip Tom DeLay

53. This seems to have been the formula for enacting the Brady bill regulating handgun sales in late 1993.

54. "But many believe that it was primarily the unflagging determination of Meehan and Shays to make the argument for banning 'soft money'—at late hours of the night, when they were nearly alone on the House floor but with a relatively large C-Span audience tuned in—that turned what was a dead issue earlier this year into one that is expected to go with considerable momentum to a reluctant Senate." Mary Leonard, "After Months, a Triumph for Meehan," *Boston Globe*, August 4, 1998, p. A10. See also Bob Hohler, "Shays Feels GOP Heat over Campaign Bill," *Boston Globe*, July 22, 1998, pp. A1, A13; Elizabeth Drew, *The Corruption of American Politics: What Went Wrong and Why* (Secaucus, N.J.: Carol Publishing Group, 1999), ch. 11.

55. "Over the past fortnight or so, Senator Joe Lieberman, the Democrat who greatly added to the tide of opinion now running against Mr. Clinton, has reminded the country of the moral force of a speech delivered from the Senate floor." "What Clinton Hath Wrought," *The Economist*, September 19, 1998, p. 27.

pressed for Clinton's impeachment anyway, and achieved it, although the attendant political turmoil also brought down Gingrich's successor, Bob Livingston (R-La.). Later in the Senate, party leaders Trent Lott and Tom Daschle, aided by a timely plan broached by Phil Gramm and Edward M. Kennedy, managed to reach bipartisan agreement on procedures for a trial.[56] Once that was under way, junior Republican Congressmen Lindsey Graham and Asa Hutchinson (R-Ark.), two of the so-called House managers, made particularly effective cases for the prosecution,[57] Senator Susan M. Collins (R-Maine) advanced a compromise initiative that drew notice,[58] and Senate patriarch Robert C. Byrd (D-W.Va.) loomed as a random variable. But in fact the trial ran down the tracks to a largely party-line destination.

Also in 1999, Senator McCain took the lead in pressing for use of NATO ground troops in Kosovo.[59] Congressmen Christopher Cox (R-Calif.) and Norm Dicks (D-Wash.) led a House committee that brought in a unanimous, much-noticed report documenting leakage of U.S. nuclear technology to China.[60] In the wake of the school massacre in Littleton, Colo-

56. Nancy Gibbs, "Order in the Court," *Time,* January 18, 1999, pp. 26–31; Anne E. Kornblut, "An Unlikely Alliance [Kennedy and Gramm] Breaks Impeachment Stalemate," *Boston Globe,* January 9, 1999, pp. A1, A9.

57. Guy Gugliotta and Eric Pianin, "Strong Case Made, Both Sides Say; Democrats Implore White House Lawyers to Rebut Evidence," *Washington Post,* January 17, 1999, p. A27. "If any speaker moved votes, it was probably Rep. Lindsey Graham." David Von Drehle, "Same Side, Different Approaches; While Hyde Reached to Lofty Tradition, Graham Displayed a Folksy Effectiveness," *Washington Post,* January 17, 1999, quotation at p. A26.

58. Anne E. Kornblut, "Suddenly, Collins Is in Limelight," *Boston Globe,* February 5, 1999, p. A23.

59. "Almost ubiquitous on television news shows, Mr. McCain, an Arizona Republican, steadily makes the case from which President Clinton shies away—that America can no longer afford to rule out the use of ground troops in Kosovo." Alison Mitchell, "McCain Keeps Pressing Case for Troops," *New York Times,* April 4, 1999, p. 7.

60. "While the House was torn asunder over impeachment, the five Republicans

rado, Senator Gordon H. Smith (R-Oreg.) reversed his position on aspects of gun control, bringing the Senate with him,[61] and three Democratic congresswomen, Rosa DeLauro (D-Conn.), Nita M. Lowey (D-N.Y.), and Carolyn McCarthy (D-N.Y.) pressed that issue publicly: "Almost every day, the three lawmakers hold a news conference, resurrecting the same pleas and plaints and seeming never to tire of their mantras. . . . Sometimes other Democrats join them, sometimes not, but these three are always there, perhaps the most insistent voices and the most public faces attached to their party's battle in the House for new restrictions on firearms."[62]

By way of moves like these is a kind of history made.

and four Democrats on the investigating panel, led by Representative Christopher Cox, secretly and unanimously achieved consensus." Jeff Gerth and Tim Weiner, "Tracking Suspicions About China's Atom Spying," *New York Times*, May 23, 1999, pp. 1, 12. See also Francis X. Clines, "Shepherding a China Report Past the Partisan Routines," *New York Times*, May 24, 1999, p. A18.

61. Robin Toner, "'Feeling Ashamed' on Gun Issue, Senator Is Moved to Act," *New York Times*, May 17, 1999, p. A12.

62. Frank Bruni, "3 Democratic Women Lead on Gun Control," *New York Times*, June 14, 1999, p. A18.

Mathew A
   Wasniewski,
Black Americans
      in Congress

INDEX

Ackerman, Bruce, 28n48, 58n37

action bonus: for majority party, 118–22, 182–83; South, 181–84, 183n30

action careers: defined, 169; early vs. late action in, 187–92; examples of, 62–66; to index eras, 213–15; notable, xv, 168–76; variety in, 189–92; vs. full careers, 173n14

actions: abroad, 12; in Arendt, 25–27; attributes of, 41–42; coding of, xii–xiii, 31–42, 62–70, 155n38; consequentiality of, 22–23; constitutional, 26–27; dataset of, xiii, 11, 31, 56–57; by decade, 55–57; entrepreneurial, 25, 211–13; future, 224; and gender, 233–35; ideational aims of, 15–17; in ideological impulses, 197–211; inequality in, 24–25, 169; kinds of, xiii, 9–12, 19, 37–38, 42, 49n19, 53–55, 62–70, 233–35; and majority party, 116–22; multiple year or Congress, 41–42, 192–97; salience of, 42, 56–57, 70, 110, 160n43; in selected Congresses, 42–47, 55; to shape opinion, 95–102; by

staff, 85n18; in Stuart era, 124–25; unusual, 72–77

Adams, John, 9n12, 140n16, 156, 159n40

Adams, John Quincy: as House member, 9, 42, 195; as president, 152–53, 156

African-Americans in Congress, 2, 16, 23, 37, 55, 102, 134, 138, 156n38, 157, 169–71, 172n7

Aldrich, Nelson W., 53, 172, 175–76, 198, 199, 208, 230

Alsop, Joseph, 192n36, 239n46

Amar, Vikram David, 142n20

Ames, Fisher, 4, 5n4, 91

Anderson, Thornton, 14n18

antislavery: petitions, 9, 42, 195; speeches, 10, 14, 16, 98, 231

appointments, presidential: making, 67, 81–83, 96n37, 128, 242; patronage jobs, 27, 115, 145–47, 195; taking, 68, 73–74, 103, 135–42, 191

Arendt, Hannah, 25–26

Arnold, R. Douglas, 97n38

Ashworth, John, 98n41, 176n19